HENRY T. KING.

Sketches of Pitt County

North Carolina

A Brief History of the County

1704-1910

Henry T. King

HERITAGE BOOKS
2007

HERITAGE BOOKS
AN IMPRINT OF HERITAGE BOOKS, INC.

Books, CDs, and more—Worldwide

For our listing of thousands of titles see our website
at
www.HeritageBooks.com

A Facsimile Reprint
Published 2007 by
HERITAGE BOOKS, INC.
Publishing Division
65 East Main Street
Westminster, Maryland 21157-5026

Originally published
Raleigh
Edwards & Broughton Printing Company
Printers and Binders
1911

— Publisher's Notice —
In reprints such as this, it is often not possible to remove blemishes from the original. We feel the contents of this book warrant its reissue despite these blemishes and hope you will agree and read it with pleasure.

International Standard Book Number: 978-1-55613-322-0

TO THE YOUTH OF PITT COUNTY,
DESCENDANTS OF A NOBLE ANCESTRY, WHO,
EVER FAITHFUL TO EVERY DUTY, LEFT THEM EXAMPLES
WORTHY OF IMITATION AND PRACTICE,
THIS LITTLE VOLUME IS
DEDICATED

TABLE OF CONTENTS.

CHAPTER ONE.
Early Mention of the Tar and Pamlico River Country—Lawson in Pitt—The Tuscarora Indians—Indian Localities—King Blount, 17

CHAPTER TWO.
Duvall Settles at Mount Calvert—King Blount Helped—"Black Beard," or Teach—King Blount Given Land in Bertie—Other Settlements Along Tar River—George Moye and the Indian—Edward Salter—Edgecombe—Tar—Precincts Made Counties... 23

CHAPTER THREE.
Edgecombe County—Tobacco Inspection—Military Census—John Hardy—Hugh McAden, a Presbyterian Preacher—His Trip—Tells of his Meetings.................................... 29

CHAPTER FOUR.
Something About Early Settlers—Entering Land—Quit-rents—Building Regulations—Overseers and Slaves—Marking Stock—The Established Church—Wild Animals—Liquor Question—How People Lived—Court-houses......................... 34

CHAPTER FIVE.
High Life—Education—Marriage—Domestic Life—Mail—Amusements and Pleasure—"High Betty Martin"—The Children..... 38

CHAPTER SIX.
John Simpson—Petition to Divide Beaufort County—Pitt County Formed—Boundaries—Court-house—Named for William Pitt—Alexander Stewart—Taxes—Jurors—Ministerial Jealousy—Line Between Pitt and Dobbs—Salter and Moye—Red Banks Ferry—Masonic Lodge—The Assembly............................ 41

CHAPTER SEVEN.
Courts—William Moore Complained of Simpson—Simpson Censured and Reprimanded—Mail Route—Regulators—March to Alamance—Pitt Company Under Captain Salter—Sheriff's Arrears —Martinborough 47

CHAPTER EIGHT.
Official Corruption—Blue Laws—County Officers—The "John and Elizabeth" Schooner Affair—Few Taxes Paid—Militia Officers—Martinborough—Revolutionary Proceedings—Pitt Freeholders Issue a Declaration of Rights—Standing Committee Appointed, 51

CONTENTS.

CHAPTER NINE.

Help for Boston—Donations Asked—Committee Elected as Directed by the Continental Congress—Members—The Salt Question—Provincial Congress at New Bern—Court-house—Vermin...... 56

CHAPTER TEN.

Committee of Safety Proceedings—Deputies to Provincial Congress Elected—Three Obstructionists—Acts of Continental Congress Approved—John Tison, Tory—Help for Boston—Provincial Congress and Assembly—Second Declaration of Rights—Rev. Mr. Blount—Patrollers—Atkinson and Sheppard................ 60

CHAPTER ELEVEN.

Negro Insurrection—Measures to Prevent it—White Man Instigator —No Lives Lost, but Negroes Whipped—Delegates to Hillsboro —Raising Troops—Military Districts and Officers—Justices Qualify—Trouble About Rev. Mr. Blount.................. 65

CHAPTER TWELVE.

Committee Meets—Hillsborough Resolves—John Tison, Patriot—Delegates to Provincial Congress—Committee of Secrecy, Intelligence and Observation — Pay for Provisions — Ammunition Bought—Salt—Pay for Ammunition—Allowances to Troops—Preparations for War....................................... 69

CHAPTER THIRTEEN.

Pitt Members of District Committee—Capt. James Armstrong—Test and Pledge—Supplies Bought—Pitt at Battle of Moore's Creek —More Patrollers—Salt—Delinquents—Daniel Fore—Bounty Money—Arthur Moore—Mr. Carson, Dancing Master—Delegates to Halifax—Instructions for Independence—John Simpson.... 73

CHAPTER FOURTEEN.

Provincial Council—Pitt Company at Wilmington—Officers—Returns of Men—Independence—John Hunter—Delegates to Halifax—More Troops—Equipment of Soldiers—James Salter—Enlistments in Other States—Justices of the Peace—Royalists Plot —Lack of Arms—Two Vagabond Young Men—Protest Against General Moore—The Assembly............................ 78

CHAPTER FIFTEEN.

No Senator—Supplies—Insolvents—Pitt's Quota—Sheriffs Fined—Simpson Succeeds Robeson—Falconer Succeeds Ascue—More Troops—Members of Assembly—Robert Salter—Robert Williams, Surgeon—Field Officers—Colonel Armstrong Wounded—Day of Fasting—Charleston—Money—Continental Army...... 82

CONTENTS. 7

CHAPTER SIXTEEN.

Guilford Court-house—Pitt Militia—Joel Truss—Old British Road—British Pass Through Pitt—Cattle and Provisions Captured—Skirmishes—Men and Guns at Martinborough—Troubles South of Pitt—Call for Troops—Prisoners in Jail—Buck's Barn—Leniency 86

CHAPTER SEVENTEEN.

Peace and Independence—Part of Pitt Given to Beaufort—John Simpson—Negro Burned for Murder—Acts of the Assembly—Armstrong and Salter, State Officers—Justices Resign—Part of Craven Given to Pitt—Armstrong, Brigadier-General—Pitt Academy—Greenville—William Blount—Greenville Ferry—Simpson Paid.. 90

CHAPTER EIGHTEEN.

Constitution Rejected—Motions and Vote Thereon—Location of Capital—Constitution Adopted—Amendments Recommended—The University—Foreign State—New Court-house—John Simpson Dead—Bounties for Manufactures—Pitt Iron Mines—Pitt in the Revolution—Governor Caswell's Opinion..................... 95

CHAPTER NINETEEN.

Tory Pardons—Vote on the Capital Bill—William Blount—First Census—Washington's Tour—Impressions in Pitt—Old People—James Armstrong Dead—Second Census—Peace and Progress—Schools and Houses—Mail Facilities—Modes of Conveyance—Good Old Times... 99

CHAPTER TWENTY.

Third Census—Yankee Hall—Second War with England—Two Pitt Companies at Beacon Island—Their Pay-roll—Retreat and Amusing Incident—Fourth Census—Occupations—Bridge at Greenville—Greenville Academies—Fifth Census—John Joyner, 104

CHAPTER TWENTY-ONE.

Steamboats—Constitutional Convention of 1835—Delegates—Important Votes—Baptist State Convention—Greenville Gazette—Presidential Election—Loss in Population—Flat Boats—Dr. Williams Dead—Harris and Yellowly Duel—Harris Killed—Academy Incorporated 109

CHAPTER TWENTY-TWO.

Plank Road—Seventh Census—Plank Road Stockholders Organized—Cold Spring—Court-house Burned—Great Loss—Common Schools and Progress—County Superintendent—Apportionment—Journal of Education—Very Old Man..................... 113

CONTENTS.

CHAPTER TWENTY-THREE.

Military Spirit—Good Old Muster Days—Eighth Census—Elections—Fort Sumter—President Calls for Volunteers—Governor Ellis Calls for Volunteers for State's Defense—Secession Convention—Pitt's Members—G. B. Singeltary Raises First Company—Tar River Boys—Marlboro Guards—Disbursing and Safety Committee—War Funds—Third Regiment.................. 118

CHAPTER TWENTY-FOUR.

Major Grimes—Wyatt Killed—Disposition of Pitt Companies and Men—Hatteras Captured—Pitt County Boys Prisoners—Surgeon Brown and Madison—Yellowly's Call for Volunteers—Officers of Twenty-seventh Regiment—Chicamacomico—Promotions 122

CHAPTER TWENTY-FIVE.

Enlistments—Military Board—Capture of Roanoke Island—Companies and Officers—Forty-fourth Regiment—Seventeenth—Grimes, Lieutenant-Colonel—Fifty-fifth—Tranter's Creek Skirmish—Fight a Few Days Later—Colonel Singeltary Killed—Movements—Seventy-fifth 126

CHAPTER TWENTY-SIX.

Vance Elected Governor—State Census—Yellowly for Congress—Fifty-fifth at Kinston—General Clingman's Complaint—Maryland Campaign—Captain Joyner Killed—Heavy Losses—Singeltary's Reply—Movement of Troops—Haddock's Cross-roads—Federals Capture Greenville—Other Events................. 130

CHAPTER TWENTY-SEVEN.

Emancipation Proclamation—Movements of Troops—Colonel Griffin in Pitt—His Picket Lines—Tithe Gatherers—Colonel Hammond—His Predicament—Conversation—Escape—Chancellorsville—Jackson Killed—In Virginia....................... 134

CHAPTER TWENTY-EIGHT.

Gettysburg—Farthest At—Severe Losses—Potter's Raid—At Greenville—Videttes Fired Upon—Return from Tarboro—Skirmish at Otter's Creek Bridge—Lieutenant Sharpe—Escape of Raiders—Their Route—At Scuffleton—Demoralization of Followers..... 138

CHAPTER TWENTY-NINE.

The Eighth—Major Yellowly—Forty-fourth and Sixty-sixth—Bristoe Station—Losses—Cas Laughinghouse—Duel That Never Occurred—War Prices—Capture at Haddock's Cross-roads—Red Banks Affair—Other Events............................. 142

CHAPTER THIRTY.

County Matters—Sixty-seventh—Movements of Other Regiments—Plymouth Captured—Great Victory—Heavy Losses—Taxes—The Wilderness—Remarkable Fighting—Spottsylvania—General Daniel Wounded and Grimes in Command—Drewry's Bluff—Captains Jarvis and Hines Wounded—Thomas King—Juniors—Cold Harbor—Captain Anderson Killed...................... 145

CHAPTER THIRTY-ONE.

Grimes, Brigadier-General—Losses Around Petersburg—A Great Capture by Fleming, James, Cherry and Coggins—Regiment of Juniors—Davis Farm—Reams Station—Hard Times in Richmond—Short Rations—Winchester—Grimes in Command of Division—Other Fighting—Peace Party—Pitt Officers of Juniors—Fort Fisher 150

CHAPTER THIRTY-TWO.

Deeds of Daring by Harris and Bland—Losses and Promotions—Around Petersburg—Fall of Fort Fisher—Wise's Fork—Southwest Creek—Bentonsville—Juniors—Struggling Against Odds.. 154

CHAPTER THIRTY-THREE.

Lee's Lines Broken at Petersburg—Retreat—Incidents—Johnston and Sherman—Appomattox—Last Charge—Surrender—Johnston Surrenders to Sherman—Pitt's Parole at Appomattox—Men Furnished—Officers 157

CHAPTER THIRTY-FOUR.

"Wheelers"—Dupree Kills Federal—Amnesty—Holden Provisional Governor—Delegates to Convention—Acts—Worth Elected Governor—School Matters—War-time School Books—Curious Lessons 161

CHAPTER THIRTY-FIVE.

War-time School Books—Geographical Reader for Dixie Children—-Description of the State—Its People—Patriotic—South Carolina—Review—Questions and Answers—Confederate Prowess Taught 165

CHAPTER THIRTY-SIX.

Carpetbaggers—Legislature of 1866—Pensions—Thirteenth Amendment—Reconstruction—Military Government—Cotton Planter—Education—Willis Briley Murdered—Two of the Murderers Hanged—Negro Militia—Laflin and Rich—Misguided Missionaries 169

CONTENTS.

CHAPTER THIRTY-SEVEN.

Riddick Carney—Attempt to Capture—Federal Lieutenant Killed—Second Attempt to Capture—Major Lyman and Negro Militia—Two Negroes Killed—Both Carneys Die—Horrible Tragedy—Ku Klux—Negro Officers—Specimens...................... 174

CHAPTER THIRTY-EIGHT.

Ninth Census—Things Improving—Convention of 1875—Delegates—Vance and Jarvis Elected—Jarvis Becomes Governor—Newspapers—Jarvis Elected Governor—Latham Elected to Congress—General Grimes Assassinated—A Lynching................ 179

CHAPTER THIRTY-NINE.

Tenth Census—County Towns—Education—Evolutions of the Old Male Academy—Prominent Teachers—Latham Defeated—Yellowly Dead—Jarvis Minister to Brazil—Fine Babies—Earthquake—Latham Elected—Railroad 183

CHAPTER FORTY.

Eleventh Census—Growth in Country and Towns—More Towns—Education—County Superintendents—Tobacco—Market Opened—Farmer Governor—Daily Reflector—King's Weekly—Jarvis Appointed U. S. Senator—Harry Skinner Elected to Congress—Great Fire—Telephones—Skinner Re-elected—Latham Dead—Records for Postmasters 188

CHAPTER FORTY-ONE.

Spanish-American War—Greenville Guards—Officers—Mustered in at Raleigh—Go to Tybee—Storm—Mustered Out—Skinner Defeated—Greenville Fair—Second Great Fire—Tingle Succeeded by Ragsdale—Bryan Grimes Elected Secretary of State—Railroad — Telephone Matters — Amendment — Twelfth Census — Towns—Dr. O'Hagan Dead.................................. 193

CHAPTER FORTY-TWO.

First Four-weeks Teachers' Institute in State—Rural Free Delivery—Harry Skinner Appointed United States District Attorney—Special Taxes for Schools—Teachers Organize—County Board of Education—Full-time Superintendent — Houses — Medals — Grimes Re-elected—Skinner Re-appointed—Railroads—Public Building—Steel Bridges—Grimes Elected Third Time—Training School—Pitt Dry..................................... 198

CHAPTER FORTY-THREE.

Laughinghouse Superintendent of Penitentiary—Post-office Site—Training School Opened—Its History—Senator Fleming Dead—Big Fire—Court-house Burned——Records Saved—Greenville Post-office Advanced to Second Class........................ 203

ADDENDA 206

CONTENTS.

CONCLUSION 207

MAPS.

Map of Indian Locations.......................................	18
Map of Early Settlements along Tar River......................	27
Map of Pitt County in 1760....................................	41
Map of Pitt County in 1787....................................	92
Map of Pitt County, showing Townships.........................	201

INTRODUCTION.

These Sketches are the result of years of inquiry, research and compilation. They are intended to give such traditions and facts as could be had from reliable sources and records. An earnest endeavor has been made to get the truth and put it in form to place before the public, that the heritage of a glorious past, and the achievements of the present, may be the pride of posterity.

Efforts have been made to be as correct as possible, but with matter, written and unwritten, traditions and reminiscences, errors are unavoidable. From diversity of statement and difference of opinion, accuracy has been sought. Criticism is legitimate, but it should not minimize the true. The criticism that may eliminate errors in the future will be duly appreciated.

Acknowledgments are made to the late Dr. W. M. B. Brown, the late Dr. C. J. O'Hagan, Hon. A. L. Blow, Hon. W. R. Williams, Hon. J. Bryan Grimes, and to many others, who have at various times rendered valuable aid in the collection and preservation of historical matter; and to them is due much credit for the production of these Sketches.

These Sketches are not intended as a biography, genealogy or advertisement, but the demand for sketches of many of Pitt's prominent men, both of the past and the present, has made necessary the addition of a second part, where many such sketches may be found. And from a financial standpoint, it has been found well to allow advertisements or a directory of some of the County and Towns. But all are parts, separate and distinct, and not confusing.

With a consciousness that much matter of historical value is here preserved, that should be a source of patriotic pride to the people of the County, and simply asking credit for whatever merit may be found in them, these Sketches of Pitt County are respectfully submitted.

Greenville, N. C.,   HENRY T. KING.
January, 1910.

SKETCHES OF PITT COUNTY. 15

To cite authorities for much of the matter herein recorded would demand more space than can be allotted in a work like this. It would be difficult to cite authorities where a fact has been the result of a variety of fragmentary evidence. Such has often been the case. They will be furnished when necessary.

The following works have been consulted:

NORTH CAROLINA WORKS:

Colonial and State Records, Regimental Histories, Foote's Sketches, Moore, Wheeler, Hawks, Williamson, Jones's Defense, Lawson, Wiley, Grimes's Notes, Sketches of Eastern Carolina, Handbooks of Department of Agriculture, Moore's Roster, Roster of North Carolina Troops in Spanish-American War, Acts of Legislature, North Carolina Booklet, Report of Fraud Commission, Publications of Historical Society, Letters of General Grimes, Life of Vance, etc.

HISTORIES OF UNITED STATES:

Stephens, Willard, Lee, Grimshaw, and others.

MISCELLANEOUS:

County Records, Congressional Directory, United States Government Reports of the Civil War (Land and Naval), Dictionary of American History, Census Reports, Files of Newspapers, Almanacs, and numerous Personal and Private Letters and Papers of the author.

CHAPTER ONE.

Early Mention of the Tar and Pamlico River Country—Lawson in Pitt—The Tuscarora Indians—Indian Localities—King Blount.

As early as 1681 mention is found of the Pamlico River. The commission of Captain Henry Wilkinson, as Governor of Albemarle, issued that year, gave him jurisdiction over "that part of the province of Carolina, that lyes five miles south of the river Pemplico, and from thence to Virginia." Settlers were slow to cross the Albemarle Sound, and as the country of the Pamlico was possessed of so few good harbors, in 1694 Governor Archdale was instructed to offer moderate quit rents and taxes to settlers there. These inducements must have had some effect, for in 1696 the country had enough inhabitants to be erected into the county of Bath.

How far up Tar River any settlement had been made is unknown. The whole river was then known as the Pamlico, and what is now Pitt County was then a part of the Pamlico country. Traders had no doubt ascended to the head of navigation and a stray squatter may have been settled on its banks. Pirates were plentiful in Carolina waters and its rivers and harbors often furnished them safety, after a return from cruising on the high seas.

In 1700, John Lawson, an English surveyor, arrived at Charleston, South Carolina, and began a tour of survey and exploration. About 1704 he reached what is now Pitt County. He came from the central part of the province and entered Pitt County from Greene. He must have entered somewhere in the Marlboro section, and then have followed an Indian trail, on and across Contentnea Creek, a little below Tyson's bridges, on the Forbes and Moye lands, to the Randolph landing on Tar River. There an Indian, who had hidden a canoe, took them all across. Lawson then went down the river, by land, about six miles, where he spent the night under a very large spreading oak. During the night there was a very heavy snow storm, with thunder and lightning. He states that he was then twelve miles from the English settlements, and that about half way he crossed a

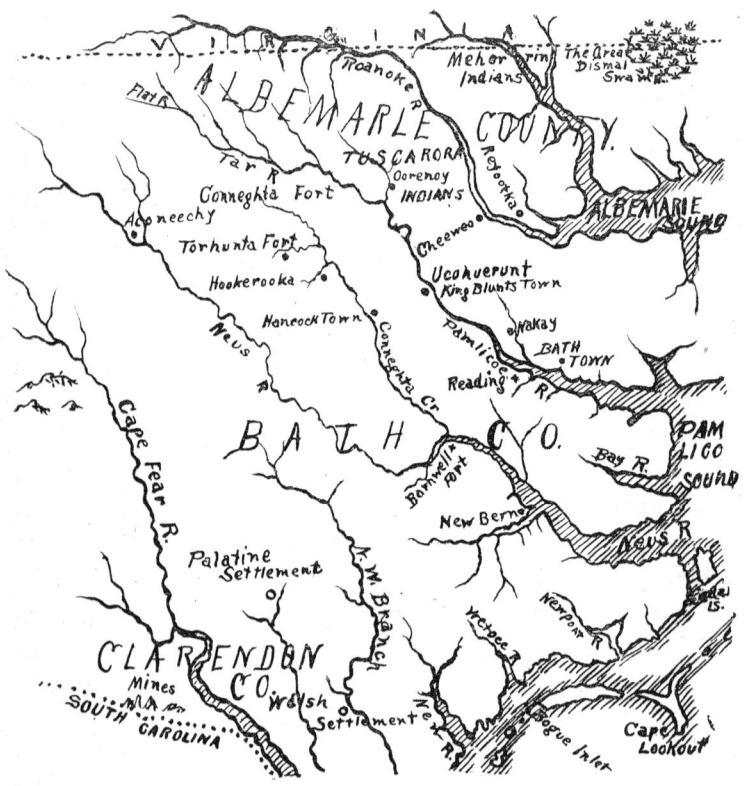

INDIAN LOCATION.
From an old map by Eman Bowen, now in office of the Secretary of State.
From pen sketch by H. T. K., 1909.

very deep creek,* "and came safe to Mr. Richard Smith's, of Pampticough."

The origin of the name of Tar River is undoubtedly unknown. Many writers are inclined to "Taw" as the original.

---

*Tranter's Creek.

INDIAN VILLAGE.

INDIAN CHIEFS

Hawks thought its Indian name "Torpœo." It was often spelled "Tau." How it became "Tar" is equally unknown. Many claim it a corruption of "Taw" or 'Tau." Hawks says it is a corruption of the first syllable of Torpœo and should be written and spelled "Tor." That its meaning was health is doubtful. At what time it became known as Tar is too, unknown.

At this time the Tuscaroras were the most numerous Indians in Eastern Carolina. Their principal towns were on the Big Contentnea, and Pitt County was, in part, somewhat their frontier. Those frontier Indians lived on such terms with the whites that in the bloody Tuscarora War of 1711, they remained friendly and gave some aid to the whites. But the whites felt the fury of the enraged Indians and near 300 were massacred in a most cruel and brutal manner. It is tradition that the house of John Porter, at the head of Chocowinity Bay, was the first attacked. In 1712, Tqm Blunt, a half breed and a minor chief and five other subordinate chiefs, who had taken little part in the war, made a treaty with Governor Pollock, by which they gave up all right to hunt below Bear Creek and made war with the English against the other hostile Indians.

About two miles above Bear Creek, on the General Grimes farm, was an Indian fort, which was known as Indian Fort Branch. About the fort was a field of about ten acres, cleared by the Indians. This ten acres is now a part of a seventy-five-acre field and is still in cultivation. Ucohuerunt, on Tar River, was one of Blunt's chief towns. Uneray was his upper town. The location of King Blunt's Town is very uncertain. On an early map of Indian locations, Ocohuerunt is shown on the west side of Tar River, apparently several miles above Greenville. It is said that there was an Indian town about where Old Sparta now is and that Town Creek got its name from this. On the same old map is shown "Ooneroy," about where Fishing Creek empties into the river, or some above that place. This may have been King Blunt's Upper Town,

"Uneray." King Blunt's Old Town must have been on the west side of Tar River, near Penny Hill, perhaps on the Governor Elias Carr plantation or about Old Sparta. Tradition gives Mabry's Bridge, across Fishing Creek or a little above, as the lacation of an Indian town, probably Urenay.

Just over in Edgecombe from Penny Hill is a place of woods known as "Indian Ridge," and there are evidences of Indian occupation of the vicinity on both sides of the river. In Bethel Township are many evidences of Indian habitation. Tradition says there was an Indian camp or town on the old James homestead, right near Grindool. A mile or two west of Grindool have been found many Indian relics, among them pottery in large broken pieces, arrow heads, etc. Indian Well Swamp was a favorite watering place of the Indians. All along its banks were water holes, dug by the Indians. At its head there was in earlier times, a large pond, always full of water, and this was known as "Indian Well." It took its name from this pond and these holes or wells. Just above the junction of Clay Root Swamp and Swift Creek was an Indian town. Many relics have been found in that section, including pottery, arrow heads, tomahawks and various others. There are also indications that on the Arthur Forbes place, about three miles above Greenville, there was once an Indian town or camp. Many relics have been found in Carolina township near the Martin line. In other parts of the County, there are evidences of Indian towns or camps in the far past.

After the Tuscarora war, most of those Indians went north and joined the Five Nations in New York. Blunt and some who had been faithful to the English remained. He was made their king and given lands between the Neuse and Tar rivers and above Bear Creek. Thus with peace restored and no Indians to fear, settlements began to multiply and grow up along Tar River and other streams.

CHAPTER TWO.

Duvall Settles at Mount Calvert—King Blount Helped—"Black Beard," or Teach—King Blount Given Land in Bertie—Other Settlements Along Tar River—George Moye and the Indian—Edward Salter—Edgecombe—Tar—Precincts Made Counties.

The first man to "patent" land in what is now Pitt County, was Lewis Duvall. It was at or very near the present Boyd's Ferry and he named it "Mount Calvert and Mount Pleasant." That was in 1714. That year and the next he patented 1,648 acres, in three tracts. Duvall died, and some years later his daughter sold the land to Edward Salter, who had settled at "Tuscarora," the farm now owned by Mrs. F. C. Saunders.

The Tuscarora war ended in 1715, and as one of the aids returned King Blunt for his help, he was given one hundred bushels of corn out of the "Publick Store."

During these years the pirate Teach, or "Black Beard," was a frequenter of Carolina waters. A sister, Susie White, lived near Boyd's Ferry, on the Grimes farm. Tradition says that Teach very often visited her. When he would return from a cruise and wanted to take a rest or vacation, he would visit his sister. Not far away, in the lowgrounds, stands a cypress, once famed as the lookout of Teach. It was known as "Table Top," being much taller than any of the surrounding trees and had a large flat top, very thick. Into its body were driven spikes, or were cut notches, so that it was not difficult to climb. From its top could be had a splendid view of the river to, and below Washington. There Teach resorted to see if the river was clear of a hostile boat, or to watch them, and then act according as circumstances demanded. A few years ago a storm broke off the top of this cypress, but the body is still standing.

INDIANS FISHING.

INDIANS MAKING CANOE.

Many and wonderful are the tales told of Teach's buried treasure in this section, and almost as many are the attempts that have been made to find it. In the lands on both sides of the river many a hole has been dug, but there is no record of the treasure being found. It has not been so very long ago that the grave of Susie White was disturbed by unknown midnight treasure seekers.

The outbreak of the Indians in South Carolina seemed to have excited the fears of King Blunt and his Indians that they might suffer, and "fearing harm on account of the Indian War in 1717," they asked a settlement on the Roanoke River and were given 53,000 acres of land in Bertie County, to which they soon moved. There they lived many years, King Tom Blunt being succeeded by his son James. Later they removed to New York, but still held their lands in Bertie and long received rents for them.

Settlements continued to grow along the river. In the next few years they had even passed beyond the Pitt limits and above was rapidly being settled. Capt. John Spier settled at Red Banks, and it is said there was a warehouse there as early as 1725 for the inspection of tobacco. George Moye had settled below Pactolus, and we find that this year he made complaint to the Governor's Council, at Edenton, that an Indian, belonging to King Blunt's town, had fired into his house and wounded two of his children. The Council found that as the Indian was drunk and had no malice, and that as the children were likely to do well, he should be fined twelve buckskins and twelve doe skins, to be paid Robert West, collector, for George Moye. This was in May, and the skins were to be paid in August. Then the Indian was to be given back his gun. Moye complained at the October sitting of the Council that the fine had not been paid, and the Indian was ordered to appear before the Council.

Settlers were now pushing into the interior. In 1727 Robert Williams bought from the Earl of Granville all the lands on the south side of Tar River, between Otter's and

Tyson's Creeks, extending several miles inland. Settlements had become many higher up the country, and in 1730 the people between the Roanoke River and Contentnea Creek, above what is now Pitt County, petitioned to form the precinct of Edgecombe.

Edward Salter was one of the Commissioners of Peace for Beaufort Precinct in 1731. The same year he was a mem-

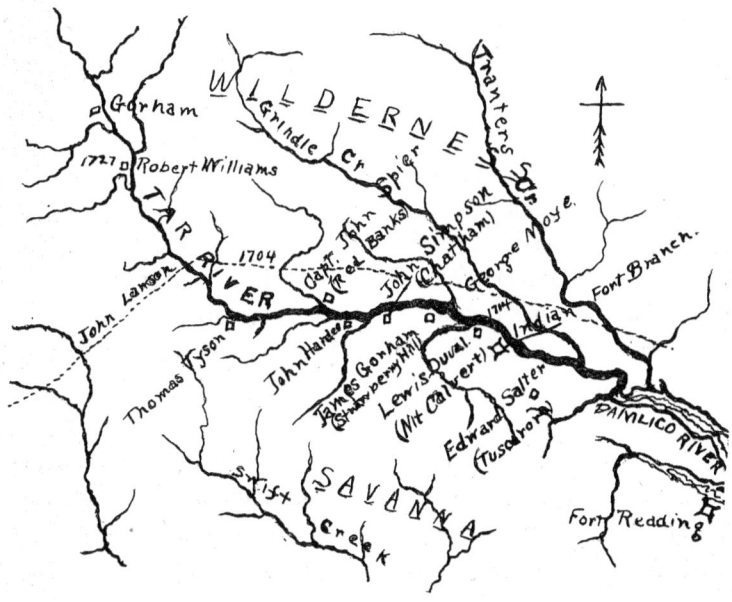

EARLY SETTLERS ALONG TAR RIVER AND PROBABLE ROUTE OF
JOHN LAWSON THROUGH THE COUNTY, 1704.
From pen sketch by H. T. K., 1909.

ber of the Lower House of the Assembly. At this session he was one of the committee to confer with the Committee of the Upper House, on the bill to ascertain and regulate the payment of quit rents and fees of the officers of the government.

In 1732 Governor Burrington established the precinct of Edgecombe, it being all that territory west of a line beginning at the mouth of Conoconaro Creek on Roanoke River, and thence in a straight line down to King Blunt's old town on Tar River, then continuing to Neuse River, and then to the northeast branch of the Cape Fear River. Later in the same year, upon petition of the people, the line was changed to run down the Roanoke River to Hoskin's line at Rainbow Banks, and then in a straight line to King Blunt's old town on Tar River. Justices of the Peace for Edgecombe were appointed by the Governor, and it sent representatives to the Assembly, but the Assembly refused to concur with the Governor in establishing the precinct. It killed the bill for establishing it in February, 1735, though that section continued to be known as Edgecombe.

Edward Salter was again a member of the Assembly for Beaufort in the year 1734.

Tar was now an important article of export, and North Carolina produced more than all the other colonies. Pitt County was a forest of the long leaf pines and furnished a large share of this product. The inhabitants of Tar River numbered twenty families in 1735, and it is said that 1,000 hogsheads of tobacco were raised in the county at this time.

In 1738, the old division of three counties, Albemarle, Bath and Clarendon, was abolished and each of the precincts became counties. Bath County had comprised four precincts—Beaufort, Craven, Carteret and Hyde. Beaufort comprised about what is now Beaufort and Pitt counties, and the court-house was at Bath.

CHAPTER THREE.

EDGECOMBE COUNTY—TOBACCO INSPECTION—MILITARY CENSUS—JOHN HARDY—HUGH MCADEN, A PRESBYTERIAN PREACHER—HIS TRIP—TELLS OF HIS MEETINGS.

After several years the people of Edgecombe Precinct succeeded in getting Edgecombe County established by the Assembly of 1741. As its southeastern boundary was the northwest boundary of Beaufort, and later became the boundary of Pitt, it is of interest. It began on Roanoke River at Jenkins Henry's upper corner tree, from there a straight line along the lines of Tyrrell and Beaufort counties to the mouth of Cheek's Mill Creek on Tar River; then from across the river opposite the mouth of the creek, in a straight line unto the middle grounds between the Tar and Neuse rivers. At this time it was more settled than Pitt.

The importance of tobacco as a staple of commerce, and no doubt the weakness of many to ship inferior tobacco as good, led to the establishment of warehouses for its inspection by the authorities. An act of 1743 provided for two warehouses for Beaufort County, one at Bath and one at Red Banks. The rivers and creeks were about the only means of transportation and communication. Their importance was realized so fully that an act of 1745 provided for Commissioners to "make, mend and repair all roads, bridges, cuts and water courses." For Beaufort County, on the north side of Tar River, above Tranter's Creek to the Edgecombe line, Seth Pilkinton, George Moye, Sr., William Mace, John Burney and James Barrow, were the Commissioners; on the south side, from Chocowinity to the Edgecombe line, they were Edward Salter, Thomas Tyson and John Hardee. In 1752 their duties were enlarged to include clearing rivers and creeks for navigation.

INDIANS COOKING FISH.

A military census was taken in 1754 by order of Governor Dobbs. Beaufort showed up with one regiment of seven companies, with a total of 587 men. Officers recommended were, Colonel, John Boyd; Lieutenant-Colonel, William Caruthers; Major, ... Buck; Captain, John Hardee. John Alderson was recommended for Captain in place of Captain Newsome. The first three officers were promotions of one grade each. It was shown that there were no Indians in the county and also no arms. In the public storehouse was about fifty pounds of powder and one hundred and fifty pounds of large shot.

John Hardee was a member of the Assembly this year.

The next year the returns of the militia and taxables showed: Militia, 680: taxables—whites, 771; blacks, 567; total, 1,383; a gain of 14 whites and 18 blacks. The population of the colony at this time was, by returns, about 45,000, but more than 80,000 were claimed.

Preachers were scarce in the colony this early. Hugh McAden, the first Presbyterian missionary in the colony, visited this section this year. He was a native of Pennsylvania and licensed by the Pennsylvania Presbytery. He came to Western Carolina early in this year. After much travel, he went to Wilmington and from there came to this section through Dobbs County. Beginning with his Journal in that county the following is an extract:

"The next morning, set out upon my journey for Pamlico, and rode about ten miles, to Major McWain's, where I had the opportunity of seeing and conversing with Governor Dobbs, who is a very sociable gentleman."

That night he lodged at Petter's Ferry,* on Contentney, about twenty miles, it being too late to go farther. The next day he rode about forty miles to Salter's Ferry on Tar River. The next day, being Saturday, he came to Thomas Little's, where he remained over Sabbath, April 4th. This man had not heard a Presbyterian minister in the twenty-

---

* This place was later known as Blount's Ferry; then Bell's Ferry, and is now Grifton.

INDIANS COOKING CORN.

eight years he had lived in Carolina, and took the opportunity of sending around for his neighbors, and collected a congregation; and kept him till Wednesday to preach again. Of this meeting he said, "I found some few amongst them that I trust are God's dear children, who seemed much refreshed by my coming."

On the 7th day of April, Wednesday, after the sermon, he rode to Mr. Barrow's, about five miles, and the next day, about five or six miles, to Red Banks, "where I preached to a pretty large company of various sorts of people, but fewer Presbyterians. In the evening, rode up the river, ten miles, to Mr. Mace's, who is a man of considerable note, and a Presbyterian." Here he remained till Sabbath, the 11th, and preached in the neighborhood.

On Tuesday, April 13th, he set out homeward, and rode twenty miles, to Mr. Toole's, on Tar River; this man he describes as unhappy in his notions of unbelief. On Wednesday he rode thirty miles, to Edgecombe Court House.

The increase in the production of tobacco made several more warehouses necessary for its inspection, and in 1758 warehouses were established at all the principal places in the colony. Those in Beaufort were now Bath, William Spier's, Travers, Grist's, Tranter's Creek, Chocowinity, Congleton's, Red Banks, Blount's Creek, Mill's, Salter's, Durham's Creek, and South Dividing Creek.

Those in that part now Pitt were Spiers, below Red Banks; Grists, on Bear Creek; Tranter's Creek, near its mouth; Congleton's, near the mill on Tranter's Creek; and Salters, now Boyd's Ferry. Travers was on Tranter's Creek near its mouth.

CHAPTER FOUR.

Something About Early Settlers—Entering Land—Quit-rents—Building Regulations—Overseers and Slaves—Marking Stock—The Established Church—Wild Animals—Liquor Question—How People Lived—Court-houses.

*The early settlers took up the richest and nearest lands on the rivers and navigable streams. Laws were passed to prevent one man from taking too much land on the rivers, to the exclusion of others. So he was allowed only 640 acres in one tract, and not another in two miles of this, unless by special warrant. They lived principally on the streams and every family had its boat of some kind for travel and transportation of produce. To prevent non-residents entering land for speculation, it was required that one should reside in the province two years before he could sell his lands and rights. For entering lands, a quit rent of one shilling for every fifty acres was required, and three years were allowed for building a habitable house, clearing, fencing and planting at least one acre.

The Council at its March, 1726, meeting passed the following: "For saving of lands for the future, every house shall be fifteen feet long, ten feet Broad, Made tight and habitable of Clapboards or Logs squared, with a roof and chimney-place and a Door-place. The whole acre cleared well, the major part of it broke up and planted with either fruite, trees or grain." Those who remember the log cabin, with its clay-daubed walls, board roof, door with wooden hinges, square hole in the wall for a window, and its stick or dirt chimney, have a good idea of the houses of many of the early settlers and of the homes of slaves and their overseers. The overseers were often bond-servants and the slaves were

---

*Much of this chapter is from Grimes' Notes on North Carolina, as is also much of the next chapter.

negroes, mulattoes and Indians. Land, slaves and stock comprised the wealth of the planter. He had little use for gold and silver, but to purchase slaves.

Horses were branded and cattle and hogs were marked in their ears, as is the custom to-day. For altering or defacing brands or mismarking of stock there was a penalty of ten pounds proclamation money over and above the value of the animal, and "forty lashes on his bare back well laid on; and for the second offense, in addition to the price mentioned, standing in the pillory two hours and branding in the left hand with a red hot iron with the letter "T" was added. Slaves, for the first offense, had both ears cut off and were publicly whipped, and for the second offense suffered death.

The Church of England (Episcopal) was established by law, though other forms were allowed. In fact there was freedom of worship. An act of 1705 required that to sit in the House of Commons, in Carolina, the member should have received the Sacrament according to the Rites of the Church of England in less than twelve months, or show good reason why he had not, or swear that such action was from no dislike for that church, and that he had not been in communion with any other church within that time. If he refused to thus qualify himself, his seat was declared vacant and an election ordered to fill the vacancy.

Wolves, bears, panthers, wild cats, foxes and many other wild animals were very numerous and did much damage to crops and domestic animals. Beginning with 1705, many acts for destroying these were passed. They were called "vermin" in those acts. Bounties were offered for them. Squirrels did considerable damage, were very numerous, and many acts were passed for destroying them.

The liquor question also troubled the colony. The law was similar to that of to-day, requiring license, and allowing a man to sell "cyder or other liquors, the produce of his own plantation, at any time hereafter by full and Lawful measures (the same not being drunk in the cellar, house or plantation"). The prices for "Drink, Dyet, Lodging, Fodder, Provender, Corn or Pasturage" was fixed by the Justices of the County Court.

The poor landowners were reduced to the primitive methods of the Indians, using stone hand mortars for pounding or grinding their grain, but the better class used hand mills brought from England. Nails were made in blacksmith shops and all ironware was brought from England.

Each large planter had his own saw pit, carpenter, cooper, blacksmith, tanner, etc. He raised wool and cotton enough to clothe his own people, carded, spun, and wove his own cloth and made his own clothes. Each such plantation was a miniature republic in itself, raising its own beef, pork, horses, grain, tobacco, wool, cotton, gardens and other necessities, having its own mechanics, manufacturers, laborers and rulers. Many of these planters owned vessels that traded with England, the West Indies and sometimes with Europe. Slaves made tar and turpentine in the spring and summer, and cleared land in the fall and winter; the women and children did most of the farm work. One slave on a plantation was allowed to carry a gun for the protection of stock and to kill game for the table. When it became necessary to execute a slave, his owner was paid his value as assessed by the Justices and allowed by the Assembly. A planter starting life with modest beginnings could, by the increase of his stock, slaves and buying more land, which was cheap, soon become wealthy.

New precincts or counties were formed as the increasing population demanded. All court-houses built in the various precincts or counties were required to be not less than twenty-four feet long and sixteen feet wide. Prisons and stocks were also provided for the punishment of those convicted of crimes.

Such were some of the rules and custom, laws and government, and manners and conditions in the province of Carolina about the middle of the eighteenth century, under which our forefathers were building up this great Commonwealth. And the pioneers of Pitt County were bearing their share of those burdens, reaping the attendant blessings and building for future generations.

CHAPTER FIVE.

High Life—Education—Marriage—Domestic Life—Mail—Amusements and Pleasure—"High Betty Martin"—The Children.

Among the planters were some who brought the customs and manners of their English homes, and they lived as much after the style of their former homes as conditions would admit. Some, who came as officials, brought their friends, retainers and tenants. Many of them belonged to the gentry and were highly educated. They had good houses and were supplied with many conveniences, unknown to the poorer classes. They vied with each other in having the best homes and furnishings.

Educational advantages were very poor. The rich were educated in England or at Williamsburg, Virginia, or Charleston, South Carolina; some were taught at home. The girls were generally taught by their mothers or placed with those who undertook to educate them. The poorer classes had so few advantages that few learned much. There were no common schools as we have. Servants were sometimes taught to read and write by their mistresses.

The rich got their clothes mostly from England, or other colonies, and dressed well. All kinds of manufacturing in the colonies was discouraged by England, and the hand-loom was long the only means of making cloth.

At first no one but a minister of the Church of England was allowed to perform the marriage ceremony, but owing to the scarcity of those ministers laws were passed giving others that right also. There were laws against the marriage of Indians and whites and of whites and negroes or mulattoes, yet these latter seem to have been rather frequent, especially between whites and Indians.

Domestic life was much like that of ante-bellum days of slavery, in the homes of the rich. The men attended to the affairs of the farm or other business while the women, with a lot of servants, did the work of the house, weaving, spinning, sewing, etc. It was an independent, self-reliant life, that grew and trained the heroes of later history.

There were at this time no mail facilities. Letters and other mail came at any time there came any one to bring them. They were dispatched in the same manner. As most of the planters lived on the rivers, mail was often brought or carried by some chance boatman. Official letters were required to be forwarded from plantation to plantation, and so on to the destination, a severe penalty being prescribed for any one who caused delay. The General Assembly provided for payment of the costs thus incurred to those who forwarded such mail.

Amusements and pleasure were not as rare as the reader might suspect. There were games and plays and outdoor amusements in many forms. Indoors, there were music, cards, dancing and many games; outdoors, there were hunting, fishing, bowling, perhaps horse racing, cock-fighting and other things. Boating and sailing were also much indulged in. Singing was also an accomplishment possessed by many to a high degree. There were social duties that took some time of the more wealthy. Some of their social functions would have done credit to a later period. In most of these pleasures and amusements there was little distinction of class, a common safety making all neighbors, the richer and the poorer sharing alike in them. There were many social and family games, plays and dances.

"High Betty Martin" was thus early a favorite. It came to North Carolina from Maryland, where it was composed in honor of Miss Elizabeth Martin, grandmother of Governor Richard Caswell. It ran thus:

> "High Betty Martin, tip-toe, tip-toe,
> High Betty Martin, tip-toe fine;
> She couldn't get a shoe,
> She couldn't get a stocking,

> She couldn't get a husband
> To suit her mind.
> > High Betty Martin, tip-toe, tip-toe," etc.

The children had their games, playing soldier, Indian, ball, etc., the girls having their playthings after the manner of to-day, if not up-to-date as now. With all its trials, troubles and disadvantages, it may be said to have been a life close to nature, simple and not so full of hardships, as is generally supposed.

CHAPTER SIX.

John Simpson—Petition to Divide Beaufort County—Pitt County Formed—Boundaries—Court-house—Named for William Pitt—Alexander Stewart—Taxes—Jurors—Ministerial Jealousy—Line Between Pitt and Dobbs—Salter and Moye—Red Banks Ferry—Masonic Lodge—The Assembly.

John Simpson, who came from Massachusetts and settled on Tar River, about six miles below Greenville, calling his place "Chatham," was a member of the Assembly for Beaufort County in 1760. The Assembly met at Newbern. On Friday, May 9th, a petition of sundry inhabitants of Beau-

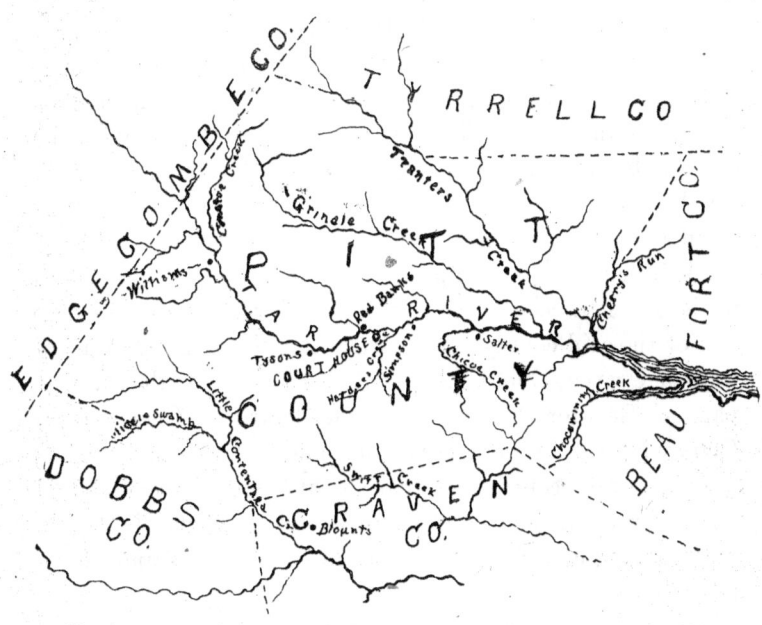

PITT COUNTY, AS FORMED 1760.
From pen sketch by H. T. K., 1910.

fort was presented asking for a division of the county, saying that the county was "in extent one hundred miles or more and divided by a boisterous and tempestuous river," etc. A petition against dividing the county and declaring the above untrue, was also presented. By a majority vote, the matter was referred to the next session of the Assembly, which met in November, the same year.

November 19th the committee to examine the petitions for the division of Beaufort County reported a great majority in favor of the proposed division, and recommended it. John Simpson was ordered to prepare a bill for such division, which he did the same day and introduced. It provided for erecting the "upper part of Beaufort County into a county and parish, by the name of Pitt County and St. Michael's Parish." The bill passed the Lower House that day and was sent to the Upper House. On the 25th it passed the Upper House and was ordered engrossed.

It provided that on and after the first day of January, 1761, "the upper part of the said county of Beaufort, beginning at the line between the said county and Tyrrell, running south, southwest to Cherry's Run, where the main road crosses the said run; thence down the said run to Tranter's Creek; thence down the said creek to Pamlico River; thence down the said river to the Fork Point, on the south side of the said river; thence up the Chocowinity Bay and Creek to the head thereof; thence south, southwest, to the dividing line of the said county and Craven; thence along the dividing lines of Craven, Dobbs, Edgecomb and Tyrrel; so that all that part of Beaufort County to the westward of Cherry Run, Chocowinity Bay and Creek, shall and is hereby declared to be a separate county and parish, and shall be called and known by the name of Pitt County and St. Michael's Parish, with all and every the rights, privileges, benefits and advantages," etc.

John Hardee, John Simpson, William Spier, George Moy and Isaac Buck were made commissioners for building a court-house, prison, pillory and stocks, on the lands of John Hardee, on the south side of Tar River near Hardee's Chapel. A tax of two shillings on each taxable poll in the county was levied for two years, to pay for the building of the court-house, stocks, prison and pillory. Courts were to be held at the house of John Hardee until a court-house could be built. The freeholders of the county were to meet at his house on next Easter to elect twelve vestrymen for the county.

The county was named in honor of William Pitt, the elder, Earl of Chatham, who was then Prime Minister of England, and under whose administration England was successful in every quarter of the globe. William Pitt, Earl of Chatham, was born November 15th, 1708, and was the son of Robert Pitt, Esquire, of Cornwall. He served long in Parliament, was vice-treasurer of Ireland, treasurer and paymaster of the army, privy counsellor, and secretary of State. On the downfall of the Rockingham administration he was appointed Lord Privy Seal and raised to the peerage, with the title of Earl of Chatham. He was a great friend of America and nobly plead its cause in Parliament. While rising to speak in the House of Lords he was stricken with a convulsive fit and died about five weeks later, on May 11th, 1778. He was one of England's great men. His second son, William, was born May 28th, 1759, became Prime Minister of England in 1783, and died January 23d, 1806. In history he is too often confused with his father and credited with being the friend of America, while he did not enter upon his career until independence was practically won. That John Simpson was a great admirer of Pitt, and had much to do with giving the county its name, may be judged from the fact that he named his home "Chatham."

The formation of Pitt was a blow to Beaufort, whose people felt it. Alexander Stewart, missionary at Bath, wrote the next year that his parish had lost "the better half of my white parishioners, so that the whole number of whites in St. Thomas' Parish is not now quite 1,000, besides about 400 taxable negroes."

A report on Tar River about this time said that it was navigable for about one hundred miles.

THE JOHN EASON HOUSE,

Said to have been used for the Colonial Court House. It is still standing on the lands where John Hardee died. On the chimney are the letters "I. H. S." Inside between the chimneys is a brick vault.

It seems there were no county commissioners at that time as we have to-day, and that the Assembly passed upon matters now within their jurisdiction. The formation of Pitt caused some confusion about the collection of taxes, and the Assembly of 1762 allowed Thomas Bonner, late sheriff of Beaufort, to collect the taxes for 1760. The Assembly also released John Brown from all public duties and taxes.

Pitt was in the New Bern Superior Court District and sent six jurors to that court. It seems that the juries were composed of twenty-four men. The county courts were held quarterly in February, May, August and November, and was presided over by Justices of the Peace.

Pitt had no minister after its separation from Beaufort, but the Rev. Mr. Stewart continued to make visits. This did not satisfy the people and they employed a Presbyterian minister. There was some friction between this Presbyterian, Rev. John Alexander and Rev. Mr. Stewart and he (Rev. John Alexander) left the colony, Rev. Mr. Stewart warning others that he was "an unworthy person."

The Assembly of 1763 provided for running the line between Pitt and Dobbs counties, which had never been done. Richard Caswell, John Simpson and William Wilson were appointed commissioners to run it. It was to begin from "Blount's Ford on Little Contentney Creek to Luke White's, then up the Middle Swamp to William Wilson's, and from thence to the nearest part of Edgecomb County."

The Governor's Council met at Wilmington in 1764. On February 28th, Edward Salter presented a "remonstrance" against the "illegal conduct in office" of John Hardee, John Tyson, George Moye and Abraham Tyson, Justices of the Peace. George Moye thereupon made a counter "remonstrance" against Edward Salter, who was also a Justice of the Peace. The matter was referred to the Court of the Justices at New Bern and nothing more was heard of it.

Among the acts of the Assembly this year were those for a ferry at Red Banks, for running the line between Pitt and

Dobbs counties and for making William Spier's, Simpson's and Salter's landings, places for the inspection of tobacco.

The tax returns for 1765 showed 750 white men taxable and 429 blacks and mulattoes, male and female. Beaufort's return showed 411 whites and 476 blacks.

The first Masonic Lodge in North Carolina was at Crown Point, in Pitt County. It is not known when it was established. In 1766 St. John's Grand Lodge of Massachusetts issued a dispensation to Thomas Cooper, of the Pitt County Lodge, to act as Deputy Grand Master of North Carolina. Reports of this Lodge for the years 1766 and 1767 are on file in the archives of the Grand Lodge of Massachusetts, at Boston. The Greenville Lodge now possesses a certificate of membership of one, Clement Holliday, in that Crown Point Lodge, dated March 27th, 1768.

Crown Point was an important stopping place on the road to Newbern. It was just on the south side of Turkey Cock Swamp, and its inn was popular in colonial days. Wilmington claims to have had a Masonic Lodge as early as 1735, but the proof is not so conclusive as that of the Pitt Crown Point Lodge.

The tax returns this year showed 798 whites and 470 blacks and mulattoes.

Among the acts of the Assembly this year were those for preventing the wanton destruction of fish in Neuse and Tar rivers and Fishing Creek; for a post from Suffolk, Virginia, to the boundary house on the South Carolina line; and the various counties were made coextensive with the parishes, 100 pounds being appropriated per year for a minister, under the Lord Bishop of England. Rev. Mr. Stewart reported that in one day he baptized 124 "white and black children" in Pitt.

CHAPTER SEVEN.

Courts—William Moore Complained of Simpson—Simpson Censured and Reprimanded—Mail Route—Regulators—March to Alamance—Pitt Company Under Captain Salter—Sheriff's Arrears—Martinborough.

In the organization of Superior Courts, Pitt County had been placed in the district composed of Craven, Dobbs, Beaufort, Hyde and Pitt. Court was held twice a year by the Chief Justice of the colony and the Associate of the district, jointly or separately. The oppression of taxation that later caused the trouble between Governor Tryon and the Regulators was beginning in this part of the colony.

In the Assembly on November 20th, 1768, John Ashe presented the affidavit of William Moore, setting forth that he was present at the court-house in Pitt County on the fourth Tuesday in October, it being a term of the Inferior Court, and that it was a "general topic of discourse" with the Justices that they could do no business, and the reason was that they did not want a "list of taxables returned to the court because if it was they were apprehensive of being without a sheriff as there was hardly any one who would choose to accept of that office on account of the difficulty and hazard that attended the collection of ye taxes." The affidavit further stated that the above stated reason was given at the court or before by John Simpson and John Tyson.

A committee, with powers to enquire into all the facts connected with the matter, was appointed, and after diligent enquiry it reported that facts set forth in the affidavit were true. The report was made on the 24th and the House declared Mr. Simpson guilty of a "high misdemeanor, and that his conduct in preventing the sitting of the Inferior Court of Pitt County is greatly injurious to the Public and detestable to this House." He was ordered to appear at the bar of the

House (of which he was then a member) and receive a "severe censure and reprimand" from the Speaker for his conduct. This being done, the matter was over. Shortly thereafter he was granted "leave of absence" for the session.

A mail route was established through the Colony in 1768, in acordance with an act of 1766. It was the link between Williamsburg, Virginia, and Charleston, South Carolina. From Suffolk, Virginia, it went to Cotton's Ferry, on the Chowan, 40 miles; then to Appletree's, on the Roanoke, 30 miles; then to Salter's, on Tar River, 35 miles; then to Kemp's on the Neuse, 28 miles; then to New Bern, 10 miles; and on by Wilmington, Brunswick and the Boundary House into South Carolina and to Charleston.

Though John Simpson was in sympathy with the Regulators of Pitt County, he was loyal to the governor, and when Robert Salter reported that he had just come from Tarboro, where he learned that the Regulators of Bute and Johnston counties were preparing to go to New Bern to prevent Colonel Fanning taking his seat in the Assembly of 1770, he (Simpson) readily ordered the militia to meet at the court-house, to be in readiness to march to New Bern to be at the governor's service. He was colonel of the Pitt Regiment of militia. December 5th Colonel Simpson notified Governor Tryon that he had 358 men, with six days provisions, ready to march to New Bern, if required.

They were not required at New Bern. But they seem to have been held somewhat in readiness, as the trouble grew and a revolution was imminent in the western counties. April 13th, 1771, Colonel Simpson paid Captain Robert Salter one hundred pounds, to be applied to raising a company of infantry to join Governor Tryon's expedition against the Regulators. Benjamin Randall was paid forty shillings, as bounty on the service against the Regulators. Having determined to march against the Regulators, Governor Tryon left New Bern April 22d, and arrived at Colonel Bryan's, 100 miles from New Bern, May 1st, with the troops from the eastern counties. There he was joined by the troops from the Wilmington District on the 3d. The next day he reviewed them in the meadow at Smith's Ferry, one company from Pitt under Capt. Robert Salter being among them. On the 4th, the march was taken up for Hillsborough, going by way of Johnston Court-house. On the night of the 7th, the Pitt Company served as pickets, and next day as baggage guard. On the 15th, they were at Camp Alamance and line of battle was formed for the morrow. In the assignments of surgeons, the Pitt company, with those of Beaufort, Carteret, Craven, Dobbs, and the Rangers, was under Dr. Haslin. The next day, May 16th, 1771, was fought the battle of Alamance. The Pitt Company was very probably with the others from the New Bern District, under Colonel Leach, occupying the right on the front line. Governor Tryon had about 1,100 men, the Regulators being estimated at something like 2,000, with few guns, most of them having clubs, or unwieldly and useless weapons. The fight continued for some time, but could only result in the defeat of the Regulators, who lost more than 100 killed and wounded, while the troops lost nine killed and about sixty wounded. Thus was fought the first battle of Liberty—was shed the first blood for Liberty—in the colonies, and Pitt County, which was afterwards so devoted to the cause of Liberty, fought on the side of royalty.

Officers were not much better in collecting and turning in public moneys then than are some now. In the report for 1771 is found that 66,443 pounds and 9 pence are due the Colony. Of this amount Pitt was behind by sheriffs as follows: Abraham Tyson, 518 pounds, 13 shillings and 3 pence for 1765 (judgment and execution); George Moye, 61 pounds, 7 shillings and 9 pence for 1766 (execution); William Moore, 230 pounds and 3 shillings for 1769 and 301 pounds for 1770; making 1010 pounds and 3 shillings for Pitt County.

Pitt had now grown to such importance that a permanent town and good court-house were wanted. Richard Evans and Alex. Stewart were its members in the Assembly, and on the 3d of January, 1771, Mr. Evans introduced a bill for a town on his lands. It failed at this session, but was passed at the December, following, session. In transmitting a report of the laws of the session to Lord Hillsborough, Governor Martin said, "The place is considered to be convenient for trade and a town being in request among the people of the county I was induced to pass this act for its erection and to accept the compliment designed to me by its name." The town was named Martinborough.

CHAPTER EIGHT.

OFFICIAL CORRUPTION—BLUE LAWS—COUNTY OFFICERS—THE "JOHN AND ELIZABETH" SCHOONER AFFAIR—FEW TAXES PAID—MILITIA OFFICERS—MARTINBOROUGH—REVOLUTIONARY PROCEEDINGS—PITT FREEHOLDERS ISSUE A DECLARATION OF RIGHTS—STANDING COMMITTEE APPOINTED.

During the beginning of Governor Josiah Martin's administration, the same troubles that caused the trouble and battle of Alamance continued, though not so greatly as during that of Governor Tryon. Officers continued to collect unlawful fees, though Governor Martin issued proclamations against it and forbid such.

In order to aid the promotion of religion, virtue, morality and upbuild, he also issued a proclamation, demanding the "discovery and effectual prosecution of all persons who shall be guilty of drunkenness, blasphemy, profane swearing and cursing, lewdness, profanation of the Lord's day, or other dissolute, immoral or disorderly practices." Despite all efforts to stop oppression, it continued and the people were growing more and more in opposition to the royal government.

A list of the officers for Pitt County at this time shows that Edward Salter was clerk of the court; John Simpson, register, and also colonel of the militia; Dempsey Grimes, coroner.

In 1769 John Simpson's schooner, the "John and Elizabeth," sailed from Port Royal, Jamaica, for home, with a valuable cargo. Bad weather drove it to Vera Cruz, Mexico, where it was seized by the Spaniards and held until February 6th, 1772, when it was ordered to leave. Reaching Havana, the crew embarked on another ship, the sloop "Sally," for North Carolina, arriving in Pasquotank in April. They told a tale of suffering, imprisonment and robbery, and

BLOUNT'S HALL,
Home of Wm. Blount, still standing in Pitt County.

Simpson asked the governor to have these wrongs redressed. The crew seems to have returned with much money and that aroused suspicion. Ebenezer Fuller, the master of the schooner, soon left the Colony. Ichabod Simpson, brother to John Simpson, was mate. The result of the investigation was an incrimination of the crew and Simpson never recovered any damages.

A report to the Assembly at New Bern, March 5th, 1773, showed that 892 pounds and 18 shillings were still due from the sheriffs of Pitt County on the public taxes, as follows: George Moye, 61 pounds, 7 shillings and 9 pence; William Moore, 333 pounds and 8 shillings; Robert Salter, 498 pounds, 2 shillings and 3 pence. These, in a measure, show the opposition of the people to the burdensome taxes of those times. The Receiver General's, (John Rutherford) report showed that Pitt County had paid no quit rents, arrears of quit rents, fines, forfeitures, and other incomes, from March 25th, 1772, to the same date 1773. Another report showed none collected for the two years previous.

The field return of the regiment of Pitt militia at a general muster on the 18th of November, 1773, showed seven companies present with 566 men. One company was not represented. Three companies reported 30 men absent. The commissioned officers were John Tyson, Colonel; Amos Atkinson, Lieutenant-Colonel, and Aaron Tyson, Major. The returns were signed by John Simpson, Colonel, and John Leslie, Adjutant.

The act for a town on the lands of Richard Evans on Tar River had never been carried out, and in 1774 a supplementary act was passed providing for that town, by the name of Martinborough. The act also provided for the sale of lots by lottery and the removal of the court-house, prison and stocks and making it the county town.

During all these times the feelings between the colonies and England were growing more bitter. A meeting was held in Wilmington, July 21st, 1774, and a call issued for a general meeting to be held at Johnston court-house on the 20th of August. Some counties appointed delegates to that meeting, but it was not held. Counties began holding revolutionary meetings, Rowan holding the first, August 8th, with Craven following on August 9th, Johnston on the 12th, Pitt and Granville on the 15th, and others soon thereafter, all appointing delegates to a general convention of the colony to be held at New Bern on the 25th. Governor Martin protested against these meetings as "derogatory to the dignity of his Majesty and his Parliament, and tending to excite Clamour, and discontent among the King's subjects." He also issued a proclamation, requiring all officers to prohibit and prevent such meetings and especially that to be held at New Bern.

The *Minutes of the meeting at Martinborough are as follows:

"NORTH CAROLINA,
"PITT COUNTY, August 15th, 1774.

"At a general meeting of the freeholders of the county aforesaid at the town of Martinborough, John Hardee, Esq., in the chair,

"*Resolved,* That as the Constitutional Assembly of this Colony are prevented from exercising their rights of providing for the security of the liberties of the people, that right again reverts to the people as the foundation from whence all power and legislation flow.

"*Resolved,* That John Simpson and Edward Salter, Esqrs., do attend at the town of New Bern on the 25th instant in general Convention of this Province and there to exert their utmost abilities preventing the growing system of ministerial Despotism which now threatens the destruction of American Liberties, and that you our deputies may be acquainted with the sentiments of the people of this county, it is their opinion, that you proceed to choose proper persons to represent this Province in a General Congress of America to

---
*The Minutes of the proceedings of the Committee of Safety were long on file in the Court House, but have disappeared. Some years ago this writer made a copy for his own use, and has preserved them.

meet at such time and place as may be hereafter agreed on. That these delegates be instructed to a declaration of American rights setting forth that British America and all its inhabitants shall be and remain in due subjection to the Crown of England and to the illustrious family of the throne, Submitting by their own voluntary act, and enjoying all their free chartered rights and liberties as British free subjects. That it is the first law of Legislation and of the British Constitution that no man be taxed but by his consent, Expressed by himself or by his legal Representatives.

"On motion the said meeting was then dissolved."

October 4th, another meeting was held and a standing committee for the county was appointed, consisting of John Hardee, John Simpson, Robert Salter, Edward Salter, William Bryant, Edmond Williams, Benjamin May, George Evans and Amos Atkinson, any five of whom were to be a quorum for the transaction of business. The committee met again on the 27th and elected John Hardee chairman, and Edward Salter, clerk. They adjourned to meet the first Thursday in November.

CHAPTER NINE.

HELP FOR BOSTON—DONATIONS ASKED—COMMITTEE ELECTED AS DIRECTED BY THE CONTINENTAL CONGRESS—MEMBERS—THE SALT QUESTION—PROVINCIAL CONGRESS AT NEW BERN—COURT-HOUSE—VERMIN.

The first business that occupied the committee at its November meeting was the condition of the people of Boston, and "On motion, the Committee Considering the present un-

THE WILLIAMS HOUSE,
Where President Washington dined when in Greenville on his southern tour.

happy situation of the inhabitants of the town of Boston, and the miserable distress the poor inhabitants of said town are reduced to by the effects of the late acts of Parliament blocking up the port and harbor of the said town of Boston, and the poor of said town can not exist nor support themselves and families without the assistance of the neighboring collinys, in order to relieve and support said poor of Boston, as far as our situation and circumstances admit, we appoint John Hardee, Esq., Wm. Bryant, John Knoles, Jr., James Gorham, Samuel Calhoun, John Page, John Williams, Henry Ellis, George Evans, George Moye, William Travis, James Armstrong, Robert Salter, James Latham, David Perkins, Godfrey Stansel, John Tison, Allen Sugg, Aaron Tison, Charles Forbes, James Brooks, Jacob Blount and Laz Paine to assist the gentlemen of the vestry of St. Michael's Parish in collecting for the support of the said sufferers in said town of Boston, from such generous persons of this county as may give by subscription for support of said sufferers, such persons with the vestry to have subscription for that purpose, payable to the committee heretofore mentioned, them or either of them, they and each of them keeping a plain and regular acount of what they receive and to give each person a receipt for said donation, and to furnish this committee of this county with a copy or the original of each of their accounts for their inspection and correction, which donations are to be collected from each receiver by the direction of the said committee, to be shipped for the benefit of said Poore of Boston to any port on the continent, that the committee may think most Beneficial all the net proceeds thereof to be ordered into the hands of the committee appointed to receive the several donations from the different countys, towns, etc., on the continent in said town of Boston.

"*Resolved,* That this committee wil be thankful to any person or persons for any advice that may be of service to the committee in general.

"*Resolved,* That the proceedings of this committee be open for the inspection of any Inhabitants of this county, they, he or she being a friend to the freedom of American Liberty.

"Ordered that John Hardee, John Simpson, and Edward Salter acquaint the standing committee of this province, that a committee of this county hath formed themselves, and are ready to communicate and receive advice from them.

"The committee then adjourned till this day two weeks."

The Committee met again on the 17th. An abstract of the proceedings of the Continental Congress, recently held at Philadelphia, was presented and read. Another meeting was called and advertised for December 9th, for electing a number of persons as a "committee" as required by a resolution of the Continental Congress. At the December, 9th, meeting the following were elected to constitute that committee, agreeable to the directions of the congress: John Hardee, James Lockhart, Benjamin May, William Travis, James Armstrong, Frederick Gibble, Amos Atkinson, William Robson, Edmond Williams, John Knowles, James Gorham, John Simpson, James Lanier, George Evans, Ichabod Simpson, Edward Salter, Peter Rives, William Bryant, Robert Salter, David Perkins, James Latham and Joseph Gainer.

The newly elected Committee then met on same day. John Simpson was elected chairman. The following is the account of their proceedings:

"The Association of the Continental Congress held at the Cittie of Philada. on 20th, Oct. Past was exhibited and read—

"*Resolved,* That this committee doth approve of said Assotiation.

"WHEREAS there is many complaints that the Trading Vessels and others have raised on the price of Salt, occasioned by the scarcity of that article, which is contrary to the resolution of the Continental Congress that traders are not to take an advantage of the scarcity of Goods—the committee therefore recommend that salt should not be sold for more than three shillings four pence per bushel at Gorham's landing and above and below that place in proportion with freight and loss; any person acting contrary to the same will be deemed an enemie to his country.

"The committee adjourned till 28th day of Jan Next."

The first Provincial Congress in North Carolina met at New Bern, August 25th, with a majority of the counties represented. It was in session three days. After many indictments of the English colonial governments, though professing all due allegiance to the King, all the rights and privileges of British subjects were demanded, and unless granted it was resolved that after January, 1775. to import nothing from England, and that after November, 1775, to export nothing to that country, and declared it would "break" with any colony that refused to obey the Continental Congress. It elected William Hooper, Joseph Howes and Richard Caswell delegates to the Continental Congress, to meet at Philadelphia.

The Assembly this year appointed George Evans, Charles Forbes, Henry Ellis, Benjamin May and William Roberson, commissioners to contract with workmen for the removal of the court-house, prison and stocks to Martinborough. Courts were to be held at the house of John Leslie, in Martinborough, until the removal could be completed.

The act for destroying "vermin" was extended to Pitt and other counties, not before included.

The close of the year 1774 saw practically a state of conflict between the people and the royal governments in the colonies. Though there had been no bloodshed, indications were that it might be shed at any time and the people of North Carolina, the people of Pitt County, were preparing for what might follow.

CHAPTER TEN.

COMMITTEE OF SAFETY PROCEEDINGS—DEPUTIES TO PROVINCIAL CONGRESS ELECTED—THREE OBSTRUCTIONISTS—ACTS OF CONTINENTAL CONGRESS APPROVED—JOHN TISON, TORY—HELP FOR BOSTON—PROVINCIAL CONGRESS AND ASSEMBLY—SECOND DECLARATION OF RIGHTS—REV. MR. BLOUNT—PATROLLERS—ATKINSON AND SHEPPARD.

There is no record of a meeting of the Committee of Safety January 28th, 1775, according to the adjournment of the meeting of December 9th, 1774, the next meeting of record being on February 11th, 1775. The only business of this meeting was to authorize John Simpson to write North for a vessel to carry the donations from the county to Boston, and to call and advertise for a meeting for March 10th, next, to elect deputies to represent the county in the next Provincial Congress.

At that meeting John Simpson, Edward Salter, James Gorham, James Lanier and William Robson were elected deputies. The "Resolves" of the committee for Craven County were read and approved. The Committee having been informed that Amos Atkinson, Solomon Sheppard and John Tison had "in many Instances Obstructed the Contribution for the Relief of the poore of Boston, etc., Ordered that the Chairman Address the Sd Gentlemen, so they may appear at the next Meet'g of the Committee, and Justifie Themselves in that Particular.

"Adjourned till the 24th of this month."

The Committee met on the 24th and adjourned on the 20th of April, of which, if there was a meeting, there is no record, the next being that of May 1st, of which the following is the acount of the proceedings:—

"The association of the Continental Congress lately held at Philadelphia was produced and read.

"Resolved unanimously by every member of this committee that we and every one of us do highly approve and will strictly observe the said Resolves in Testimony whereof Each Member subscribes the same.

Youre most Obt Servts
Wm Blount

"It having been represented to this committee that John Tison hath frequently spoken disrespectfully of the proceedings of the Congress in general and of this committee in particular, on a supposition that such charge is true, it must be owned that the said Tison highly deserves to be stigmatized, but as it is not yet reduced to a certainty whether he is guilty or not or if he is, may have proceeded from unguarded heat or Ignorance and as it is the firm attention of this committee to proceed in their censures with charity and circumspection, it is therefore ordered that Mr. George Evans, Mr. James Lockhart and Mr. Benjamin May or either two of them do attend the said John Tison to remonstrate, cite him to appear before this committee when it shall next sit on the 13th day of this present Inst. then and there to answer the above charge." The committee met on the 13th and simply adjourned to the 20th, at which time it met and among other business

"Resolved that John Tison be advertised in the public papers."

At the meeting May 27th, the chairman received for the use of the town of Boston from William Robeson 12 shillings, William Bryant and Avent Pope 20 shillings, James Robeson 1 shilling.

To the Provincial Congress that met in New Bern, April 3d, Pitt sent James Gorham, James Lanier, William Robeson, John Simpson and Edward Salter. This Congress "most Heartily" approved of the acts of the Continental Congress and pledged its support for all measures advocated by it. William Hooper, Joseph Hewes and Richard Caswell were appointed delegates to the General Congress to be held at Philadelphia on the 10th of May, and it was recommended that each county raise the sum of twenty pounds for the purpose of paying the expenses of the delegates.

The Assembly met at New Bern on the 4th of April. To this Assembly Pitt sent John Simpson and Edward Salter. Thus these two men were, at the same time, members of two different Assemblies that were opposed or hostile to each other in intent.

The Committee met June 10th and called a meeting for the 23d, for the purpose of electing such persons as might be deemed proper, to carry into execution the "Resolves" of the General Congress. The "Resolves" of the Craven County Committee were read and approved. At the meeting of the 23d, held at the house of John Leslie, many members were added to the committee, to assist in carrying out the resolves of Congress.

The Committee met next on July 1st and passed the following resolution:

"We the freeholders and inhabitants of the county of Pitt and town of Martinborough, being deeply affected with the present alarming state of this Province and all America—Do Resolve that we will pay all due allegiance to his majesty King George the third and endeavor to continue the succession of his crown in the Illustrious house of Hanover as by law established, against the present or any future wicked ministry, or arbitrary set of men whatsoever, at the same time we are determined to assert our rights as men and sensible that by the late acts of Parliament the most valuable Liberties and privileges of America are invaded and endeavor to be violated and destroyed and that under God the preservation of them depends on a firm union of the inhabitants and a sturdy spirited observation of the Resolutions of the General Congress, being shocked at the cruel scenes now acting in the Massachusetts Bay and determined never to become slaves to any power upon earth, we do hereby agree and associate under all tyes of Religion, Honour, and regard for Posterity that we will adopt and endeavor to execute the measures which the General Congress now sitting at Philadelphia conclude on for preserving our constitution and opposing the execution of the several arbitrary Illegal acts of the British Parliament and that we will readily observe The Directions of our General Committee for the purpose aforesaid, the Preservation of Peace and Good Order and Security of Individuals and private property," which was signed by

87 members. The committee also adopted rules of order for conduct of its meetings. Patrolers were appointed for the proper control of slaves. Any slave found off his master's premises without a pass, was liable to thirty-nine lashes or perhaps less. It was resolved that the Rev. Mr. Blount should "preach in the Court-House of Martinborough on................." it was also resolved "That the 20th day of this Inst., be Observed as a day of Publick Fasting and Humiliation agreeable to the appointment of the Continental Congress & that Reverend Mr. Blount by desire of the chairman to Preach a Sermon at the Court House in Martinborough Suitable to the Occasion."

The Committee met July 8th, and authorized the patrolers to shoot any number of negroes who were armed and did not readily submit and gave them discretionary power to shoot any number of negroes above four who were off their master's plantation and would not submit. Any negro so killed was to be paid for out of a poll tax on all the taxable negroes in the county.

At the meeting of July 17th, Amos Atkinson and Solomon Sheppard appeared and acquitted themselves of the accusations of disloyalty charged against them at the meeting of March 10th. Some of the companies previously organized reported the election of officers.

CHAPTER ELEVEN.

Negro Insurrection—Measures to Prevent It—White Man Instigator—No Lives Lost, but Negroes Whipped—Delegates to Hillsboro—Raising Troops—Military Districts and Officers—Justices Qualify—Trouble About Rev. Mr. Blount.

While preparations were being so actively made to meet a foreign foe, as England was then considered, a worse foe was to be found at home. It was a slave insurrection, no doubt fostered and welcomed by the enemies of American liberty. Accounts of it are meagre, and as it did not really occur, it is best told in a letter of John Simpson to Richard Cogdell, chairman of the Craven County Committee, under date of July 15th, 1775. He wrote as follows: "* * * Our Committee met the .... Inst., when the Express arrived from Mr. Edward Salter giving us account of a discovery that was made in Beaufort County by one of Mr. Dayner and one of Captain Respess negro men unto Capt. Thomas Respess of an intended insurrection of the negroes against the whole people which was to be put into execution that night. We immediately sent off an Express to Tarborough to alarm the inhabitants there, we then proceeded to busines and appointed upwards of one hundred men as patrolers and passed a resolve that any negroes that should be destroyed by them or any person in company with them in apprehending should be paid for by a tax on the negroes in this county. We then separated to sound the alarm through this county and apprehend the suspected heads. By night we had in custody and in goal near forty under proper guard. Sunday the committee sett and proceeded to examine into the affair and find it a deep laid Horrid Tragick Plan laid for destroying the inhabitants of this province without respect of persons, age or sex. By negro evidence it appears that Capt. .... Johnson of

White Haven, who hath just loaded his Brigg with Naval Stores for that port, in consort with Merrick, a negro man slave who formerly belonged to Major Clark a Pilot at Okacock but now to Capt. Nath Blinn of Bath Town propagated the contagion. * * * The contagion has spread beyond the waters. There are five negroes * * * were whipt this day by order.

"Monday—The Committee sat. Ordered several to be severely whipt and sentenced several to receive 80 lashes each to have both Ears crap'd which was executed in the presence of the Committee and a great number of spectators. In the afternoon we received by express from Coll. Blount * * * of * * * negroes being in arms on the line of Craven and Pitt and prayed assistance of men and ammunition which we readily granted. We posted guards upon the roads for several miles that night. Just as I got home came one of Mr. Nelson's sons from Pometo (near Mr. Harlan's mill) and informed me of 250 negroes that had been pursued for several days but none taken nor seen tho' they were several times fired at. Had he been at Martinborough he would have received pay for his negroes. On Tuesday we sent off two companies of Light Horse, one to Lower and one to Upper Swift Creek Bridge in order to find from whence the report arose and found the author to be a negro wench of William Taylor's on Clay Root, with design to kill her master and mistress and Lay it upon those negroes. She has received severe correction. Since that we have remained as quiet as we could from the nature of things. We keep taking up, examining and scourging more or less every day; From whichever part of the County they come they all confess nearly the same thing, viz, that they were one and all on the night of the 8th inst to fall on and destroy the family where they lived, then to proceed from House to House (Burning as they went) until they arrived in the back country where they were to be received with by a number of Persons there appointed and armed by the Government for their protection, and as a further reward they were to be settled in a free government of their own.

"Capt. Johnson its said was heard to say that he'd return in the fall and take choice of the Plantations upon this River."

In a postscript to the letter he said considerable ammunition was found when disarming the negroes. Thus was timely checked a plot of murder and rapine that might have been worse than that of the Indians of 1712.

The Committee met on the 21st of July and adjourned to the 29th.

To the Provincial Congress at Hillsboro Pitt sent John Simpson, Robert Salter, William Bryan, James Gorham and James Latham. This Congress professed loyalty to the King, but denied the right of taxation without representation and made preparations for war. A provisional government was organized and the control of the colony passed from that of the royalists to that of the people. Samuel Johnston, by virtue of being chairman of the Provincial Council was *de facto* Governor.

The Congress at Hillsboro ordered two regiments, of five hundred men each, to be raised. In each district ten companies, of fifty men each, were ordered raised, these ten companies to form a battalion and to be known as Minute Men. In the New Bern District Richard Caswell was made Colonel; William Bryan, Lieutenant Colonel; James Gorham, Major. William Bryan was from Craven; James Gorham was from Pitt. Robert Salter was appointed Commissary for the New Bern District. The colony had some time before been divided into six Superior Court Districts and these military and other districts were the same as the old Superior Court Districts. The Militia Field Officers of Pitt were John Simpson, Colonel; Robert Salter, Lieutenant Colonel; George Evans, First Major; James Armstrong, Second Major. In proportioning the Minute Men to be raised, one Company was to be from Pitt, out of sixty to be raised in the colony. Committees of Safety for each District were appointed and Edward Salter was a member for the New Bern District.

When the people of Pitt became so active in their opposition to the Royal Government, Governor Martin appointed new Justices of the Peace for the County. Those new appointees refused to recognize themselves as Justices, and the need of them, to carry on the business of the courts and other public duties, made the Provincial Congress recommend that they qualify, which of course they then did.

At a meeting of the Committee some time in August, some of those who had "Received Apart" subscriptions for the relief of Boston, were ordered to refund to those who had donated. The matter of the employment of Rev. Nathaniel Blount to serve the parish for twenty years was giving trouble, and he was given notice that he could withdraw from the agreement. There were perhaps too few of his members for the other churches to be satisfied. His withdrawal was considered "the only method to Unite the People of the County." At a meeting on the 23d, over eighty new members signed or pledged themselves to abide by the acts of the Committee.

SKETCHES OF PITT COUNTY.   69

CHAPTER TWELVE.

COMMITTEE MEETS—HILLSBOROUGH RESOLVES—JOHN TISON, PATRIOT—DELEGATES TO PROVINCIAL CONGRESS—COMMITTEE OF SECRECY, INTELLIGENCE AND OBSERVATION—PAY FOR PROVISIONS—AMMUNITION BOUGHT—SALT—PAY FOR AMMUNITION—ALLOWANCES TO TROOPS—PREPARATIONS FOR WAR.

The Committee met September 9th. John Tison, Esq., was notified to attend the next meeting to answer the different allegations made against him. Some new patrolers were appointed, and it was ordered that "no Parson Act in any Publick Cappassity without signing the Association."

The Committee met on the 23d and had the Resolves of the Hillsboro Congress entered upon the Minutes, which recommended that a complete census of the inhabitants, giving age, color, sex, polls, etc., be taken. The freeholders were advertised to meet on the third Tuesday in October to elect not more than five persons to represent the county in the next Provincial Congress, and also to elect twenty-one or more persons to act as a Committee for the County. John Tison, who had been notified to appear before the Committee, to answer charges of disloyalty and disrespect to the Committee, appeared, and swore allegiance.

At the meeting on the 24th Benjamin Bowers presented a list of those elected at an election held on the 17th. Those elected organized by electing John Simpson, chairman and Thomas Wolfenden, clerk. Sheriff Bowers also showed that by the returns of the same election that John Simpson, Edward Salter, and William Robeson were elected delegates to represent the County in the Provincial Congress for the ensuing year.

At the meeting on the 25th some action was taken regarding the neglect of duties by the road overseers. Permission was given Captain John Cooper to sue John Knox and to warrant Patrick Robeson. A "Select Committee of Secrecy, Intelligence and Observation" was appointed. It consisted of John Simpson, Arthur Forbes, William Robeson, George Evans, Simon Pope, Robert Salter and Thomas Wolfenden.

The Provincial Council met at the court house in Johnston County, this month (October). Among its resolutions was "Resolved that the Treasurers or either of them pay into the hands of Mr. Robert Salter Commissary of New Bern district the sum of five hundred pounds proclamation money to enable him to purchase provisions for the troops and that they be allowed in their Accounts with the Public."

At the meeting of November 11th, the chairman gave the information that a quantity of powder and ball had been received. It was turned over to that "Committee of Secrecy, Intelligence and Observation." It seems the vessel bringing the powder and ball had been seized and the full amount was not delivered. At the next meeting, December 16th, Captain Paule White, whose vessel was seized and who sold the powder and ball, presenting his *account as follows:

					£450	0	0
To 717 lbs of powder @ 5s	£179	5	0				
To 1,782 lbs of Lead @ 63s	56	2	6				
To 8 casks for the Lead @ 2s	16	0					
To 2 hogsheads for the powder@11s	1	2	0				
	237	5	1				
75 pr ct advance pr agreement	177	19	2				
					£415	4	8
					£865	4	8

The account was allowed and a copy ordered sent to the Provincial Council for approval. On complaint of John Bowers that John Brady owed him, but had left the County, and that James Brady and William Brady owed John Brady enough to pay the debt, it was ordered that they pay

---

*This account is a copy of the original.

Bowers. Merchants were solicited not to sell salt above five shillings a bushel except under certain circumstances. Being informed that Captain Paule White had a quantity of powder, Colonel Robert Salter and Arthur Forbes were instructed to secure it.

The Provincial Council met at the court house in Johnston, on the 18th of December. Among the first business was the payment to John Simpson, Edward and Robert Salter, the sum of £864 4s 8d for the Captain White account. It seems that Captain White got to Ocracoke with the powder and lead, when he was captured by a British warship, but he succeeded in getting away with some of his cargo, which was brought to Martinborough and bought by the committee.

In addition to the rations already allowed the troops, the Continental Congress recommended that the following be allowed additional: "Three pints of peas or beans per week, or vegetables equivalent, rating the peas or beans at a dollar per Bushel; one pint of milk per day, or at the rate of 1/12 of a dollar per pint; half a pint of rice or one pint of Indian Meal per man per week; one quart of spruce beer or cyder per man or nine gallons of Molasses per Company of one hundred men per week; three pounds of candles to one hundred men per week for Guards; twenty-four pounds soft, or eight pounds of hard soap per one hundred men per week." All this was allowed and in addition, the sum of two pence per day to each man, to be paid by the commissaries and allowed them in settlements.

This has been an eventful year with the people of Pitt County. Always professing allegiance to the King of England, they had steadily prepared to absolve that allegiance. They had practically made the first Declaration of Independence, and had taken charge of the county affairs. The Committee of Safety had grown from a few men to two hundred or more, and more names were being added at nearly every meeting. Its men had met every question of State and were taking part in the birth of a new nation that was to become great, greater, and at last the greatest of all nations.

Robert Salter was Commissary of the New Bern District; James Gorham, Major of the Minute Men for the same district; Edward Salter was a member of the Committee of Safety for the same district. The County Committee had taken charge of the County affairs and it would seem that a new era had already dawned. The people, through their representatives had pledged themselves to stand by the declarations of the Provincial Congress, and that Congress had pledged itself to stand by the declarations of the Continental Congress. So Independence was practically had, though no formal declaration had been made by any duly delegated authorities, except that of Mecklenburg and quasi resolves of other counties.

There was no mistaking war. At Lexington the first blood had been shed, and in our own North Carolina patriotic blood was hot for the conflict. North Carolina soldiers were camping in other States. And the people of Pitt County were with the foremost in the struggle that was at hand.

SKETCHES OF PITT COUNTY.   73

CHAPTER THIRTEEN.

Pitt Members of District Committee—Capt. James
    Armstrong—Test and Pledge—Supplies Bought—
    Pitt at Battle of Moore's Creek—More Patrollers
    —Salt—Delinquents—Daniel Fore—Bounty Money
    —Arthur Moore—Mr. Carson, Dancing Master—
    Delegates to Halifax—Instructions for Independ-
    ence—John Simpson.

The principal events in the County during 1776 were the meetings of the Committee and preparations for resisting British power. The Committee seems to have become or to have been succeeded, by a regular county government by the end of the year.

A meeting of the District Committee was held at New Bern, beginning January 16th. Edward Salter was the member from Pitt. Roger Ormond, of Beaufort, having died, John Simpson was elected in his stead, thus giving Pitt two members on the Committee. Salt was a very important article and difficult to get. The Committee had control of its distribution and sale. The District Committee ordered eight hundred bushels sent to Martinborough, to be sold by the County Committee.

The County Committee met on the 23d. A "certificate" was issued to Captain James Armstrong, who had raised a Company of Minute Men. Major George Evans was authorized to raise a Company, which should choose its own officers and after twelve months training, be placed under the authority of the Provincial Congress, which should provide for them and pay for their services. The chairman was ordered to receipt for arms received from Robert Jameson, for the use of the Continental Army. The Captains of the militia were ordered to see that the people signed the pledge and test to the committee. The chairman laid before the Committee a letter from District Committee relating to John Tison, which was ordered filed. He also produced receipt from Majors Batton and Gorham for a quantity of ammunition. He reported that he had received 150 1-2 yards of _____ and was ordered to pay Rother Leathem 16d per yard. Also a letter and receipt for powder, from the Edenton District Committee. Mr. Pettit and Mr. Kennady were ordered to choose persons to settle their affairs.

Donald McDonald, a Scottish Highlander, who had settled in Cumberland County, received a commission from Governor Martin, who was aboard the British ship of war, Cruiser, at Wilmington, raised the royal standard and soon had about fifteen hundred men enlisted. They were from the Cape Fear section. Learning this, an emergency meeting of the New Bern District was held February 10th. It seems that the members from Pitt did not know of this meeting, as neither attended. Colonel Caswell was ordered to march immediately with the Minute Men under his command, and join other forces that might be on the same expedition to suppress the insurrection. The Colonels of Dobbs, Johnston, Craven and Pitt, were ordered to enlist as many of the militia as was necessary and join the Minute Men under Colonel Caswell. The committees of Dobbs and Pitt were instructed to furnish Colonel Caswell as much powder and lead as they could.

The battle of Moore's Creek was fought February 27th, 1776, and was the first American victory for Independence. Richard Caswell, who commanded the Minute Men and militia from the eastern counties mentions those from New Bern, Craven, Johnston, Dobbs and Wake, but says nothing of those from Pitt under Captain John Salter, who joined his army, and are next mentioned in the defense of Wilmington. In this battle about 1,100 Americans fought 1,600 Tories. The Americans were on the south side of the creek and had removed the planks of the bridge. The Tories attempted to cross and many were killed. The Americans then forded the creek and attacked in the rear, making a complete victory, killing about thirty, taking 900 prisoners, among whom was General McDonald, 2,000 stands of arms and £15,000 in gold.

The Committee for the County met February 13th, appointed many more patrollers and attended to other matters; among them the salt sent up by the District Committee was ordered sold in small quantities at five shillings per bushel, by Thomas Wolfenden, who had the power to swear any one whom he suspected of applying for more than their necessity demanded; also that he deliver Colonel Robert Salter one hundred bushels for the use of the army and no salt was to be sold any one who had not signed the "Test" or did it before the delivery of the salt.

The Committee was probably in session several days, but the next meeting of record was on the 17th. Lists of men drafted under the recent orders from the District Committee, to meet the Minute Men of Dobbs, were presented and the clerk was instructed to furnish to the officers of the several companies, the names of the delinquents that they might be summoned to appear at Martinborough on the second Saturday in March, to show cause for their action—why they did not join the other troops under Lieutenant Robert Salter, agreeable to orders.

The Committee adjourned to March 2d, when all the business seems to have been to order Daniel Fore before the Committee to answer some expression he had made. It then adjourned to the 16th, when it was ordered that the salt sent by the District Committee be sold in small quantities "at Publick Vandue" on the 26th.

The defense of New Bern being a matter of much concern to several of the District Committee, they held two "emergency" meetings, one on the 10th and another on the 15th, both of which were approved by the full Committee on the 22d. Robert Jamison having advanced one hundred and twenty-five pounds, bounty money, to the Minute Men of Captain James Armstrong's Company, the public treasurer was ordered to pay it.

At the meeting of the 23d, Arthur Moore was ordered sent to Halifax to answer some charges against him. Captain Bowers was allowed to take bond for Moore, who was then in jail. Major Gorham presented a petition in behalf of the County for the discharge of Mr. Carson, from teaching dancing. He also asked that the families of the militia and Minute Men be supplied with corn at 13s. 4d. per barrel. Both petitions were granted.

At the April (29th) meeting, leave to bring suits was granted to several and Daniel Fore appeared before the Committee and was acquitted.

The Provincial Congress met at Halifax, April 4th. Pitt sent John Simpson, Edward Salter and William Robeson. This was one of the most important assemblies ever held in North Carolina, and was held at one of the most critical periods of our history. Many able and experienced men were members.

On the 12th, the Congress instructed the delegates, William Hooper, Joseph Hewes and John Penn, to concur with the delegates from the other colonies in declaring for Independence, forming alliances, and making all provisions for maintaining Independence; but reserved the right to make its own Constitution and laws, of appointing delegates and adjusting its own affairs. The thanks of the Congress were returned to Colonel Richard Caswell and the "brave officers and soldiers under his command" for their bravery and service rendered their country at the battle of Moore's Creek. James Gorham and Benjamin May were elected officials to receive, procure and purchase firearms and ammunition, in Pitt County, for the use of the troops. It was resolved to raise 1,500 men in the four Districts of Edenton, New Bern, Halifax and Wilmington, and of these fifty were Pitt's allotment. In the election of a Committee of Safety for the State, John Simpson, with James Coor, was elected for the New Bern District.

The meeting of the County Committee on June 29th, was unimportant and little was done. The meetings of July 13th, and of August 10th, were very much like the preceding. Permission to sue was the principal business. And with these meetings the County Committee of Safety seems to have disappeared from our history. It was probably succeeded by a regular and better organized and working County government.

CHAPTER FOURTEEN.

Provincial Council—Pitt Company at Wilmington—Officers—Returns of Men—Independence—John Hunter—Delegates to Halifax—More Troops—Equipment of Soldiers—James Salter—Enlistment in Other States—Justices of the Peace—Royalists Plot—Lack of Arms—Two Vagabond Young Men—Protest Against General Moore—The Assembly.

The Provincial Committee, or Council, as it was now called, of Safety met at Wilmington, June 7th. It had much to do, and it did much. A considerable force had been concentrated about Wilmington. It was so formidable that Governor Martin had seen fit to sail with the British fleet for Charleston. A brigade from the New Bern District was there; one of its companies was from Pitt. The Council appointed John Salter, Captain; Josiah Little, Lieutenant; Luke Bates, Ensign for those from Pitt. The regiment was under the command of Brigadier-General Ashe and the returns for July 31st for Captain Robert Salter's Company were: present fit for duty, 47 men; total officers and men, 58; none sick, one deserted; 25 pounds of powder; 100 pounds of lead; guns fixed, 43. Not another company returned any powder and lead. The regiment had 659 men; but only returned 447 fit for duty.

The Provincial Council met at Halifax July 21st. On next day news of the Declaration of Independence by the Continental Congress reached the Council. The Council simply had the Declaration read and ordered it to be proclaimed in the most public manner, that the people might hear the great and good news as early as possible.

The prisoners who were considered the most dangerous to liberty were closely confined in jails. John Hunter, one who had been active in these matters, had been taken while on a cruise about Ocracoke looking for small vessels. He was then confined in Martinborough jail. He became tired of being "confined in the narrow limits of this town, deprived of all Company," and wrote the Council accordingly. There is no record of a reply. The Provincial Congress met at Halifax, November 12th. Pitt sent as its representatives, Benjamin May, William Robeson, James Gorham, George Evans and Edward Salter. Richard Caswell was made President and James Green, Secretary. This Congress formed a Constitution, provided for a permanent government and ushered the Colony of North Carolina into the State of North Carolina.

Provision was made for raising more troops, and among the officers of one of the companies to be raised in the New Bern District were James May, Captain; James Lanier, Jr., Ensign; both from Pitt. The equipments of a soldier was to consist of a "good gun, cartouch box, shot bag and powder horn, a cutlass or tomahawk"; and when the soldier was not able to equip himself it was to be done at the public expense. Robert Salter having resigned as Commissary of the Second Regiment, James Salter was elected to succeed him.

At the December meeting of the Council of Safety, the matter of the enlisting a number of soldiers, by the Continental officers, who had been sent to aid South Carolina in the regiments of that State and Georgia, was considered. By this North Carolina was robbed of the bounty advanced to them, and of that many, in making up its quota in the Continental Army and discredited with the other States. Effective steps were taken to prevent it in the future. At this time, there were one, or perhaps more, companies of Pitt County soldiers in South Carolina. Captain James Armstrong was about Charleston with his Company.

The following were appointed Justices of the Peace, by the Congress at Halifax, for the County: John Hardee, John Simpson, George Moye, Lazarus Pierce, Amos Atkinson, Peter Reaves, John Williams, Robert Salter, Edmund Williams, Frederick Gibble, John Bowers, James Lanier, David Perkins, William Hines, James Latham, and William Travis.

All officers were required to take a strict and strong oath to support the Constitution and laws of the State of North Carolina and to abide by every act of its authorities and to support the war for Independence.

Thus 1777 saw a change in conditions. There was no royal authority; it was the State of North Carolina, with a State government of its own people—self-government in truth and in fact,—with a Governor, Richard Caswell, with a Council, a Legislature of two Houses, an organized army in the field and county governments attending to local affairs.

Colonel Robert Salter was at Tarboro July 3d, where he got information that a plot had been formed in Martin and adjoining counties for the purpose of aiding the Royalists. They were, at a concerted time, to murder all the leading men and thus get possession of the State. It was feared they might get charge of the public magazines and leave the troops without ammunition. About thirty made an attempt to carry out their plan at Tarboro, but failed. Lieutenant Colonel Henry Irwin with twenty-five men captured them, disarmed them and made them take the oath of allegiance. It was said there was hardly a county in which some men were not concerned in this plot.

War was in progress over the whole country and the swarms of British troops continually landing in America made the calls for more patriot troops often and more urgent. Governor Caswell issued his call for drafts. In response to this, Colonel Simpson issued orders for a general muster of the militia at Martinborough. After this muster the militia was divided, but the trouble was the lack of arms. Some had sold them, some had had them impressed, and there were many who were unable to buy them. Colonel Simpson complained that such was not creditable to the appearance of his men. By some process of war, perhaps the disbanding of his men or other fortune of war, Major Gorham had become an officer without a command, and turned into the ranks. Colonel Simpson complained that such would be of no good, when there was a vacancy that he (Gorham) would have accepted.

In June James Spivey and sixteen others petitioned Governor Caswell for some redress against the depredations of William Lambort and Noah Smith White, "Two Vagobone young men, that Resorts our Neighborhood Near the line of Pitt and Dobbs, on little Contentney, as their manner of living is by pilfering and Stealing of Hogs, which has been proved against them, & sheep, & bells, & anything they Can, and doing Mischief to peoples Creatures, they both have been Drafted Twice, & run away, & lay out first in one County and then in the Other, till the Companyes Macht, & then they will skulk about and & be at their Mischief again." It is not known what redress was obtained.

In August there was a protest against the appointment of "a certain Doctor Hand, resident in Pennsylvania," as Brigadier General of North Carolina troops, to succeed General Moore, deceased. The protest was signed by sixteen of the Field Officers of the North Carolina troops, then at Trenton, New Jersey. Among those who signed was Colonel James Armstrong, of the Pitt Regiment. The North Carolina regiments were heavy losers in the campaigns about Philadelphia and in New Jersey. The Eighth Regiment was commanded by Colonel James Armstrong. Its losses were so heavy that it was so reduced that the remaining men were transferred to the Second Regiment under Colonel John Patten.

The first session of the first General Assembly of the State of North Carolina, was held at New Bern. It met April 7th and continued in session to May 9th. Pitt's representatives were, in the Senate, Robert Salter; in the House of Commons, William Robeson and John Williams. Robert Salter was a member of the Committee on Magazine, Stores and Provisions.

CHAPTER FIFTEEN.

No Senator—Supplies—Insolvents—Pitt's Quota—Sheriffs Fined—Simpson Succeeds Robeson—Falconer Succeeds Ascue—More Troops—Members of Assembly—Robert Salter—Robert Williams, Surgeon—Field Officers—Colonel Armstrong Wounded—Day of Fasting—Charleston—Money—Continental Army.

In the Assembly at New Bern, which met April 14th, 1778, Pitt seems to have had no representative in the Senate, as none appears on the roll. William Robeson and John Williams were again in the House.

The need of supplies of clothing for the army was very great. The matter of furnishing it was also a problem. To remedy the trouble, the Assembly passed an act requiring each county to furnish certain such supplies. The amount required of Pitt was, 25 hats, 105 yards of linen, 50 yards of woolen or double woven cotton cloth, 50 pairs of shoes and 50 pairs of stockings. This was repealed a little later, other provision having been made to secure such supplies. This Assembly allowed Benjamin Bowers, Sheriff of Pitt, seven pounds and sixteen shillings, for thirty-six insolvent taxables for the year 1774. An act was passed for completing the Continental Battalions from the State, many men still being required to fill the ranks. Pitt's part of the quota necessary under this act was 35, the whole from the State being 2,648.

At the May term of the District Superior Court, the sheriff of Pitt, and those of Beaufort, Carteret and Hyde were fined fifty pounds, each, for not attending the Court.

Having been elected Entry Taker for the County, William Robeson resigned his seat in the House of Commons and John Simpson succeeded him. A little later, John Simpson was elcted one of the Councillors of State.

Under date November 17th, John Simpson wrote Governor Caswell that Lieutenant Josiah Ascue who was unable to go with the men of the second draft, on account of a wound in his ankle, had procured a lad "to drive the cart or play the Fife," and wished to resign. He recommended the acceptance of the resignation and the appointment of George Falconer to succeed Lieutenant Ascue. The men of the second draft were to meet the next Monday and Lieutenant Falconer was wanted there at that time.

Still the need was more troops. Drafting men into service had become an every day business in all sections. In November, the Continental Congress asked for more troops. The Council advised Governor Caswell to immediately raise 1,324 men out of the militia, which, with the 2,648 already raised and the addition of the new levies and regulars then on furloughs, would complete the 5,000 required by the Congress for the aid of South Carolina and Georgia.

The Assembly met at Halifax, January 19th, 1779. The roll of members present at the opening showed Robert Salter as the Senator from Pitt, but the list of members given at the close of the session gives that of Edward Salter as the Senator. John Simpson and John Williams were again in the House. John Simpson having been elected a member of the Council of State, resigned and James Gorham was elected in his stead. The Assembly recommended Robert Salter, Recruiting Officer for Pitt (the Governor's Council having appointed him in 1777), to command the detachment of militia, which might be sent as an escort to the Commissioners for running the dividing line between North Carolina and Virginia.

Dr. Robert Williams was appointed Surgeon of the militia in March. In a requisition to Governor Caswell for medicine, he was anxious for all the medicines he could get. He was then at Camp Liberty Town.

Colonel Robert Salter, Recruiting Officer, and recommended to command the escort for the boundary Commissioners, died about May, ... John Williams, of Surry

County, immediately applied for the position, but the importance of getting some tobacco delivered at once to pay for some cannon, made Governor Caswell make the apointment without delay and Benjamin Hawkins got the place.

The State Council, at its July meeting, appointed Edward Salter, Lieutenant Colonel, in place of George Evans, who declined to serve. Benjamin May was appointed First Major and John Enloe, Second Major, as Field Officers for the County.

June 20th was fought the battle of Stono Ferry, South Carolina. About 1,200 Americans failed to dislodge about 700 British, who were advantageously posted. The American loss was something over a hundred killed and wounded, among them being some from Pitt. Of North Carolinians, ten were killed; wounded, twenty-six. Of the wounded was Col. James Armstrong. In the following November he presided over a Court of Inquiry into the conduct of Colonel Gideon Lamb at Brandywine, which acquitted Colonel Lamb "with Honor."

William Bryan, Brigadier General for the New Bern District, resigned in the spring and the Assembly nominated William Caswell and John Simpson for the vacancy. When the Assembly proceeded to an election, Caswell was elected.

At the State Council meeting at Halifax, in October, Colonel Herritage presented a certificate showing that Dr. Robert Williams, Jr., had been appointed Surgeon to the State Regiment in March last. It was then directed that he be paid from that date.

It was not a bright prospect that presented itself to the Americans at the beginning of 1780. Yet there were manly spirits and brave men who kept the fires of liberty burning and responded to every call for men and means. The cry was "more men." The response was always encouraging. In the midst of these struggles and troubles, a reliance on a Higher Power was not forgotten. The Continental Congress issued a proclamation setting apart Wednesday, April 26th,

1780, to "be observed as a day of fasting, humiliation and prayer, that we may with one heart and one voice implore the sovereign Lord of Heaven and earth to remember mercy in his judgments; to make us sincerely penitent for our transgressions; to prepare us for deliverance, and to remove the evils which he hath been pleased to visit us; to banish vice and irreligion from amongst us, and to establish piety and virtue by his divine grace; to bless all public councils throughout the United States, giving them wisdom, firmness and unanimity, and directing them to the best measures for the public good." It was generally observed.

May 12th, General Lincoln surrendered Charleston to the British, but only after a long and gallant defense. North Carolina had many troops in his army. It will be remembered that after Brandywine, when Colonel James Armstrong's command was so weakened that he was reduced, his men went into Colonel Patten's command. Colonel Patten's Battalion was included in the surrender of Charleston, and that included his Pitt County men.

As difficult as it was to obtain recruits, the matters of money with which to pay them was often as great a difficulty. The last of May Colonel James Armstrong obtained a warrant from Governor Caswell for $50,000 for the recruiting service. Soon thereafter he went on a recruiting expedition to Cross Creek. With what success he met is not told.

By act of the Continental Congress, after January 1st, next (1781), the Continental Army was to consist of four regiments of Cavalry; four of Artillery; forty-nine of Infantry, exclusive of Colonel Hazen's regiment; and one regiment of Artificers. Each regiment of Infantry should consist of nine companies, and each company should consist of sixty-four men, commissioned officers and privates.

CHAPTER SIXTEEN.

GUILFORD COURT-HOUSE—PITT MILITIA—JOEL TRUSS—OLD BRITISH ROAD—BRITISH PASS THROUGH PITT—CATTLE AND PROVISIONS CAPTURED—SKIRMISHES—MEN AND GUNS AT MARTINBOROUGH—TROUBLES SOUTH OF PITT—CALL FOR TROOPS—PRISONERS IN JAIL—BUCK'S BARN—LENIENCY.

The year 1781 did not dawn bright for the cause of liberty in North Carolina, and strong efforts were being made to raise men and money, both of which were so badly needed. Men from Pitt County were in the armies in South Carolina, in Virginia, in Pennsylvania, and elsewhere. North Carolina was being invaded by a victorious army and only a few of its militia, with some troops from some other States, could be at its front. It was a pursuit and retreat until General Greene faced about and turned back to fight Lord Cornwallis. On the 15th of March they met at Guilford Court-House, and though General Greene withdrew from the field at the end of the fight, it was practically an American victory. Pitt County had many militia under General Butler in that fight. Dr. Robert Williams was a surgeon there. There has been much written about how the militia run on that occasion. It was only a mistake in understanding orders.

An interesting incident was the action of Joel Truss, of the Pitt Militia. He was a giant in size and strength, being near seven feet tall. It seems that the "running" was the result of an order to fall back to a certain position beyond a fence. Some did this, among them being Joel Truss. In his hurry to reach the fence, he had somehow become separated from his gun. Once behind the fence he found others likewise without guns. And, too, he was fighting mad, and delivered himself something like this: "Boys, just look yonder what guns they have. Why, I can put my thumb in one and turn it all about. (His thumb was almost as large as a lady's wrist, and he was alluding to some small cannon.) Then bursting into a volume of oaths and curses, he added, "D——'m, if they will throw down those guns and fight fair, I'll whip half dozen of them myself," emphasizing it with ominous shakings of his club-like fists. And then, with others, he retreated rather hurriedly.

Lord Cornwallis retreated to Wilmington, and on April 25th left there for Virginia. After threatening New Bern, his army divided and took parallel routes to Halifax. One division went by or near to Kinston and on through Greene County. That division or a detachment crossed the Moccasin River, below the present site of Snow Hill. The signs of an old road, known as the British road, may yet be seen across some parts of the Streeter place and the John Bynum place in Greene County. It crossed the Middle Swamp back of the Noah Joyner place and the Noah Joyner house was built in that road. It can not be traced further north. But there was an Indian or early crossing place on Little Contentnea between theFarmville and Tyson bridges, in an almost direct line for a continuation of this old road northward, and it must have been where this old road crossed that creek. That detachment must have passed through the county along the present road to Tarboro, and on to Halifax. Another passed by way of Peacock's bridge, where a skirmish was had with 400 Americans, under General Gorham,* who were routed by the 800 British, under Tarleton.

There must have been some fighting in the neighborhood of the line between Pitt and Edgecombe in what is known as the Otter's Creek section. Only a few years ago some lumbermen found some very large pines, with balls near the hearts. They were shot into the trees when they were young and years of growth had covered them.

Another incident of the passage of the British army is

---

* This was no doubt James Gorham of Pitt, and the 400 Pitt militia with Governor Nash, at Halifax, to meet Lord Cornwallis, must have been the same men and commanded by him (Gorham).

worth recording. There were many Tories in Edgecombe, and when they heard of Lord Cornwallis coming, they proceeded to collect all the cattle, hogs and general supplies they could for his army. In collecting little attention was paid the rights of others, but they were careful about their own. Lieutenant-Colonel Edward Salter, getting information of such proceedings, marched up there with the Minute Men under him and captured the entire camp and supplies, and the poor British had none of them. It seems that later other supplies were collected, but not in such quantities. Again they were captured. Captain Tilman, with thirty horses from this county and a few from Craven went up and captured Benjamin Vichous, one of the ringleaders, and twenty-one head of cattle.*

During his march from Wilmington an American force, though small, was on his rear and front. Though no battle was fought, he was confronted at Swift Creek and also Fishing Creek, and at Halifax there was gathering a large force. Governor Nash was there with 400 from Pitt, and a larger number from Edgecombe, and General Allen Jones with the militia of Northampton. At each place there was some skirmishing without results.

On May 26th, Colonel James Armstrong wrote General Sumner that there were about fifty men at Martinborough and about thirty guns in good order and twenty more that would be repaired. He was also hoping to increase both the number of men and that of guns. He had been reduced to half pay some time about the first of the year and had since resigned, to be recommended to be retired on half pay.

Some British and Tories became troublesome in the country south of the Neuse River. General William Caswell expected them to pass through Pitt, and in September ordered the entire militia of the county to be collected and to skirmish towards Neuse River, in front of the enemy. There the

---

*These expeditions may have been one and the same. The first account is tradition by an aged and respected citizen from contemporaries of those times. The latter is from the State Records.

militia was to join his command. General Caswell was at Kingston and reported that he had heard heavy firing to the northward some days previous. If a battle or skirmish was fought northward of Kingston, there is no record of it.

The Assembly, at Halifax, early in the year, made an urgent call for troops for the army about Wilmington, which was still ocupied by the British. Pitt's quota for this purpose was 150. Gen. William Caswell resigned as Brigadier General of the New Bern District and Col. James Armstrong was elected to succeed him, but General Caswell was reinstated.

The war was now drawing to a close. The year 1782 was one of more anxiety than events, yet there were no less war preparations. Disaffection was still found among some people. Deserters and Royalists who were too active were often confined in the common jails. Pitt jail was often used for this purpose and there was a house used for the same purpose on Tar River, at what was later known as the "Lower Taft Landing." It was a large house, built of hewed logs and known as "Buck's Barn," having been built for a barn. It was standing long after the Revolution. On January 14th, Col. James Armstrong sent Captain Mound a discharge for Thomas Davis, claiming that Davis had reenlisted since his desertion, and asked that Davis and twenty others who fled from the action at Guilford Court-House be sent to Halifax. Job Tyson, a young man, who had enlisted, after the fall of Charleston, for the defense of the State, accepted a parole from Lord Cornwallis, when he passed through. Becoming uneasy for his safety, he fled to South Carolina, and not knowing, could not avail himself of the proclamations of conditional pardon. Having never taken up arms against the State, when he returned many of the most prominent citizens of the county petitioned Governor Burke for his pardon, which was no doubt granted.

CHAPTER SEVENTEEN.

PEACE AND INDEPENDENCE—PART OF PITT GIVEN TO BEAUFORT—JOHN SIMPSON—NEGRO BURNED FOR MURDER—ACTS OF THE ASSEMBLY—ARMSTRONG AND SALTER, STATE OFFICERS—JUSTICES RESIGN—PART OF CRAVEN GIVEN TO PITT—ARMSTRONG, BRIGADIER-GENERAL—PITT ACADEMY—GREENVILLE—WILLIAM BLOUNT—GREENVILLE FERRY—SIMPSON PAID.

Peace, with the Independence of the United States of America, was concluded in February, 1783. With no foreign foe to contend against, civil matters and rebuilding the losses of the country in so long and disastrous a war began to occupy the attention of the people. Pitt County had lost many of its good citizens, but had suffered much less than some other counties that were in or nearer the scenes of conflict.

At this time all of Chocowinity "Neck" was a part of Pitt County. There was no road from Washington on the south of the river. An act this year provided for "a ferry across Pamplico River at the town of Washington, and the clearing a road and making a causeway through the swamp and marsh opposite to the said town, into the old road the nearest and best way." The court of Pitt County had charge of the ferry and fixed the fees.

John Simpson complained to the Assembly that he had lost some certificates and wanted the Assembly to make them good. This was refused.

Some time about the close of the war, perhaps this year or the last, an awful thing was done in Pitt County. It was publicly burning a negro by virtue of the sentence of the court. Her name was Rose and she had murdered her mistress, being aided by another slave. The facts as learned about it, are that John Tyson, and Sibbey, his wife or sister, lived on the north side of Contentnea Creek, about opposite the W. A. Barrett place, near Farmville. They had two slaves, Shade and Rose. Sibbey was very cruel to them and treated them very badly. With the help of Shade, Rose murdered Sibbey. It was premeditated and cold-blooded. When it was found that Rose and Shade had committed the crime, they were arrested. Shade being a very valuable negro and only aided and abetted Rose in the crime, was sent south and sold. Rose was taken to jail, tried, convicted and sentenced to be burned at the stake, which sentence was carried out by the sheriff at or near the town of Martinborough.*

Among the acts of the Assembly for 1784 were those for cleaning out Tar River and Fishing Creek, in the counties of Pitt and Edgecombe, for the purpose of opening them for navigation; making Martinborough, Lanier's (on Tranter's Creek), Edward Salter's, Dupre's and Ellis's Landings (just above Blue Banks, now public landing), places for the inspection of tobacco; and the repeal of the "Cession Act"† of the year before. Against this many members of the House protested, among them being John Jordan and Richard Moye, Pitt's representatives. It had been the custom to allow each member of the Assembly traveling expenses for one day for each county passed through in attending the sessions, but this session changed it to the mileage system. Colonel James Armstrong was elected a member of the State Council and Colonel Salter State tax-collector for the County.

Benjamin May and Robert Moye resigned as Justices of the Peace, this year.

One of the principal acts of 1785 relating to Pitt County was giving Beaufort a good part of its eastern portion. The act made the new line as follows:

"Beginning at the Craven County line where it crosses Creeping Swamp and running with Creeping Swamp and

---

* The account of this crime and its punishment is from an honored citizen, who was well versed in the history of his section.

†At the close of the Revolution the Colonial Government was badly in debt, and States ceded their public lands to the National Government to assist in paying those debts. Among them was North Carolina, which, by an act of the Assembly at Hillsboro, April, 1784, ceded all its lands now comprising the State of Tennessee. The National Government did not accept this cession at once, and the Assembly of October, 1784, at New Bern, repealed the Cession Act.

Chicod Swamp to the mouth of Round Island Branch, then a direct course to the mouth of Pitch Hole Branch, then with the Swamp to Bear Creek, then down Bear Creek to Tar River, then down the River on the north side to the mouth of Tranter's Creek, then up said Creek to Martin County line, then with Martin, Beaufort and Craven lines to the beginning," all the territory therein being added to and made a part of Beaufort County.

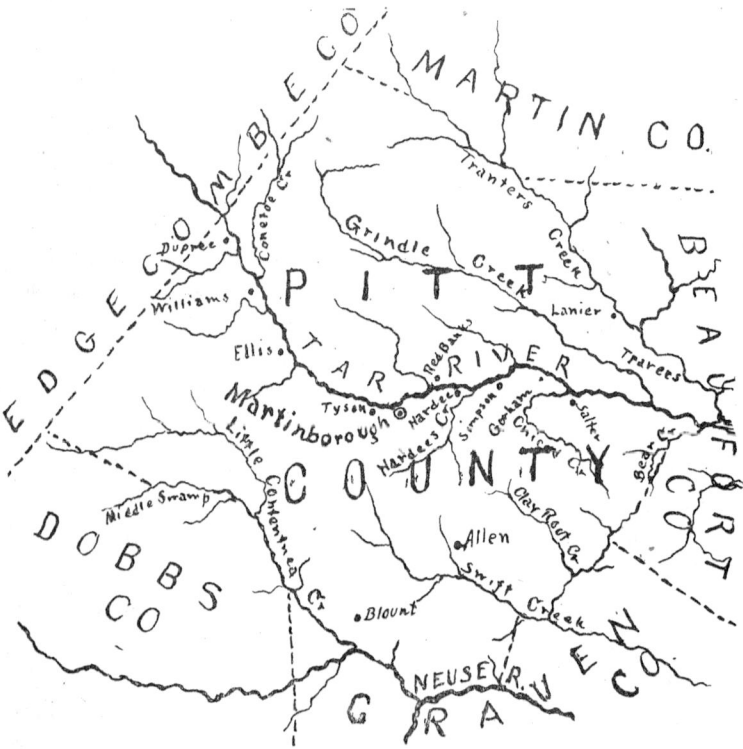

PITT COUNTY, AFTER CESSION TO BEAFORT 1785—FROM CRAVEN 1786.
From pen sketch by H. T. K., 1910.

Richard Evans died without making title to many of the lots, sold by the lottery in Martinborough, and the Martinborough act was amended for the purpose of having the titles made.

The Assembly also elected Colonel James Armstrong Brigadier General for the New Bern District.

The two most important events of 1786 to Pitt were, the incorporation of the Pitt Academy, to be established at Martinborough. (It had as trustees, some of the most prominent men of the State. They were Governor Richard Caswell, Hugh Williamson, William Blount, John Simpson, James Armstrong, James Gorham, John Hawkes, John Williams, Robert Williams, Arthur Forbes, Benjamin May, John May and Reading Blount); and the annexing a part of Craven to Pitt, making the new line as follows:

"Beginning at the Pitt line where Creeping Swamp intersects the same, thence down the run or middle of the Clay Root Swamp to the run of Swift's Creek Swamp, thence up the run of the same to Isaac Gardner's Ford, or path across the same, thence a direct line to the lower landing on Grindal Creek, which is in about half a mile of said Creek, thence down the said Grindal Creek to the River Neuse, thence up the meanders of the River Neuse to the mouth of Great Contentney Creek, thence up the said Creek to the mouth of Little Contentney Creek, thence up the same to the line of the County of Pitt, be and the same is hereby annexed to Pitt." Within this territory is very nearly all of Swift Creek township, and the lower parts of Chicod and Contentnea.

The same act that incorporated Pitt Academy changed the name of Martinborough to that of "Greenesville," said to have been in honor of General Nathaniel Greene, the hero of Guilford Court-House.

Nathaniel Greene was born in Rhode Island in 1742. He entered the army in 1774; was made a Brigadier General in 1775 and a Major General in 1776. In 1780 he was appointed to succeed Benedict Arnold in command at West Point and a short time thereafter appointed to the command of the armies of the South to succeed General Gates. After a series of marches and masterly maneuvres, he fought the Battle of Guilford Court-House, March 15th, 1781, having a force of 4,400, much of it being raw militia, with Lord Cornwallis, who had a veteran force of 2,200 and practically won a notable victory that led up to Lord Cornwallis's defeat at Yorktown. He then began a brilliant and successful campaign in South Carolina, and after the war was over returned to Rhode Island. He soon moved to Georgia, where he died in 1786.

In the territory annexed from Craven lived William Blount, who had been a member of the Continental Congress since 1782, and several times a member of the Assembly. He had landed interests in what is now Tennessee, and being charged with purchasing land from the Indians contrary to custom, he made a denial of the same to Governor Caswell by letter. He was a member of the Continental Congress for 1787 and in the Assembly from Pitt, in the Senate, in 1789.

A free ferry was established at Greenville in 1787 by the Assembly, and a small tax provided for its maintenance. It is supposed to have been about where the bridge now stands.

The Assembly this year settled with John Simpson a matter which had been standing since 1781. He had turned his vouchers over to the Auditors, who lost them, and it took all that long time to get the matter adjusted and to find that the State was indebted to him. He had never received part of his pay as a member of the Assembly of 1782.

The delegates of the several States having framed a Constitution, it was read, and considered some time in December, but not adopted at this session.

CHAPTER EIGHTEEN.

Constitution Rejected—Motions and Vote Thereon—Location of Capital—Constitution Adopted—Amendments Recommended—The University—Foreign State—New Court-house—John Simpson Dead—Bounties for Manufactures—Pitt Iron Mines—Pitt in the Revolution—Governor Caswell's Opinion.

The Convention for considering the Federal Constitution, as proposed by the Continental Convention at Philadelphia, met at Hillsboro, July 21st, 1788. Pitt sent Sterling Dupree, Robert Williams, Richard Moye, Arthur Forbes and David Perkins. All but David Perkins were present on the opening day. He did not get there till August 1st.

The report of the Committee of the Whole said that a Declaration of Rights, together with amendments, ought to be laid before Congress and a Convention of the States, before North Carolina should ratify the Constitution.

James Iredell, seconded by John Skinner, moved the adoption of the Constitution and recommended six amendments. This was lost by a vote of 84 yeas to 184 nays. Pitt's delegates, except David Perkins, who voted yea, voted no. Then the Report of the Committee of the Whole was adopted by a vote of 184 to 83, Pitt's delegates voting as on first question. This Convention selected the farm of Isaac Hunter, in Wake County, or any place within ten miles thereof, as the location for establishing the State Capital.

The year 1789 was notable for two important and long steps in progress by North Carolina. They were the adoption of the Federal Constitution and the establishment of the University.

The Convention that adopted the Constitution, met at Fayetteville, in November. In it were many of the men who had been members of the Hillsborough Convention the year before, which rejected the same Constitution. Pitt's delegates were William Blount, Shadrach Allen, James Armstrong, Samuel Simpson and James Bell, all of whom were present at the opening. On the fifth day a resolution, rejecting the Constitution until certain amendments were added, was lost by a vote of 82 to 187, all of Pitt's delegates voting against it. The question was then on the adoption of it. It passed by a vote of 195 to 77, Pitt's delegates voting for it.

Thus North Carolina became the twelfth member of the United States of America—the American Union. And it was unanimously recommended that its representatives in Congress endeavor to obtain the adoption of the amendments recommended by this Convention.

The Assembly passed the act for establishing the University. It provided all the machinery for its establishment, and among its trustees was William Blount. The University was not opened for the reception of students until 1795.

During the period between the rejection of the constitution by the Convention at Hillsboro, in August, 1788, and its adoption by the Convention at Fayetteville, in November, 1789, North Carolina was referred to by the papers and in many other ways as a "Foreign State." The new government had been organized and put into effect with the inauguration of George Washington, April 30th, 1789.

Another act of 1789 was that for the building of a courthouse, prison and stocks at Greenville, and for keeping the same in repair, for which a tax of not exceeding eight pence on every hundred acres of land and not exceeding two shillings, "like money," on every taxable person, and a tax of two shillings on every hundred pounds value of town property in said county, was laid. James Armstrong, Shadrach Allen, John Moye, Arthur Forbes, Samuel Simpson, Benjamin Bell and William Blount were appointed the commissioners to have charge of the money raised for this purpose, have the building erected and sell the old court-house and prison.

Samuel Simpson, member of the Fayetteville Convention, was a son of John Simpson. John Simpson died March 1st, 1788, lacking seven days of being sixty years old. He had figured very prominently in Pitt's affairs and also in those of the Colony and State. He had filled almost every office, from Justice of the Peace to Councillor of State in civil affairs, and from private to Brigadier General of Militia, in military affairs. He had offered his services to the Royal Governor when he heard that Regulators were marching to New Bern to prevent Fanning from taking a seat in the Colonial Assembly; and he was among the first to make open resistance to that same authority when the rights of his people were in jeopardy. He was a great and useful man, and had not death claimed him so early he would have reached higher and greater honors in the State and nation.

At the beginning of the Revolution, bounties were offered for manufacturing enterprises that would supply the necessities for domestic use and materials for war. Iron foundries were badly needed. Iron ore was not so plentiful as now and many mines were worked that have long since been abandoned as not paying. It is said that some ore from Pitt was used during the war for manufacturing various articles. In several places in Chicod Township, an ore, containing iron is found, though not in large quantities. In fact the ore is poor, but it is said it sufficed for many purposes in those times. Another bed of the same quality of ore is on Tranter's Creek, in Pactolus township. This is some better than that of Chicod. Both were no doubt used in those days.

The people of Pitt were true patriots, and there is no record of any Tories being found in it at any time, except Tison and one or two others, unless some were included in the plot of 1777, which ended with the capture of thirty by Colonel Henry Irwin, at Tarboro. If any were concerned in it, it is yet to be learned. In 1765, there were 750 taxable men in the county; in 1790, there were 1,461; so there must have been about 1,100 in 1776. From these numbers there must have been near 1,000 who enlisted and fought in the war. Before specifying any quota, four companies had been formed. The first was under the call of August, 1774. Then James Armstrong and George Evans were authorized to raise a company each. There was one or more under Robert Salter that joined Colonel Caswell on the march to Moore's Creek, and next are heard of at Wilmington. Then followed calls for Pitt's quota for the Continental Army, those calls being for 50, 35, 50 and 150 men, respectively. It is not doubted that they were promptly furnished. Then there were 400 with Governor Nash at Halifax, in 1781. All of which shows that Pitt County did its full duty in those days "that tried men's souls." In 1786, Governor Caswell, in having the militia organized, issued commissions for four field officers and thirty-six for captains, lieutenants and ensigns of twelve companies. At that time there was some dissatisfaction about military matters in the county, and in deprecating it he said, "and am much concerned about the Pitt militia, which I always considered as equal, at least, to any in the State." The record of Pitt in the Revolution is one to be proud of.

CHAPTER NINETEEN.

Tory Pardons—Vote on the Capital Bill—William Blount—First Census—Washington's Tour—Impressions in Pitt—Old People—James Armstrong Dead—Second Census—Peace and Progress—Schools and Houses—Mail Facilities—Modes of Conveyance—Good Old Times.

North Carolina was now a part of that new nation born of blood and sacrifices. With 1790 came an era that promised peace and prosperity. The Assembly passed acts of pardon for many offenses committed during the past, especially those of the long war for Independence. Among the beneficiaries of those acts were a number of the inhabitants of Pitt, Martin and Edgecombe, but it is to be doubted if many were from Pitt; if so, they were living on the borders along the Martin and Edgecombe lines.

The bill for establishing the capital as recommended by the convention passed the House by a vote of 52 to 51. It was a tie and the Speaker voted for it, thus giving it one majority. Shadrach Allen and Samuel Simpson were Pitt's representatives in that branch, and they both voted for the bill.

William Blount was in the Senate from Pitt in 1789, and at the time of the meeting of the Assembly was west of the mountains, being engaged in some affairs connected with the Indians. Returning for the meeting of the Assembly, he charged mileage from there. The clerk refused to allow it and the Assembly of this year (1790) complimented him on his action in so doing. Therefore Mr. Blount only received mileage from Pitt.

This year the first National Census was taken. The nation then had only 3,929,214 population; North Carolina, 393,751; Pitt County, 8,275. Pitt's population is thus given: Males over 16 years of age, 1,461; males under 16,

1,507; females, 2,915; total whites, 5,883; slaves, 2,367; all others, 25; grand total, 8,275.

Having previously made a tour of the New England States, in March 1791 President Washington started on a Southern tour. He came by way of Petersburg, Virginia, and his first stop in North Carolina was at Halifax, where he spent the night.

His route took him through Pitt and the following is found in his diary, relating to that part of his tour:

"TUESDAY, APRIL 19TH.

"At 6 o'clock I left Tarborough, accompanied by some of the most respectable people of the place for a few miles--dined at a trifling place called Greenville, 25 miles distant—and lodged at one Allan's,* 14 miles further, a very indifferent house without stabling which for the first time since I commenced my Journey were obliged to stand without a cover.

"Greenville is on Tar River and the exports the same as from Tarborough with a greater proportion of Tar—for the lower down the greater number of Tar makers are there—this article is contrary to all ideas one would entertain on the subject, rolled as Tobacco by an axis which goes through both heads—one horse draws two barrels in this manner.

"WEDNESDAY, APRIL 20.

"Left Allan's before breakfast and under a misapprehension went to a Colonel Allan's, supposing it to be a public house; where we were kindly and well entertained without knowing

---

*This was Shadrach Allen, and his place was known as Crown Point. It was just south of Turkey Cock Swamp, and there are no remains of buildings now there. It was also the place of the first Masonic Lodge in North Carolina. The Colonel Allen, with whom he got breakfast, was Colonel John Allen, brother to Shadrach and lived near Pitch Kettle, in Craven County. Arriving at Col. John Allen's, and thinking it a public house or inn, President Washington asked if he could get breakfast. Mrs. Allen said she would have to see Col. Allen. Finding that the man who wanted breakfast was President Washington, a big breakfast was prepared. A pig, chicken, turkey and other things were upon the table. President Washington ate only some eggs and drank some rum, touching nothing else. Either here or at Col. Shade Allen's, there was a young girl to whom President Washington became attracted, took her to New Bern with him and to the ball in his honor at the palace that night. At New Bern he was entertained and slept in the house on Middle street, now owned and occupied by James A. Bryan.

it was at his expense, until it was too late to rectify the mistake. After breakfasting and feeding our horses here, we proceeded on and crossed the River Neuse 11 miles further, arrived in Newbern to dinner. At this ferry which is 10 miles from Newbern, we were met by a small party of Horse; the district Judge (Mr. Sitgreaves*) and many of the principal Inhabitants of Newbern, who conducted us into town to exceeding good lodgings.

"It ought to have been mentioned that another small party of Horse under one Simpson† met us at Greenville, and in spite of every endeavor which could comport with decent civility to excuse myself from it, they would attend me to Newbern. Colonel Allen did the same."

The house in which he is said to have dined in Greenville is still standing and known as the Dr. Dick Williams house, now occupied by his children. On the weatherboarding near the front door can yet be seen some marks, which are what time has left of President Washington's name, said to have been written by him on that occasion. But a very highly respected citizen of Greenville, who died only a few years ago, told this writer that the Williams house was not the house which he had been told was the house at which President Washington dined, but that it was a house long since removed, that stood about where the southern end of the old Macon House now stands. This gentleman also stated that Dr. Robert Williams, then one of the most prominent men in the county and who lived very near the road by which President Washington came from Tarboro, afterwards said he never heard of the President's visit until years after and doubted the truth of the statement that such a visit was made.

That Pitt was a good county in which to live, and that its people lived well and long, is shown by the fact that in 1794 there were then living in the county, William Taylor 114

---

* John Sitgreaves, Judge of the United States District Court.

† Samuel Simpson was ordered to escort President Washington from Greenville to New Bern, by Thomas Blount, and this was in all probability the Simpson alluded to.

years old; Lancelot James and John Banks, each over 100 years old; and William Howard, 108 years old. William Howard was a native of Ocracocke Island, but had lived on the banks of Tar River 91 years.

Some time about 1794 or 1795, James Armstrong died. He had been a soldier of the Revolution and had filled every position from private to Brigadier General. He had been an officer of the militia, and when his country called for men to resist oppression, he was one of the first to respond.

The Census of 1800 showed that Pitt County had a population of 9,084, all told, being an increase of 809, or about ten per cent in ten years.

This was an era of peace and progress. The National Government was no longer an experiment, there were no international complications to disturb the people and the Indian wars had become of no great importance. Internal affairs were uppermost and the rush of people to the new Nation, promised to make a great Nation of many people. Conditions then existing in the State applied to Pitt County. It might be called a primitive age, an age of simplicity. At this time there was not a public school in the State. The great mass of the people could neither read nor write, education being the accomplishment of the few and wealthy. There were few private schools. The school house was built of logs, with a dirt chimney; a log was sawed out at one side for a window; the seats were made of split logs, the split side being somewhat smoothed and supported on round legs driven in holes bored in the under side, and such seats had no backs; a shelf built to one side of the house answered for a desk for writing, the pupil sitting on one of the benches; the floor was of rough-hewn timber, with many and large holes that let in the cold in winter. The teacher was held in little esteem and was practically a servant and nurse for the smaller children. The teacher was generally a woman, practically imported from New England, and generally ended her career in the school room by marrying the son of the house and causing a row in the family. The teacher's pay was a pittance.

There was little letter writing. Postage was not less than twenty-five cents on each letter, and it took weeks and sometimes months to get a reply where now it is only a question of a day or two. Comforts were few and simple. There were no stoves, no coal, no gas, no matches. The fire in the great fireplace, pine torches and tallow candles were the producers of heat and light on all occasions.

There were few vehicles of any kind; the roads were very bad and often impassable. Everybody rode horseback, and sometimes a family of four were mounted on one horse. Almost every woman could spin, weave, knit, sew, cut and make all the wearing apparel for the household. There was little money in circulation. Hogs, cattle and turkeys were driven to the markets of Virginia. Tobacco was rolled to market in hogsheads, an axle being put through the hogshead and shafts being attached.

Courts were jolly times. Drinking, fighting, gambling and their attendant vices, were its prominent features. Drunkenness was a common vice from which the preachers were not always exempt. Lotteries for raising money for churches, schools and the disposal of town lots, were licensed by law. The whole population practically lived in the country and knew nothing of the attractions of towns and cities. Swift justice was often visited upon the criminal. The life of those times meant health and strength. It was a lot of hardy, honest men and women, who seemed to believe in hanging as all or most punishment for the present, a brimstone hell for future punishment and calomel for all the ills of the present life.

CHAPTER TWENTY.

THIRD CENSUS—YANKEE HALL—SECOND WAR WITH ENGLAND—TWO PITT COMPANIES AT BEACON ISLAND—THEIR PAY-ROLL—RETREAT AND AMUSING INCIDENT—FOURTH CENSUS—OCCUPATIONS—BRIDGE AT GREENVILLE—GREENVILLE ACADEMIES—FIFTH CENSUS—JOHN JOYNER.

The Census of 1810 showed little increase of Pitt's population from 1800, it being only 85, the total being 9,169.

About this time some New England tradesmen settled on Tar River at Yankee Hall, and it soon became a center of business for much of the country to the north thereof.

There is little record of the men of Pitt in the second war with England. North Carolina being far removed from the main seats of the war, perhaps not so many of her men took part, and of those who did, their history is lost in that of others. North Carolina was invaded in 1813 and in response to Governor Hawkins' call for troops, two companies from Pitt, about 125 men and officers, were enlisted.

Of one company, George Eason was Captain; Sumner Adams, Lieutenant; Samuel Albritton, Ensign; John Allen, Peter Adams, Josiah Daniel, Moses Hatton, Sergeants; Thomas Adams, Levin Hall, Samuel Johnston, George Knox, Corporals. Of the second, Samuel Vines was Captain; Isaac Downs, Lieutenant; William Rountree, Ensign; Benjamin Bell, Elias Carr, Willie Clements, Sergeants; Benjamin Johnston, Levy Pearscen, Nathaniel Pettit, Moses Turnage, Corporals.

The field officers were, Hardy Smith, Brigadier General; Howell Cobb, Lieutenant Colonel Commander; William Pugh, Second Major.

The privates were, of Captain Eason's Company: Ambrose Arnold, Watson W. Anderson, Levin Adams, William W. Andrews, John Baldwin, Miles Britton, Noah Buck, William Bryan, Noah Beddard, Henry Barnhill, Jonathan Briley,

William Brooks, Reading Bell, Stephen Careney, Willie Bell, William Cammel, Charles Crisp, William Crawford, William Downs, Jesse Dudley, Frederick Dinkins, William Elks, Henry Fulford, Stephen Fulford, Reuben Flake, William Galloway, William Highsmith, Thomas Holliday, Matthew James, George Killebrew, William Little, Benjamin Leggett, Josiah Mills, William Manning, Allen Moore, Asia Moore,

OLD BRICKELL CANNON

One of the cannons with which Joseph Brickell armed his trading vessels about 1797 for defense against French encroachments on American commerce. Brickell lived at Greenville and this cannon in now in the cemetery.

While being used to celebrate the election of John Spiers to the legislature in 1836, a premature discharge killed two negroes and injured several other people.

William Moore, Noah Magowns, William Mitchel, Samuel Nobles, Alfred Nelson, William J. Parkston, James Robertson, Reuben Rollins, Richard Eaton Rivers, Henry Smith, Luther Spain, Benjamin Shivers, John Tison, Jacob Turner, Isaac Turner, William Teal, Willoughby Whitehurst, Garison Williams, Solomon Whichard, Calven Herrington.

The privates of Captain Vines' Company were: Richard Albritton, William Albritton, Samuel Allen, Robert Barr, Abednego Briley, Nathan Brady, Benjamin Briley, Aaron Cox, William Edwards, Thomas Flanagan, John Fowler, Jordan Fulford, Ancos Garriss, David Hattoway, Harry Hadison, Joseph English, Isaac Joiner, William Lang, John Little, Dread Little, William Moore, Thomas Mills, John Moye, Abraham Mills, Simpson Meeks, Benjamin Nobles, James Pearce, Turner Pollard, John Pope, William Peebles, Jr., Isaac Parker, Henry Rodgers, Richard Shingleton, Benjamin Smith, Jethro Sermon, Arden Tucker, Harman Walston, Benjamin Ward, Burrel White, John Wilson.

These two companies were a part of the garrison of Beacon Island, in Pamlico Sound, at Ocracoke Inlet. It was for the defense of the inlet and Portsmouth; but when the British fleet appeared, the entire garrison abandoned its post and fled in boats for the mainland, arriving there safely. The British were too many for them and flight was their only safety. After plundering Portsmouth, taking all the cattle, hogs and provisions to be found, the British sailed away. There was another company at Beacon Island, under Captain Sadler. It seems to have been there later and to have garrisoned the Island after the others left. It was also from Pitt County.

It seems these companies were not prepared for defense, but were doing a picket service. On each projecting headland on to Washington, were signal corps, with a barrel of rosin, bottle of spirits of turpentine, ball of oakum and a flint and steel for striking fire. On the approach of the British fleet, these signal corps were to successively light their signals. And it is said that within two hours after the appearance of the fleet, the signal had reached Washington and the long roll was beaten for assembling the militia. The militia assembled and was led by Captain Mallison to an old entrenchment a little east of the town. Calling to his men to follow and be ready to defend their country, Captain Mallison leaped into the entrenchments. He landed on the head of a long-horned cow and, grabbing a horn with each hand, he thought the British had him and that he was between two bayonets; so he hastened to yell, "I surrender."

The use of the signals were to be by night, the fire, and by day, the smoke. (The cow incident is not vouched for, but came of good authority.)

The Greenville Academy was incorporated in 1814.

Yankee Hall must have become an important point of business on the river and also to have done a good shipping business. In 1816 two sea-going ships were built there.

The census of 1820 showed good growth in population for Pitt. The population was 10,001, as follows:

Whites, under 16 years of age—males, 1,368; females, 1,320.

Whites, between 16 and 45; males, 1,143; females, 1,163.

Whites, over 45, males, 353; females, 384.

Total whites, males, 2,864; females, 2,867.

Total, both sexes, 5,731.

Slaves—males, 2,213; females, 2,028.

Free negroes—males, 18; females, 11.

Total, 29.

Summary—Whites, 5,731.
    Slaves, 4,241.
    Free negroes, 29.
    Total, 10,001.

The county had no incorporated town and the population of Greenville was not given.

Those given as engaged in the various occupations were: Agriculture, 3,205; Commerce, 25; Manufacturers, 61; total, 3,291.

Sometime in the twenties, very probably the latter, a bridge was built over Tar River at Greenville, and the old ferry, so long in use, discontinued. In 1828 land was bought from

John Cherry, about five miles southeast of Greenville, and a poor-house or County Home established.

The Greenville Female Academy was chartered in 1830. The incorporators were Gen. W. Clark, Archibald Parker, John C. Gorham, Richard Evans, and Absalom Saunders.

The Census of 1830 showed a good increase in Pitt's population, it being 12,093, an increase of 2,092 over that of ten years before.

From the schools chartered, a spirit of education must have come over the people about this time, and several academies were chartered. Clemmons's Academy was chartered in 1831, with Willie Gurganus, Thomas E. Chance, Edmund Andrews and William Clemmons, Trustees. Contentnea Academy was incorporated the same year with Moses Turnage, Lewis Turnage, Abram Baker, Elbert Moye, William D. Moye and Alfred Moye, Trustees. Jordan Plain Academy was incorporated the next year with Hugh Telfair, Thomas Jordan, Valentine Jordan, Benjamin F. Eborn, James Little and Churchill Perkins, Trustees. While this looks like educational progress, yet it seems that the people were not yet ready for or in favor of general education, for it is said that John Joyner, one of the prominent men of the county and several times a member of the legislature, was "turned out of" his church for sending one of his boys, Noah, off to college.

These schools seem to have passed out of the memory of those living. Clemmons's was in Carolina, near the Martin line. Contentnea was near the Moye Cross Roads, being on the road to Farmville, a little north of A. P. Turnage's present home, but not so far as the late Moye school house. Jordan Plains was about two miles north of Pactolus, on the Williamston road.

CHAPTER TWENTY-ONE.

Steamboats—Constitutional Convention of 1835—Delegates—Important Votes—Baptist State Convention—Greenville Gazette—Presidential Election—Loss in Population—Flat Boats—Dr. Williams Dead—Harris and Yellowly Duel—Harris Killed—Academy Incorporated.

The first steamboats appeared on Tar River in the early thirties, but as business ventures were failures.

The year 1830 was the year of the organization of the North Carolina Baptist State Convention. It took place in Greenville, a few prominent members of that church meeting in what is now known as the Ricks House and organizing with Patrick Dowd, President, and Samuel Wait, Corresponding Secretary.

To the Constitutional Convention of 1835 Pitt sent Dr. Robert Williams and John Joyner. They were both good representatives, but little given to speech-making. Both voted for biennial sessions of the legislature; for giving Edenton, New Bern, Wilmington and Fayetteville, Borough representation in the legislature; and against the election of the governor by the popular vote of the people, and giving the free negroes the right to vote. On the question of substituting the word "Christian" for the word "Protestant" in the thirty-second Article of the Constitution, Williams voted for and Joyner against. On the question of a property qualification for negroes for voting, Williams voted against it and Joyner for it. The Constitution proved to be very unpopular with the East and not one Eastern county voted for its ratification. Pitt voted thirty-two for, to seven hundred and ten against it. This was about the way the other Eastern counties voted, but the Western counties voted as solidly for it and it was ratified by a majority of 5,165.

Before this Constitution was adopted, Catholics were forbidden to hold office, though public sentiment had never allowed its enforcement. William Gaston, a Catholic, was a member of this Convention and had held many offices and only the year before had been elected a Judge of the Supreme Court. If the law had been strictly enforced he would have been barred.

About this time, too, was published the first newspaper ever published in Greenville or the county. It was the Greenville *Gazette,* published by John Brown, known as "Printer Brown." It was a small paper and did not long exist. The town was too small to support even a small paper.

In the Presidential election in 1840, William Henry Harrison, Whig, received 627 votes and Martin Van Buren, Loco Foco, 391 in Pitt.

The county seems to have gone backwards between 1830 and 1840 in some way, for the Census of the latter year showed a population of only 11,806, a loss of 287 in ten years.

The year 1842 is remembered as the year of a great flood. Some old people claim it the largest flood and rise in the river ever known.

It seems there was not enough business on the river in those days to make steamboats profitable, and they gave way to float boats. Though they were slow they did a profitable business and were long on the river, even after steamboating began.

October first, 1847, H. F. Harris, a member of the legislature, fell in a duel with E. C. Yellowly. Both were young lawyers of the Greenville bar. They were close friends, rivals at the bar and also for the graces of an only daughter of a wealthy planter. A case in court caused the first difficulty. Harris had the first speech to the jury and severely criticised the management of the case by Yellowly. In his reply, Yellowly more severely criticised Harris. After court,

Harris made an attack on Yellowly. Friends prevented anything serious then. Harris challenged Yellowly to meet him on the field of honor, which challenge was acepted. However, both were arrested and put under heavy bonds to keep the peace one year. On the day the bond was out Harris renewed the challenge, which was again accepted.

On October first, 1847, they met on the North Carolina and Virginia State line, on the Dismal Swamp Canal, about four miles from the "Half-way House." Before fighting, Yellowly sent his second to see if the duel could then be stopped. Harris was obstinate and demanded that the duel proceed. In the first shot, Harris's shot went wild, and Yellowly fired up into the air. Again Yellowly attempted a reconciliation, but Harris said he went there for blood and would have it before he left. In the second shot Harris's shot again went wild. This time Yellowly's shot went true and Harris fell, pierced by the ball, nearly in the center of his forehead, a little over the right eye. Seeing Harris fall, Yellowly said to his second, "Go to him for God's sake, for I don't want to kill him." Harris was dead when the second reached him. Yellowly and his party left at once, but was arrested in Virginia, though the magistrate did not hold him.*

---

*NOTE.—J. E. Wilkins, an eye-witness to part of the duel, gave this writer the following account of the affair. He said: "I was a small boy on a visit to my uncle, William Wallace, who lived at Culpepper Locks, on the Dismal Swamp Canal, in Virginia. I was in possession of my first gun and with a crowd of boys, some larger, my cousin, W. T. Wallace, son of my uncle, being in the crowd. Returning home, we came up the east bank of the canal and ahead of us saw two carriages and several men, walking about mixed up. A man came running meeting us, stopped us and told us to remain where we were. We were then about one hundred yards from the men and carriages. Soon there were pistol shots and again the men were busy getting about. Soon there were other pistol shots and again the men stirred about. A tall, small man and two or three others got into the carriage and drove off. The boys were much excited, and passing on up the canal bank by where the shooting had taken place, they saw a man lying next the woods on the bank, with a red handkerchief over his face. The boys went on to

Both Harris and Yellowly were brave, fearless men. Harris was an expert with the pistol. Both had practiced for the occasion, though Yellowly did not want to fight. Dr. W. J. Blow was Yellowly's second, and also surgeon to both.

The steamboat "Amidas" was built and placed on Tar River in 1849 by John Meyers and Sons, of Washington, and became a paying enterprise.

The Midway Male and Female Academy was incorporated this year, with Churchill Perkins, Henry I. Toole, William Grimes, Godfrey Langley, Benjamin Daniel, Valentine S. Jordan and David Langley, as trustees. This school was at or near Pactolus.

William Wallace's and told that a man had been killed on the canal bank and gave particulars. William Wallace was a magistrate. A warrant was issued and the party in the carriage containing the tall, small man were arrested at Deep Creek and had a hearing before three magistrates. After the hearing all the parties signed the paper and were released and left. The trial was held in the little inn at Deep Creek, kept by Major Sam Foreman. The body of the dead man was taken to Deep Creek and a coffin got from a wheelwright who kept them."

CHAPTER TWENTY-TWO.

Plank Road—Seventh Census—Plank Road Stockholders Organized—Cold Spring—Court-house Burned—Great Loss—Common Schools and Progress—County Superintendent—Apportionment—Journal of Education—Very Old Man.

The legislature of 1850 chartered the Greenville and Raleigh plank road. A provision in the charter provided that any white person who should travel on the road after built, should pay a fine of five dollars, unless the proper tolls had been paid. If a slave should be the offender, the penalty was not more than twenty lashes.

The census of this year gave Pitt County 13,397 population, divided as follows: Whites, 6,677; slaves, 6,633; free negroes, 87. The vote for Governor was, David S. Reid, Democrat, 583; Charles Manly, Whig, 591.

On the 20th of February, 1851, the stockholders of the Greenville and Raleigh plank road, met in Greenville and organized. Benjamin F. Hanks, of Washington, was made chairman, and John A. Selby, of Greenville, secretary. John Meyers, E. J. Warren, Gould Hoyt and F. B. Satterthwaite were appointed a committee to see how much stock was represented. R. L. Meyers, E. J. Warren, F. B. Satterthwaite and W. J. Blow were appointed a committee to draft a set of by-laws. The following shares were reported represented: Raleigh, 30 shares; Wilson, 64; Washington, 1,016; Greenville, 1,329; total, 2,359. Alfred Moye was elected president by a vote of 1,391 to 887 for R. L. Meyers. Nine directors were elected. They were Joseph Potts, Benjamin F. Hanks, B. F. Havens, R. L. Meyers, of Beaufort; Thomas Hanrahan, William Bernard, Sr., F. B. Sattherthwaite, of Pitt; John W. Farmer, of Edgecombe; Thomas D. Hogg, of Wake.

The plank road was a great enterprise and did much for the upbuilding of the county. The arrival and departure of the old stage-coaches were almost as great events as that of daily trains now. Crowds were always waiting for it. Along the route it was the same. Stores were built along the road, and the village of Marlboro was one of its results. It became a place of much importance and soon boasted a male and female academy that was the pride of that section. The steamer "Morehead" was built and placed on the river to run in connection with the coaches.

The spring of 1856 was a noted cold one. Snow began falling Sunday night, April 26th, and continued to Tuesday night, when there was a general freeze. The oldest inhabitant remembered nothing of the kind before. All the fruit and vegetation were completely killed, as were all growing crops. Whole fields of wheat, nearing the heading state, were killed and presented a curious sight.

Pitt County sustained an irreparable loss in 1858 by the burning of the court-house. It was a complete loss, with many of the records. On the fly-leaf of the appearance docket, which was saved, is the following memorandum of the event: "On Friday morning, about 4 o'clock on the 7th February, 1858, the court-house in Greenville, Pitt County, was discovered to be on fire, and was entirely consumed, with all the records, except the books in the office of the register, the trial and appearance dockets of the Superior Court, and the trial docket from the office of the clerk of the county court."

The court-house is supposed to have been burned by a man from Tennessee, to destroy a will. He had made a copy of the will and changed some words. Finding this, the clerk refused to certify it a true copy. This Tennesseean was interested in some property left by the will and it was not as he wanted it. Circumstantial evidence was so strong that the grand jury found a true bill against him for the burning, but he was never brought to trial for it.

A portion of the first court-house ever built in the county is yet standing and is used as a tenant house. It is about three miles east of Greenville, on the Washington road. It was built on the lands of John Hardee, which once had prospects of being in a town. But the present site of Greenville was more attractive and in 1771 Martinborough was established and in a few years a court-house was built. It stood on the lot in front of the present court-house, a little north of the

THE WHICHARD SCHOOL HOUSE, GREENVILLE.
This was a pioneer school, long conducted as a pay school, by Mrs Violet Whichard. Later was used as printing office by her sons. Now moved and remodeled for dining room and kitchen.

site of the old market-house of a few years ago. There is no record of what became of that court-house. In 1789 William Blount got a bill through the legislature for a new one and the court-house that stood in and across Evans street just above Third, and which was burned in 1858, is supposed to be the one built under Blount's bill.

After years of effort a common school system was now partly in force in the State. Though Archibald D. Murphey threw sparks of life into the cause of common education in

1816-17, no lasting results were had. But the act creating the "Literary Fund" in 1825 was a revival of interest that by 1840 had over $100,000 in the treasury for school purposes. A new life was now put into the school matters, but strange to say the independent and indifferent action of many counties required more legislation to force the matter upon the people. In 1852, Calvin H. Wiley was elected the first State Superintendent of Public Instruction. He entered upon the work with a zeal and determination, that in a few short years found the schools on a surer foundation and the system somewhat on the order of to-day. The Literary Fund was divided among the counties, and where other taxes were added a reasonable school term was the result. Pitt's share of that fund as early as 1856 was $1,289.40.

At a meeting of the County Superintendents in 1858, Alfred Moye was elected chairman. The other Superintendents were John S. Daniel and Willis Whichard. Their duties were the same as those of our present Board of Education. The chairman had to give bond in the sum of $6,000 for the faithful performance of his duties. E. C. Yellowly, James Murray and Alfred Moye were elected examiners of teachers and allowed five dollars per year each. This meeting was held in April. In July they made an apportionment of 50 cents, "surplus," to be divided among the white children of each district. There were thirty-eight districts in the county. The school committees were elected by the popular vote of the districts and when no election was held the Superintendents appointed them. The next year the apportionment was 55 cents. Under an act of the legislature of this year, the Superintendents subscribed, out of the school funds, for the *North Carolina Journal of Education,* published by the State Educational Society, for each school district in the county.

In 1860 there died in Pitt County, where he had spent most of his life, Charles Harris, aged 122 years. He was born in England in 1738 and came to America when twenty-two years of age. He was a veteran of three wars: the Revolution, the second war with England and some Indian wars. He married Loany McLawhon and they had nine children, none dying younger than eighty-six years. At the age of 107, in 1845, he joined the Free Will Baptist Church and was baptized in Swift Creek.

CHAPTER TWENTY-THREE.

Military Spirit—Good Old Muster Days—Eighth Census—Elections—Fort Sumter—President Calls for Volunteers—Governor Ellis Calls for Volunteers for State's Defense—Secession Convention—Pitt's Members—G. B. Singeltary Raises First Company—Tar River Boys—Marlboro Guards—Disbursing and Safety Committee—War Funds—Third Regiment.

The questions of slavery and States Rights had agitated the country almost from its very beginning. The agitation had grown with time, and now at the close of 1859, and the beginning of the next year, when a President was to be elected, much excitement was all over the land. The war with Mexico had not been very popular in the State, and Pitt did not furnish many of the men who followed Scott and Taylor to their great victories. However the other questions had served to keep alive the military spirit, and as many were predicting war between the North and the South, the military spirit took on new life.

The general musters were big days. In years before, perhaps led by some old Mexican veterans, to the music of the fife and drum—

>"The jay bird, he died with the whooping-cough,
>   The bullfrog, he died with the colic;
> Up jumped the toad, with his tail cut off—
>   And that was an end of their frolic,"

they had lived in the past and its glories. But now stormier times were in prospect and though hard cider and beer and sometimes things much stronger, and the usual mutual fist fights, and mellowness all around, on such days, the thought of preparation for what might come was more often than the thought of what had been. But still there were good feeling and joy, and spirits enlivened by the cider gourd, and it was tramp, tramp, as they kept step to the music of the old veterans' fife and drum playing

> "As I went down the new-cut road,
> There I met a terrapin and a toad;
> The toad, he pat, the frog, he sing,
> And the terrapin cut the piggin wing."

Those were good old times—times of peace, pleasure and plenty. But others were coming. The song of "Dixie" was to banish that of "The Star Spangled Banner." The beginning of 1860 was a sign of the times.

Pitt County now had a population of 16,440, as follows: Whites, 7,840; free negroes, 127; slaves, 8,473. Of the white population, there were only 16 foreign born. Greenville, its only town, had a population of 828.

The people were taking interest in all affairs and the election campaign was a warm one. The election was close. For Governor, John W. Ellis, Democrat, 771; John Pool, Whig, 778. In the Presidential election, Abraham Lincoln was elected over all his competitors, but getting very, very few votes in North Carolina and not enough to count in Pitt County. Talk of dissolution of the Union was begun. In Pitt, there were strong Union and strong Secession men. Discussions were warm and 1861 saw its people divided among themselves. The legislature which met in December, 1860, recommended that a volunteer force should at once be enrolled and armed for defense. General Beauregard opened fire on Fort Sumter, April 12th, 1861, and on the 14th, it was evacuated. This meant war, and President Lincoln immediately called for 75,000 volunteers. Governor Ellis refused the demand for 1,500 from North Carolina and called the legislature in extra session. He also said war was upon us and called for 20,000 volunteers for the State's defense. The legislature met May 1st and called a convention, and that convention, on May 20th, passed the Ordinance of Secession. Pitt sent to that convention, now known as the "Secession Convention," F. B. Satterthwaite and Bryan Grimes. In the election for the call of the convention, Pitt County voted 986 "for convention" to 177 votes "against convention." It was a hot campaign and Satterthwaite and Grimes, candidates without opposition, and neighbors and friends, often had hot words, as Grimes charged Satterthwaite with being a "Union" man and opposed to secession.

But the men of Pitt County had not been idle. Earlier in the year enlistments had been made. The first company was raised by George B. Singeltary, in March. He was Captain and his brother, R. W. Singeltary, First Lieutenant. It had 140 men. The next was the Tar River Boys, G. W. Johnson, Captain and R. Greene, First Lieutenant, with 100 men. In April the Marlboro Guards were organized, with Wm. H. Morrill, Captain; J. B. Barrett, First Lieutenant; 71 men. Early in May, the Third Regiment was organized at Garysburg and in its companies were 84 men from Pitt.

At the May meeting of the County Court, P. A. Atkinson, H. S. Clark, F. B. Satterthwaite, L. P. Beardsley and Churchill Perkins were appointed a Disbursing and Safety Committee for the County. P. A. Atkinson was appointed treasurer. Their first meeting was held on the 8th, when H. S. Clark was elected chairman and W. M. B. Brown, secretary. The secretary reported that subscriptions amounting to $4,399.76 had been received and that $4,367.76 had been paid out for equipping and supporting the volunteers. More funds were needed and it was decided to borrow $10,000 from the bank of Washington. The expenses of Lieutenant W. A. Bernard, Dr. C. J. O'Hagan and W. H. Shelley, to Petersburg, were paid. They had been sent there on business pertaining to military affairs of the County. The Committee appointed sub-committees in each district, whose duty it was to look after the needs and wants of the families of those who had volunteered and those otherwise destitute and needy. Of the military fund raised for equipping and providing for the soldiers, $3,840 were raised by private and voluntary subscriptions, in amounts varying from $400 down to ten cents.

That the war spirit was thoroughly aroused is seen by the active preparations made for war. Many were enlisting and going to the front. The people at home were doing great things to sustain them. At a meeting of the Justices of the County, on the 13th, it was resolved to raise $25,000 for equipping and sustaining the troops sent off to war.

Pitt County men were enlisting everywhere. Some were so anxious to get to the front that they enlisted in companies already there. They were full of the idea advanced by many hot secessionists that all the blood to be shed could be wiped up with a pocket handkerchief, and they did not want the war ended before they could take a part.

When the Third Regiment was organized, there were sixty men in Company D, from Pitt. Edward Savage, of New Hanover, was Captain. In company E, M. L. F. Redd, of Onslow, Captain, there were 21. There were also a few others in some of the other companies. In the Second Regiment were 10 men in Company A, and others in other companies.

CHAPTER TWENTY-FOUR.

Major Grimes—Wyatt Killed—Disposition of Pitt Companies and Men—Hatteras Captured—Pitt County Boys Prisoners—Surgeon Brown and Madison—Yellowly's Call for Volunteers—Officers of Twenty-seventh Regiment — Chicamacomico — Promotions.

On the organization of the Fourth Regiment, at Camp Hill, near Garysburg, Bryan Grimes was commissioned Major of that regiment. He was offered Lieutenant-Colonel of the Eighth or Major of the Fourth and chose the latter. He at once resigned as a member of the Secession Convention and was succeeded by P. A. Atkinson.

On the 10th of June was fought the battle of Big Bethel, Virginia, in which Henry L. Wyatt was killed, being the first soldier to fall in battle wearing the Gray. He was at that time a member of the Edgecombe Guards, his parents having but recently moved from Greenville to Tarboro, where he enlisted. Though born in Richmond, Virginia, most of his life was spent in Greenville, where he grew to manhood and received most of his education, all of which he received in Pitt County. Pitt has as much claim to him as a hero as has Edgecombe, as it was only a circumstance that gave him to that county.

The Twenty-seventh Regiment was organized at New Bern, June 22d, Captain Singeltary's and Captain Morrill's companies being two of its companies. Captain Singeltary was elected Colonel, and R. W. Singeltary succeeded him as Captain of the company, which was known as "H." Captain Morrill's company was "E." The Tar River Boys had been sent to Portsmouth, N. C., and in July, Captain Johnson was elected Lieutenant-Colonel of the Seventh Volunteers, and the volunteers sent to Hatteras. On the 13th, Dr. Wyatt M.

Brown was elected Surgeon of the Seventeenth Regiment. He had been a surgeon in the U. S. Army, but some time previous had resigned and located at his old home, Greenville, with his brother, the late Dr. W. M. B. Brown. Dr. C. J. O'Hagan was elected Surgeon of the Ninth. In the Thirty-third, organized this month, Pitt had 26 men in Company B.

The last recorded meeting of the Disbursing and Safety Committee was held on the 13th. The only business was allowing some accounts and only two members, L. P. Beardsley and P. A. Atkinson, and the secretary, were present.

August 28th Fort Hatteras was attacked by a large fleet. Next day the attack was resumed. In the defense of the fort, numbers 2 and 3 of the channel batteries were under the command of Lieutenant-Colonel G. W. Johnson, assisted by First-Lieutenant M. T. Moye and Second-Lieutenant G. W. Daniel. The guns of the fort could not reach the boats, while those of the boats were throwing more than twenty shells a minute into the fort, and after receiving that bombardment three hours and twenty minutes, the fort was surrendered, with many prisoners, though some of the Confederates managed to escape. Most of the Tar River Boys were taken prisoners and sent to Fort Warren. Surgeon Brown had his body servant, Madison, with him. Madison was offered his liberty, but preferring to remain with his master, was sent on a prisoner with the others.

Some time later Surgeon Brown was exchanged and made chairman of the State Examining Board of Surgeons, with headquarters at Goldsboro. Afterwards he was transferred to Mississippi. He never forgot his faithful servant Madison, and made provision for him after he was freed.

E. C. Yellowly and A. J. Hines, who had been commissioned respectively Captain and First Lieutenant, to raise a company, had enlisted 128 men by September. In July they had issued the following circular:

ONE HUNDRED MEN WANTED

For the First Regiment of State Troops.

The undersigned are now raising a company of State troops to complete the first regiment, of which Col. Stokes is in command. It is desirable that this company should be formed as speedily as practicable, that it may secure a position under so efficient and experienced an officer as Col. Stokes, and the more speedily it is formed the more speedily will it be led to meet an enemy now ready to commence its long-threatened attempt to invade our homes and subjugate a free people.

Recruits will be enlisted at Greenville, Pitt County, by the undersigned until the Company is formed.

E. C. YELLOWLY, *Capt.*
GREENVILLE, July 10, 1861. A. J. HINES, *1st. Lieut.*

However, it was not formed in time to get into the First Regiment, but got into the Eighth Regiment at Camp Macon, as Company G, on its organization on the 13th. C. D. Rountree and Walter N. Peebles were elected Lieutenants. The regiment soon left for Roanoke Island, where it arrived on the 21st.

Soon after the organization of the Twenty-seventh Regiment, four companies volunteered for the war, which reduced it to a battalion of twelve months volunteers, of which G. B. Singeltary was elected Lieutenant-Colonel. Before the close of the month four other companies had been added and it was reorganized as a regiment. G. B. Singeltary was again elected Colonel and his brother, T. C. Singeltary, of Company E, Major. R. W. Singeltary was elected Captain of Company H; J. A. Williams, First Lieutenant; G. W. Cox, Second, and C. F. Gaskins, Third.

October 4th, was the fight at Chicamacomico, in which the Eighth captured the Federal camp and 55 prisoners. On the 6th the camp at Roanoke was captured, with much camp plunder. In both of these actions Company G was engaged and did its duty.

In November Captain Morrill, having been promoted Commissary of his regiment, (27th) resigned, and was succeeded by Jason P. Joyner, as Captain of Company E. He was promoted from Adjutant. H. F. Price was elected First-Lieutenant.

In December Colonel G. B. Singeltary resigned as Colonel of the Twenty-seventh Regiment and was succeeded by John Sloan, the Lieutenant-Colonel, who was in turn succeeded by T. C. Singeltary soon thereafter.

CHAPTER TWENTY-FIVE.

ENLISTMENTS—MILITARY BOARD—CAPTURE OF ROANOKE ISLAND—COMPANIES AND OFFICERS—FORTY-FOURTH REGIMENT—SEVENTEENTH—GRIMES, LIEUTENANT-COLONEL—FIFTY-FIFTH—TRANTERS CREEK SKIRMISH—FIGHT A FEW DAYS LATER—COLONEL SINGELTARY KILLED—MOVEMENTS—SEVENTY-FIFTH.

January, 1862, found more than 500 Pitt County men enlisted and more ready. Eleven men enlisted in a company then forming in Wake, which afterwards became Company I, of the Forty-fifth Regiment. R. W. Singeltary was elected Captain of a company then forming, which afterwards became H, of the Forty-fourth Regiment. H. F. Price was elected Captain of Company H, of the Twenty-seventh, to succeed R. W. Singeltary. D. H. Smith and W. L. Cherry had each been commissioned to raise a company and were actively doing so.

February 6th, the County Court elected a Military Board for the County, John S. Smith, Dr. W. M. B. Brown and Arthur Forbes, constituting that Board.

On the 8th, the Federal fleet, which had been off Hatteras since January 23d, began an attack on Roanoke Island, and for five hours 1,400 Confederates withstood the attack of 10,000 Federals. The end was the surrender of the Confederates. They were carried as prisoners to Elizabeth City, where they were soon paroled. On the 14th, L. R. Anderson and Cornelius Stephens were commissioned Captain and Lieutenant of a company of 112 men, enlisted by them. Fifteen men from Pitt were enlisted in Company D, J. M. C. Luke, Captain, from Hertford County, Seventeenth Regiment. The Twenty-seventh Regiment was now at Fort Lane, below New Bern, where, about the last of this month, T. C. Singeltary, Lieutenant-Colonel, resigned, and R. W. Singeltary succeeded Colonel Sloan. McG. Ernul was elected First-Lieutenant of Company G, of the same regiment.

The Twenty-seventh was in a fight at New Bern, March 25th. While it did little of the fighting, it held an important position and was the last to leave the field, after which it marched to Kinston. The Forty-fourth Regiment was organized at Camp Mangum, near Raleigh, the last of this month, with G. B. Singeltary, Colonel. Abram Cox was Assistant Commissary Sergeant, Dr. J. N. Bynum, Assistant Surgeon, and W. L. Cherry, one of the Quartermasters. Companies C, W. L. Cherry, Captain; Abram Cox, First Lieutenant, 131 men; D, L. R. Anderson, Captain; C. Stephens, First Lieutenant, 116 men; and I, D. H. Smith, Captain; J. J. Bland, First Lieutenant, 120 men; and a few men in other companies were from Pitt.

In April another company, Howard Wiswall, Captain; J. H. Gray, First Lieutenant; 117 men, became K, of the Seventeenth Regiment. R. W. Singeltary was elected Lieutenant-Colonel of the Seventeenth, and that regiment went to Virginia, where it was put in General Walker's Brigade.

Early in May, Colonel Anderson, of the Fourth, was put in command of the brigade, at Williamsburg, Virginia, and Lieutenant-Colonel Grimes was in command of the regiment. In the organization of the Fifty-fifth Regiment, at Camp Mangum, J. T. Whitehead was elected Major, C. E. Jackey, Chief Musician, and J. P. Bernard, one of the musicians. Company E, J. T. Whitehead, Captain, and H. W. Brown, First Lieutenant, 90 men, were from Pitt. On the 19th, the Forty-fourth was sent to Tarboro and did picket duty in that section and Pitt, being included in the Pamlico division, under Brigadier-General Martin. First Lieutenant Brown, of Company E, Fifty-fifth Regiment, resigned, and J. A. Hanrahan succeeded him. On the 30th, a picket squad, of the Forty-fourth, had a skirmish with a few Federals at Tranter's Creek. The squad had been to Washington to exchange about 300 prisoners. Returning, it left the river at Yankee Hall and marched to Myers' Mill. A squad of sixteen Federals were then about Latham's Cross-Roads. Church Latham, a merchant there, tried to hide his books, which created some suspicion. The Federals examined them and finding nothing wrong, went on to the bridge. As they were crossing they were fired into. E. P. Fleming, of Company B, fired the first shot. There was big rise in the water and a boy was the first to give information of their approach. They crossed the bridge and went on to the mill, where the others of the squad were on guard. There they swam the creek and returned to Washington, with a loss of one killed and perhaps some wounded. Next day some of them returned and tore up the bridge. On the 31st, the Twenty-seventh Regiment, which was at Kinston, was sent to Virginia. On that day was fought the battle of Seven Pines, where Lieutenant-Colonel Grimes' Regiment got its name of the "Bloody Fourth." He was the only officer of the Regiment not either killed or wounded.

The affair at Tranter's Creek alarmed the Federals at Washington and they prepared to drive the Confederates away. A few days later the Forty-fourth and a part of the Third Cavalry were in the vicinity. On the 5th of June, about 500 Federals, the Twenty-fourth Regiment of Massachusetts Volunteers, under Lieutenant-Colonel F. A. Osborn and some cavalry, attacked the Confederates at the mill, on Tranter's Creek. They did not cross and most of the fighting was from cover, the Federals from the mill on the Beaufort side and the Confederates from the gin-house on the Pitt side. The result was seven killed and eight wounded of the Federals and six killed of the Confederates. Among the Confederates was Colonel Singeltary. It is said that seeing a Federal getting ready to shoot, he ordered one of his men to shoot, pointing at him, when a ball pierced his head, killing him almost instantly. After the fight the Federals returned to Washington and the Confederates to Tarboro.

Dr. C. J. O'Hagan was elected Surgeon of the Thirty-fifth Regiment on the 17th of June. The Twenty-seventh Regiment was in the Seven Days fight around Richmond, but its losses were light. Lieutenant-Colonel Cotten having resigned, T. C. Singeltary was elected Colonel of the Forty-fourth, which went to Virginia and was in General Pettigrew's Brigade. At Mechanicsville Lieutenant-Colonel Grimes had a horse killed under him.

In July the Seventy-first Regiment was formed by taking companies of other commands. It was also known as the Seventh Cavalry. In Company H, of which L. J. Barrett was later elected Captain, were several men from Pitt, and also a few in other companies. Captain Barrett was promoted from the ranks.

CHAPTER TWENTY-SIX.

Vance Elected Governor—State Census—Yellowly for Congress—Fifty-fifth at Kinston—General Clingman's Complaint—Maryland Campaign—Captain Joyner Killed—Heavy Losses—Singeltary's Reply—Movement of Troops—Haddock's Cross-roads—Federals Capture Greenville—Other Events.

In the August election Z. B. Vance, then Colonel of the Twenty-sixth, defeated William Johnston, of Charlotte, for Governor. Pitt's vote was 649 for Vance and 229 for Johnston. As reported by the Secretary of State, the State census gave Pitt a population of 16,793, there being 7,480 whites, 127 free negroes and 8,473 slaves. This year Captain

STATE CAPITOL, RALEIGH, N. C.

E. C. Yellowly was a candidate for representative in the Confederate Congress against the incumbent R. R. Bridgers. On the returns Bridgers was elected but Captain Yellowly's friends claimed he had been cheated out of his election, and wanted him to contest, which he refused to do.

On the 7th, the Fifty-fifth prevented the landing of troops from a gunboat at Kinston. Lieut.-Col. J. T. Whitehead, of the Fifty-fifth, being dead, Capt. M. T. Smith succeeded him.

In the summer Brig.-Gen. T. L. Clingman, who had some supervision of this section, wrote to Gen. D. H. Hill, that two companies of cavalry, one on either side of Tar River, were not sufficient to prevent intercourse between the Federals below and the people above; that the Federals got Richmond papers regularly and also other news; that Satterthwaite, a member of the State convention, lived within the Federal lines, but was allowed to go to Greenville whenever he wished, and others were allowed the same privilege. He thought such intercourse should not be allowed.

In the Maryland campaign, the Twenty-seventh formed the rear guard, and had no hard fighting in the beginning. In crossing the Potomac, on September 5th, Colonel Grimes received a severe injury by being kicked by a horse. Early in this month, the Eighth, which had been captured at Roanoke Island and later exchanged, reorganized, at Camp Mangum, and was sent east, where, about Kinston, it did picket duties, as also the Fifty-fifth was doing. In the battle of South Mountain, on the 14th, Colonel Grimes had a horse killed under him. At Sharpsburg, or Antietam, on the 17th, the Twenty-seventh lost 203 men out of 325. Company E had two-thirds of its men and officers killed or wounded, among the killed being J. P. Joyner, its Captain. It had only four men able for duty next day. When starting to make the charge in this battle, a drunken fellow on horseback rode out in front, pulled off his hat, waved it high and said, "Come on, boys, I'm leading this charge." Lieutenant-Colonel R. W. Singeltary, who was leading it, replied, "You're a liar, sir; we lead our own charges." In this battle, with only one man to a panel of fence, the Third held its position from midday of the 17th to 10 a. m. on the 18th, without so much as a drop of water, all of which time Federal artillery played "battle-door and shuttle-cock" with these fence rails. In addition to losing its Captain, Company E lost its First and Second Lieutenants killed. R. W. Joyner, brother of Captain J. P. Joyner, was elected Captain afterwards. The latter part of the month, H. G. Whitehead was promoted Captain, and J. A. Hanrahan, First Lieutenant of Company E, Fifty-fifth Regiment.

Early in October the Fifty-fifth went to Virginia and was put in the brigade of Brigadier-General J. R. Davis, of Mississippi. R. W. Singeltary resigned as Lieutenant-Colonel of the Twenty-seventh, and John R. Cooke succeeded him. C. Stephens resigned as First Lieutenant of Company D, Forty-fourth Regiment, and J. S. Eason succeeded.

This month was also noted for two expeditions into Pitt by the Federals from Washington; one to the Haddock's cross roads section was piloted by one Horner, a buffalo. Several men of Captain C. A. White's company were captured. Horner is said to have been rewarded by the Federals with the office or title of captain.

The other expedition was also from Washington, for the purpose of taking Greenville. It consisted of the steamer North State, mounting one 24-pounder Howitzer and six men; a launch with one 12-pounder Howitzer and seventeen men; a flat boat and seventeen men, in charge of Lieutenant McLane, and fourteen men with a Howitzer, in care of Gunner McDonald. The expedition left Washington on the 8th at 4:30 p. m. and arrived at Greenville the next day about ten o'clock, after having some difficulty in passing sandbars. The expedition was under Second Assistant Engineer Lay, of the U. S. Navy, who proceeded up-town under a flag of truce to demand the surrender of the town, which was done by the Mayor. Some Confederates were on the bridge when the expedition arrived. One boat went a little up the river from the wharf, and one of those on the bridge, W. C. Richardson, killed a Federal soldier on that boat. Richardson then escaped, but it had the effect of exciting the Federals to retaliation. They made many threats of vengeance, but finding it was a soldier and not a private who had killed the man, they took a lot of horses, mules, stores, and provisions and ten of the citizens and left. In the expedition were a lot of negro soldiers in uniforms with belts, swords and pistols. They drew the artillery through the streets, and when leaving gave a general invitation to all the negroes to go with them.

None went at that time. The citizens who were taken were J. S. Dancy, Hodges, Hoell, Tyce, Cobb, B. Albritton, R. Greene, Allen Tyce, James Forbes and William Stocks. They were taken to Washington, held a few days and released.

Brigadier-General Anderson, having been seriously wounded, Colonel Grimes was now in command of Anderson's Brigade and commanded it in the battle of Fredericksburg.

The latter part of the month, J. T. Williams, Lieutenant of Company E, Twenty-seventh, was promoted Captain of Company G, same regiment. About the first of December, W. L. Cherry, Captain of Company C, Forty-fourth, was promoted Assistant Quartermaster and M. G. Cherry succeeded him. On the 10th, a detachment of the Seventeenth participated in the capture of Plymouth, while another detachment helped drive the Federals from Washington. The Twenty-seventh was at Fredericksburg, but suffered little, and at Marye's Heights, was protected by a rock wall. Since reorganization, the Eighth had been in camp about Wilmington, but on the 17th, was near Goldsboro and after a several hours fight, succeeded in checking the advance of the Federals, who however, burned the bridge across Neuse River. There had been a number of changes in the officers of the Pitt companies during the last few months, most of which have been mentioned. The changes of the minor officers were very frequent.

CHAPTER TWENTY-SEVEN.

EMANCIPATION PROCLAMATION—MOVEMENTS OF TROOPS—
COLONEL GRIFFIN IN PITT—HIS PICKET LINES—TITHE
GATHERERS—COLONEL HAMMOND—HIS PREDICAMENT—
CONVERSATION—ESCAPE — CHANCELLORSVILLE — JACK-
SON KILLED—IN VIRGINIA.

Though the Confederate States were being hemmed in by great Federal armies and there was want within its confines, the great Confederate victories gave hopes of an early termination of the war; but at the same time there was more determination on the part of the North to win in the end. So, greater efforts were made to raise men and money and to cripple the South.

January 1st, 1863, gave the country President Lincoln's Emancipation Proclamation, by which he declared free all the slaves of the Confederate States. So far as the slaves themselves were concerned, it had little effect, for few of them knew of it or could profit by it. In Pitt, it may have induced a few more to run away and enter the Federal lines about New Bern and Washington. Those who remained with their masters, remained as faithful as before. During this month the Twenty-seventh had seen service around Wilmington, Charleston, Goldsboro and Kinston, at which latter place it was at this time. The Seventeenth had been brigaded under General Martin.

Colonel Grimes was relieved of the command of the brigade early in February by Brigadier-General Ramseur, and devoted his talents to increasing the efficiency of his regiment. The Eighth was now at James Island, S. C., where there were many deaths. It was also on an expedition to Savannah.

In March the Seventeenth was on duty about Fort Branch, after which it was about Kinston and Wilmington. The complaint of General Clingman seems to have been heard, for Colonel Griffin, of the Sixty-second Georgia Regiment, with three companies of North Carolina troops, with headquarters at the Avon farm, did picket duty from Blount's Creek to Williamston. Half his regiment was at the Avon. All communication and passing was forbidden between the people, across his picket lines, except to the Rev. Mr. Kenerly. Captain Gray (of Georgia) was on the north side of the river at Colonel Gray Little's, near Pactolus. Later Colonel Griffin moved up to the Clark place, on the east side of the

CONFEDERATE PLAT IN CEMETERY, GREENVILLE.
The cannon shown is the Buckell Cannon.

river, above Greenville. There it was easier to get supplies, and Mrs. S. W. Atkinson furnished him pasturage.

Pitt County now had "Tithe Gatherers," whose business was to collect one-tenth of the products of the County and forward them to the army in the field. For the Bethel section, including parts of Edgecombe and Martin counties, N. M. Hammond held the position. At one time he had a large amount of supplies on hand and the Federals heard of it. Though he had usually a squad of soldiers for a guard, at this time there were not that many on hand. There had been a detachment at the bridges across Conetoe Creek, but they had gone away a few days before. He did not sleep too well now, for he feared the supplies might be captured. Sure enough, late one night Mrs. Hammond was aroused by the tread of horses in the yard. She detected it was not the tread of Confederate horses, the Confederate and Federal cavalry drilling different. She aroused Colonel Hammond, who had really been listening too. Soon a man called and being answered, asked about getting something for his horse. Then Colonel Hammond knew it was the Federals. He told them to go to his barn, where they would find plenty of corn and fodder. Other questions were being asked and answered, when the report of a gun was heard some distance away, about where old Bethel was. The Federals got scared, and scared badly, as they were very few. Then something like the following conversation, though very hurriedly, passed between them:

Federal: Any Confederates about here?

Colonel Hammond: Yes; Colonel _____ is at the bridges, a mile or two west of here.

Federal: Any Confederates down there? (Here the report of the guns was heard).

Colonel Hammond: Yes.

Federal: How many? Are any about here?

Colonel Hammond: I don't know.

Federal: Well, you know you are our prisoner, but if you will tell us how to get away from here, —— if you mayn't go.

It is needless to say Colonel Hammond told them and they

were as glad as he was; and all the supplies were saved and soon found their way to the Confederate armies.

On May 2d and 3d was fought the battle of Chancellorsville, in which battle Gen. "Stonewall" Jackson was mortally wounded. Pitt County had many men in that battle and among the hundreds of others, had one who was of the squad that fired that fatal shot. General Jackson died on the 10th, his body was taken to Richmond and lay in state in the capitol, Company D, Forty-fourth Regiment, being the Guard of Honor. The Twenty-seventh had a fight at Gun Swamp and drove the Federals into their lines near New Bern on the 19th.

June 1st, the Twenty-seventh was ordered to Virginia and was on duty and fighting around Richmond all the summer.

At South Anna Bridge, on the 26th, the Forty-fourth suffered heavy losses. At one time the regiment was surrounded and commanded to surrender, but cut its way out. One officer, when ordered to surrender, said, "No, I'll be d—d if I do," and fought till he fell.

CHAPTER TWENTY-EIGHTH.

GETTYSBURG—FARTHEST AT—SEVERE LOSSES—POTTER'S RAID—AT GREENVILLE—VIDETTES FIRED UPON—RETURN FROM TARBORO—SKIRMISH AT OTTER'S CREEK BRIDGE—LIEUTENANT SHARPE—ESCAPE OF RAIDERS—THEIR ROUTE—AT SCUFFLETON—DEMORALIZATION OF FOLLOWERS.

July 1st, 2d and 3d was fought the great battle of Gettysburg. North Carolina had there twelve regiments and one battalion. In the Third and Fifty-fifth, Pitt County had near a company each. On the third day, the Fifty-fifth went farthest in the Federal lines, Company E, Capt. H. G. Whitehead's, being in the lead. Captain Whitehead was wounded the day before and was not in this charge. The regiment lost more than half its men, killed or wounded. The Third fought in the open on the third day and suffered very severely. Going into battle with 300 guns, it lost 220. After the battle it had only seventy-seven guns. But it lost none as prisoners or stragglers.

Potter's raid from New Bern to Tarboro and return, through Pitt, was the cause of much excitement this month. Brigadier-General E. E. Potter, with several companies of infantry and cavalry, left New Bern on the 19th. Coming by way of Vanceboro, they raided the country, and when a few miles from Greenville they captured a picket post of fifteen men, destroying their stores and tents. They were a part of Captain C. A. White's company, of Whitford's Battalion. They reached Greenville about 3 p. m. Some time was spent plundering and taking what they could use and about six p. m. they continued their raid on towards Tarboro, on the south side of the river. When nearing Tyson's Creek, they were fired upon three times by unknown and unseen parties. They reached Old Sparta the next morning and by nine o'clock were in Tarboro. A detachment was sent on to Rocky Mount and at both places much property was destroyed, consisting of bales of cotton, flour, provisions, three boats, the cotton mills at Rocky Mount, railroad and county bridges, several trains, and other property. The Tarboro raiders returned the same day. Shortly after passing Old Sparta, they were fired upon and a somewhat running skirmish was kept up to Otter's Creek, though the officers took time to get a good supper at W. B. F. Newton's, who lived at the Swain place. While there several neighbors tried to get an opportunity to shoot some of them and one James Dupree, son of Thomas Dupree, a boy about sixteen, was captured with his gun, but was released. Learning of the raid, Colonel Claiborne left Kinston with his regiment to intercept them. He met them about night at Otter's Creek bridge, about a mile from Falkland. The bridge was burned by Colonel Claiborne. Here a sharp skirmish fight occurred and the Federals finding they could not dislodge the Confederates, made a round-about march and crossed the creek at the Dupree crossing. Lieutenant V. B. Sharpe, of Company E, Forty-third, knowing the country, begged Colonel Claiborne to let him have a company to intercept them at that crossing, where he stated he could capture them all. Colonel Claiborne would not do so, so they escaped and continued on their raid. Across the creek, two citizens, Col. Walter Newton and W. B. F. Newton, were on the road with their guns. It was night and they fired into the Federals and run. They did no damage. Arriving at Colonel Newton's house they attempted to burn it, and then left by the Otter's Creek church road. The negroes put the fire out before the house was much damaged. Going on by way of the church, the Federals looted the country of all they could. Going into Greene County by way of Fieldsboro they made a circuit near Snow Hill and reached Scuffleton (Ridge Spring) next day. Whitford's Battalion was in that vicinity and a fight was expected there.

But no stand was made. Captain Edwards, of Company C, simply had the planks of the Scuffleton bridge taken up, and left, narrowly escaping capture himself. As the Federals were crossing the bridge, which they relaid, Josiah Dixon, who, with two others, was on the west side of the creek, fired into their rear. It was early in the morning and the raiders thinking they were attacked, fled, leaving some horses and baggage, which the three took.

The expedition consisted of about 300 men and officers. By the time they got back to Burney's cross roads, they had a big lot of negroes, horses, mules, wagons, provisions, and other things. There the Fiftieth Regiment from Kinston tried to intercept them. The Fiftieth opened fire on them with a small brass cannon strapped to the back of a mule, which had little effect other than to completely demoralize the followers, mostly negroes. That great mob, composed of men, women, children and babies, perched on wagons, carts, buggies, carriages, and on horseback, whipping, slashing and yelling like crazy Indians, were suddenly halted by that mule's cannon firing on some negro troops in the rear. Pandemonium reigned and the whole became a confused mass in their efforts to escape. A negro captain, driving a pair of fine gray horses, was shot dead as he attempted to pass, firing at the Confederates. Others were killed or wounded about in the woods where they were trying to escape or shoot soldiers. Scouring the woods many negroes were found and captured. Among them were many children, even babies, who had been abandoned by their mothers in their mad attempt to escape. All kinds of fine clothing, tableware and other portable things were found strewed about the vicinity. The Fiftieth captured what horses it needed and went in pursuit of the raiders, capturing more horses and property and negroes on the route. The Federals continued their way on to Street's Ferry, where some Confederates again attacked them.

At Greenville, the Federals spent several hours, raided bar-rooms, many got drunk, attempted to destroy the river bridge and had a good time. There were other Confederates of the Sixty-seventh in Black Jack vicinity when those of Captain White's Company were captured, but they left in a hurry. It was said that Colonel Whitford ordered a retreat to Contentnea bridge, and that a regular, go-as-you-please race ensued, every man looking out for self. It is not known what became of some of them, as many never reached the bridge.

CHAPTER TWENTY-NINE.

The Eighth—Major Yellowly—Forty-fourth and Sixty-sixth—Bristoe Station—Losses—Cas Laughinghouse—Duel That Never Occurred—War Prices—Capture at Haddock's Cross-roads—Red Banks Affair—Other Events.

The Eighth was still about Charleston, and while on Morris Island was at all times exposed to a murderous fire. The Fifty-fifth was doing duty about the Rapidan, in Virginia, where it remained until October.

The first of August Captain Yellowly was promoted Major of the Eighth Regiment, at which time his regiment was in Battery Wagner, where it remained some time. The Forty-fourth was now in Kirkland's Brigade, and was almost constantly fighting about Petersburg. The Sixty-sixth was organized at Kinston by combining the Eighth and Fourth battalions. Company E was mostly from Pitt County. S. S. Quinerly was Captain and I. K. Witherington, First Lieutenant. A. J. Hines was promoted Captain of Company G, Eighth Regiment.

October 14th was fought the battle of Bristoe Station, in which Cooke's Brigade lost 700 men and Kirkland's Brigade lost 560. The Twenty-seventh was in Cooke's, and lost 290 men out of 416. The Forty-fourth was cut nearly to pieces, and greatly distinguished itself. Three times was it ordered to fall back, yet it steadily advanced, and only fell back under peremptory orders; and that, too, when victory was almost won. As the color-bearer of the Twenty-seventh fell, Corporal J. B. Barrett, one of the color-guard, caught the colors. He had gone only a few steps when he was shot down and another guard caught them.

Shortly before this battle, new clothing had been distributed among some of the companies. As the Twenty-seventh was falling back up the hill, Cas Laughinghouse, of Company E, found his knapsack in his way. It was too heavy. Remembering that his new clothes were in it he would not throw it away, so he deliberately stopped and exchanged his clothes under a heavy fire, escaping unharmed.

Major Yellowly, of the Eighth, was now Lieutenant-Colonel of that regiment, having been recently promoted. For what he considered an injustice, Calhoun Mcore, of Company I, Forty-fourth, challenged his Captain, D. H. Smith, to fight a duel. Captain Smith resigned that he could accept. Then Moore refused to fight. Smith reenlisted as a private, but got a furlough home, at the expiration of which he went to New Bern and remained in the Federal lines to the close of the war. W. J. Hodges, of the same company, acted likewise. J. R. Roach succeeded Smith as Captain.

Confederate money had now greatly depreciated and prices were skyward. So scarce were many things and so much was the depreciation of the money, that a gallon of molasses was worth $8, one pound of beef 62 1-2 cents, one bushel of cornmeal $15, one pound of black pepper $8, one pound of cheese $3, a good horse $1,000, and so on. Times were getting hard. There was want in Pitt County and the County Court decided to issue $40,000 in bonds for the benefit of the poor. There was much discontent and many people were tired of the war and anxious for peace.

November 25th an expedition from New Bern under Captain Graham, of the First North Carolina Volunteers (Federals or negroes) with a number of regular troops, surrounded Whitford's Battalion near Haddock's cross-roads, captured 52, killed a Lieutenant and four men, took 100 stand of arms, a lot of horses, mules, wagons and a large amount of commissary stores. The pilot of this expedition was one Horn or Horner, who was familiar with the country. The Eighth Regiment, which was in camp near Wilmington, was now ordered to Petersburg, but before going did duty about Kinston. It was then about Petersburg till 1864.

December 30th there was a fight near Red Banks Church and the church burned. On one of their raids into Pitt from Washington, the church at Black Jack was burned, as it was sometimes used for shelter by soldiers. The Forty-first and some of a Virginia Regiment were doing duty below Greenville. One picket post was at Red Banks Church. On that night 140 Federals attacked that post. It was a general mix-up fight, hand-to-hand fight. The Federals retreated towards New Bern and the Confederates towards Greenville. The Federals reported their loss as one killed, six wounded and one missing; the Confederates as six killed, one piece of Starr's battery, caisson and horses, captured. In the darkness and close quarters, the combatants got mixed and a Federal rode off with the Confederates. At daybreak Lieutenant Slade, (Martin County) of Company K, saw he was not a Confederate, and at once he was a prisoner with the loss of his horse and arms, and his captor greatly enjoyed his prisoner's great "boo hoo." He was no doubt the one the Federals reported missing.

The past year had been one of many reverses for the Confederates, though some brilliant victories had been won. The Confederate army was being constantly depleted, while recruiting was doing little to keep the ranks filled. With the Federals were money and men and more money and more men. Yet the spirit of the Confederates was undaunted and they fought on with a determination to win. Such was the beginning of the New Year. Pitt County was doing its duty for the field and at home.

CHAPTER THIRTY.

County Matters—Sixty-seventh—Movements of Other Regiments—Plymouth Captured—Great Victory—Heavy Losses—Taxes—The Wilderness—Remarkable Fighting—Spottsylvania—General Daniel Wounded and Grimes in Command—Drewry's Bluff—Captains Jarvis and Hines Wounded—Thomas King—Juniors—Cold Harbor—Captain Anderson Killed.

At the January, 1864, meeting of the county court, the treasurer reported: receipts, from sale of bonds, $10,000; from the State, $5,592.50; from county trustee, $8,000; from sale of land, $1,634; disbursements, for military purposes, $19,657.45; balance on hand, $5,889.05.

Early in this month the Sixty-seventh Regiment was organized. Several of its companies had been in the service some time, in battalions. In the regiment were Companies D, Captain David Cogsdell, near half its men from Pitt; E, Captain C. A. White, from Pitt; G, Captain A. W. Jones, most men from Pitt; I, Captain E. F. White, from Pitt; and many men from Pitt in other companies.

February 1st, the Eighth Regiment, which had just arrived two days before, was in the fight at Bachelor's Creek, near Kinston. It returned to Petersburg on the 3d. On the 2d, the Seventeenth Regiment was in the attack on Newport, where being on the right of the brigade, assailed the Federal columns, poured over their works and captured their guns and barracks. The Federals fled to Fort Macon, but as General Pickett failed to capture New Bern, the brigade had to withdraw from Newport; thus the Seventeenth lost the advantages of its victory. The Twenty-seventh left winter quarters, where it had been picketing along the Rapidan and was sent out to repel a cavalry raid. Such were the hardships that many of the men were without shoes and many were the blood-stained tracks they left in the snows.

Preparations had been made for an attack on Plymouth. On the 18th of April Hoke's Division, arrived before Plymouth and drove in the pickets. On the 19th there was some skirmishing. Next day, the 20th, the attack was made and before night the town with 2,000 troops, a lot of fugitive negroes and a lot of stores were in the hands of the Confederates. In this fight the Eighth did effective work. At one time it charged up to the palisades and as the Federals pulled their guns out of the port holes, they thrust theirs in and fired on those in the fort, doing deadly execution. Then it burst open the gates and captured the fort. Then it attempted to storm another fort, but had to retreat with heavy loss. It had gained one great victory, but it paid dearly for it. Its loss was 154 killed and wounded, including Lieutenant D. P. Langley of Company G. General Hoke next attacked New Bern and there was every prospect of an early capture, when he was ordered to Virginia, where he arrived just in time to save Petersburg from capture. In the attack on New Bern, the Eighth and Sixty-seventh were both engaged.

At the May meeting of the County Court, the tax rate was made two and one-half per cent on the $100, and other taxes levied in proportion. It was also decided to borrow $6,000 on the "pay when we can policy." W. G. Lang was appointed a special agent and authorized to buy 500 pairs of cards and to borrow money to pay for them.

May 5th began the battle of the Wilderness, 61,000 Confederates against 118,000 Federals. The Forty-fourth made the opening charge and lost heavily. The Twenty-seventh suffered severely, its brigade losing 1,080 out of 1,753 engaged. The Fifty-fifth had 340 men and was in the center of its brigade, where in the course of three hours it was attacked seven times and each time repulsed the attack. Its loss was 34 killed and 167 wounded. It did fearful execution as 157 men lay dead in its front. The Third did much fighting with clubbed guns and with bayonets, it being a hand to hand fight, each demanding the surrender of the other. It captured two guns. Next day the Fifty-fifth was attacked early, before it had unstacked arms, and driven back, but the arrival of Kershaw's division relieved it from such a perilous position. The Third was in the fight all day and the Forty-fourth, in foiling Grant's flank movement, suffered very severely. The Fifty-fifth formed the rear guard to Spottsylvania.

The Third, Twenty-seventh, Forty-fourth and Fifty-fifth regiments were in the Spottsylvania fight and did hard fighting. On the 10th, at the Mattapony, the Fifty-fifth captured a piece of artillery and drove the Federals across the river. On the 12th, Brigadier-General Junius Daniel was mortally wounded and Colonel Grimes was placed in command of the brigade. At Drewry's Bluff, on the 17th, the Seventeenth lost 175 officers and men. It was on the right of its brigade, which occupied the right of the division. The Eighth lost near 100 officers and men in this fight, among them being Captain T. J. Jarvis of Company B and Captain A. J. Hines of Company G, wounded. C. D. Rountree, First Lieutenant, then became acting captain of Company G.

After Chancellorsville, the First and Third, which had lost so heavily, were consolidated, and as such were at Gaines's Mill, June 2d, and Cold Harbor June 3d. The Forty-fourth was also at Gaines's Mill and did much fighting. During part of this fight some of the Forty-fourth were throwing up works for defense. Minnie balls were flying thick and fast. Work was progressing slowly when Lieutenant Thomas King, of Company D, mounted the works, called others to follow and complete them. His words were scarcely ended when a ball struck him, tearing through a little Testament in his upper left vest pocket, through his clothes and stopping against his flesh. It struck him squarely over his heart and the Testament saved his life. Jumping back, he said it would be best to work as they had been doing.

June 2d was organized the Fifth Battalion of Juniors, at Goldsboro. One company was from Pitt. McD. Boyd was Captain; Ruell Anderson, J. J. Laughinghouse and B. S. Sheppard, First, Second and Third Lieutenants. There were some few men in it from Wilson and Johnston counties and

BIG TREE
On the lands of Joseph Fleming. Where the boy is standing it is about eight feet in diameter

some of the officers, not mentioned, may have been from those counties. It was composed of seventeen-year-old boys. The battalion was then ordered to Weldon.

The battle of Cold Harbor was now being fought, between General Lee, with 58,000 and General Grant with 128,000. The Third, Eighth, Seventeenth, Twenty-seventh, Forty-fourth, and Fifty-fifth regiments, in each of which Pitt County had men, were in this battle. The losses of the Third from May 31st to June 3d, were 275. The Eighth suffered severely and came out without an officer, Company G losing heavily. The Seventeenth was on the right and supported Grandy's Battery. In its front the dead were so thick that they could have been walked upon the entire extent of the regiment, without touching ground. The Eighteenth, which was also there came out with about enough men for a company. The Twenty-seventh did not suffer so much as the others. The Forty-fourth lost heavily, among it being L. R. Anderson, Captain of Company D. The Fifty-fifth was in a protected position and did deadly work. In this battle Colonel Grimes' Regiment took a conspicuous part and he had a horse killed under him.

CHAPTER THIRTY-ONE.

GRIMES BRIGADIER-GENERAL—LOSSES AROUND PETERSBURG—A GREAT CAPTURE BY FLEMING, JAMES, CHERRY AND COGGINS—REGIMENT OF JUNIORS—DAVIS FARM—REAMS STATION—HARD TIMES IN RICHMOND—SHORT RATIONS—WINCHESTER—GRIMES IN COMMAND OF DIVISION—OTHER FIGHTING—PEACE PARTY—PITT OFFICERS OF JUNIORS—FORT FISHER.

Brigadier-General Junius Daniel having been mortally wounded on May 12th, Colonel Grimes who had been in command of the brigade since, received his commission as brigadier-general, on June 5th, though it dated from May 19th.

On the 17th, the Seventeenth was at Petersburg and a part of the 20,000 Confederates who repulsed 90,000 Federals. On the 30th the Eighth was in the Fort Harrison fight and lost heavily, as also did the Forty-fourth. The Eighth came out of the Fort Harrison fight with only nine men of Company G. Out of ten color guards, only two were left and one was G. M. Mooring.

On June 2d, at Cold Harbor, Sergeant R. R. Fleming and privates M. A. James, J. H. Cherry and .... Coggins were scouting in some woods. The woods were a little thick and suddenly they found themselves very near a small field in which were drilling a company of Federals. It was a case of capture or be captured, so Sergeant Fleming jumped from the woods, yelling to the others to follow and demanded the surrender of the Federals. So sudden was the rush and thinking the woods full of Confederates, they surrendered at once, being panic stricken. The four Confederates marched their prey into the lines and turned them over to their superiors, who never thought to compliment the quartette, and others were afterwards credited with most of the honors of the exploit. When the Federals, who numbered sixty-three, found themselves prisoners in the hands of only four Confederates, they were greatly chagrined and marched into quarters a sorry looking set.

There were no braver or truer soldiers than many of those of the Twenty-seventh. These four were among the bravest and a little incident during a term of Pitt County court some years ago is worth perpetuating: Judge J. A. Gilmer was on the bench. M. A. James was on trial for some altercation with a neighbor. Judge Gilmer had the case continued, saying that knowing Mr. James as a soldier that he (the Judge) could not give him justice, for no braver or better soldier fought under Lee and Jackson than M. A. James, and he did not feel that he could allow any fine or punishment against such a man. He also specially complimented the others of the same company.

July 16th, at Weldon, the Second and Fifth Battalions were consolidated and formed the Seventy-first Regiment of Junior Reserves. During this month the Fifty-fifth was transferred to Petersburg, and assigned a position near Malvern Hill. While there many of the men heard the sounds made by the Federals digging the celebrated mine, but did not then know what was going on underground.

August 18th, the Fifty-fifth lost one-half its men in the charge at the Davis Farm fight. It went in with only 130 men. At Reams' Station on the 24th, the Twenty-seventh was in Cooke's Brigade, and with only 1,753 men, captured 2,100 and thirteen pieces of artillery. The Twenty-seventh's colors were the first on the Federal works. After this it went into the trenches for the defense of Petersburg.

There were hard times about Richmond and Petersburg. Everything was scarce and hard to get. When the Seventeenth was relieved at Petersburg about the first of September, it had been reduced from 2,200 soldiers to about 700 skeletons. One pound of pork and three pounds of meal were the rations for three days.

On the 19th at Winchester, the Third experienced both success and defeat. After having pursued the Federals most of the day, late in that day it had to retreat and seek cover. Brigadier-General Grimes was conspicuous in this fight, lost nearly all his staff, was wounded, and had a horse shot under him.

In the month of October, the Sixty-seventh was on duty in the Washington and Plymouth sections. At Cedar Creek, Major-General Ranseur was killed and Brigadier-General Grimes took command of the division. The Twenty-seventh boasted that during the summer campaign, not one man had been captured while in battle, though thirty-five had been while out on skirmish duties. At Burgess's Mill on the 27th, there was much loss. The Fifty-fifth was in the center of the brigade. The Forty-fourth was driving everything in, when a flanking movement by the Federals dealt both regiments severe losses. By a misunderstanding of orders, they were not properly supported and in falling back to their original positions, their brigades suffered severely. They were soon afterwards returned to the defenses of Petersburg.

A peace party had been growing in North Carolina. Generally, the most ardent secessionists of 1861 were the most ardent peace advocates. W. W. Holden, a well-known peace man, had been the candidate against Governor Vance for Governor this year and had been defeated. Governor Vance held it would be dishonorable for the State to take any such action not in full accord with the other Confederate States, and did all in his power to keep the men at the front in clothes and food.

On December 8th, the Seventy-first (Juniors) who had been on duty in the vicinity of Tarboro, Hamilton and Plymouth for some time, were ordered to Bellfield, Virginia. In the meantime there had been another company added and several changes otherwise. In Company G were several Pitt boys, and S. V. Laughinghouse and J. E. Clark were First and Second Lieutenants; Hugh Murray, Second Lieutenant of Company A; Captain Anderson, Company H, had become transferred to the regulars, and J. J. Laughinghouse was Captain. Arriving at Bellfield, they drove the Federals several miles and prevented them cutting the railroad, for which the legislature of North Carolina gave them a special vote of thanks. They were soon sent to Goldsboro.

It was now seen that the Federals intended an attack on Fort Fisher, below Wilmington, and the Eighth was sent to Wilmington, by way of Danville. The Seventeenth reached Wilmington on the 24th and marched to Fort Fisher. The

CAPT. J. J. LAUGHINGHOUSE.

day before an attack had been made and the Federals had succeeded in making a landing. The Seventeenth was in the fight that drove them back to their ships. For two days the forts were then attacked by land and sea by one of the most powerful fleets, but had met a resistance from an inferior force that made them take to their boats and sail away. The forts and land forces had made a gallant defense and the Seventeenth had nobly performed its part of that duty.

CHAPTER THIRTY-TWO.

Deeds of Daring by Harris and Bland—Losses and Promotions—Around Petersburg—Fall of Fort Fisher—Wise's Fork—Southwest Creek—Bentonsville—Juniors—Struggling Against Odds.

Two "deeds of daring" during this attack on Fort Fisher are worthy of perpetuation in history. They were those of Taylor Harris and C. C. Bland.

That General Butler attempted to destroy the forts by exploding the steamship Louisiana with 250 tons of powder about half a mile from the fort is well known, but that another powder scheme failed because the fuse was extinguished by a private soldier at the risk of his life, is not. Another ship or barge floating in to the shore at the fort attracted attention. It was nearing the shore when three soldiers from the fort swam out to it to see what it could be. Taylor Harris was first to reach it. Climbing aboard he found a lighted fuse just sputtering in some scattered powder and in a second or more it would be in the bulk of powder. Quickly blocking the way of the fuse with both hands he threw it overboard. It was a dangerous and daring act. He had to wade knee deep in the powder to get to the fuse and expected all to be blown up before he could reach it. Thus was an evident sister attempt to the Louisiana foiled, which, being much nearer the fort, would have done much more damage.

On the 24th, the garrison flag was shot away from its staff. The only way to get it back was to climb the pole and replace it. Volunteers were called for. C. C. Bland, Company K, Thirty-sixth regiment went forward, mounted the ramparts, seized the flag and began climbing the pole amid a hail of shot and shell. Reaching the top, he tied the flag to the pole and began descending. About half way down, he was called to, that the flag did not float right. Looking up he saw it was tied by one corner only. Climbing up again, he took off his cravat and tied the other corner to the pole and descended. When some way down he was called to, to "look out for that shell." Looking to sea he saw the shell, seemingly coming directly at him. He clung as closely as possible to the pole while the shell went by, its breeze fanning his face. He was missed. He was safe. Taking his place in the ranks, he forgot the incident in the excitement of the defense. Later he was wounded and lost a leg. He is still living, an honored citizen and a worthy minister of the Primitive Baptists.

The New Year, 1865, dawned rather gloomy for the cause of the Confederacy. Yet there was no loss of zeal for the cause. The South had suffered in the loss of thousands of its best and bravest men. The army had lost half of those who had enlisted, while there was no field for recruits. The North had lost as heavily, but had the world for recruiting, and they had more than a million veterans in the field. Pitt County had lost many of its best and noblest sons. Great changes had been made in companies and their officers. Many fell on the bloody fields, some died in hospitals and many were then in Northern prisons. Lieutenants C. D. Rountree and E. A. Moye, who had been acting Captains of Company G, Eighth Regiment, after the wounding of Captain Hines, were in prison; Lieutenant Eason died in the hospital and Lieutenants G. W. Parker and Thomas King, who had been acting Captains of Company D, Forty-fourth Regiment, had been wounded, (Parker losing a leg and King being mortally wounded, dying soon,) and J. T. Williams had been promoted Captain from Company E, Twenty-seventh Regiment; Lieutenant J. M. White had succeeded C. A. White as Captain of Company E, Sixty-seventh Regiment; Brigadier-General Grimes was acting Major-General and soon to be commissioned, and many minor officers, lieutenants, sergeants, and corporals, had met death with their faces to the enemy. There was many a vacant chair and sad home in Pitt, and mourning for loved ones who would never return. But they were patriots, every one of them patriots, and ready to make even greater sacrifices. Thus the war went on. But the end was drawing nearer.

The year opened with the Twenty-seventh, Forty-fourth, Fifty-fifth and some other regiments doing duty in the trenches around Petersburg and Richmond, with the Eighth and Seventeenth around Wilmington and vicinity, and some others scattered over the east.

On January 13th, the Federals began the second bombardment of Fort Fisher. All day and night the fight raged on the 14th and 15th, when the Federals captured the fort, at 10 p. m. Then followed the next few weeks some desultory fighting in which the Confederates would fall back towards Wilmington, and finally abandoned it. In all this fighting the Eighth and Seventeenth were constantly engaged.

At Wise's Fork, near Kinston, March 8th, Hoke's Division met the Federals and after some hard fighting, captured 1,000 prisoners and four pieces of artillery. The Seventeenth, Sixty-seventh and Sixty-eighth regiments and Junior Reserves were in this fight. The Seventeenth was on the right in advance and had the heaviest fighting. At Southwest Creek next day the Sixty-seventh and Sixty-eighth had some losses and were in the brigade which captured 700 prisoners. The Seventy-first (Juniors) were in the center and drove everything back in front of them, for which General Hoke personally complimented them. Next day, the Seventeenth, not understanding orders made an assault under the heaviest fire ever experienced by the brigade, reached the Federal works and held them until ordered to retreat. It claimed that as the only fight in which it was ever repulsed. These regiments now moved towards Goldsboro and in a fight west of that place, the division attacked a force of 35,000 Federals, driving them back and capturing three guns and 900 prisoners. This was on the 19th. At Bentonville, the Seventy-first (Juniors) were in the thickest of the fight and did gallant service.

CHAPTER THIRTY-THREE.

Lee's Lines Broken at Petersburg—Retreat—Incidents—Johnston and Sherman—Appomattox—Last Charge—Surrender—Johnston Surrenders to Sherman—Pitt's Parole at Appomattox—Men Furnished—Officers.

Around Petersburg and Richmond the end was approaching. April 1st General Sheridan avenged his re erses of the day before, and on the 2d, General Lee's lines around Petersburg were broken. On the 3d the retreat towards Appomattox began. On this retreat the Twenty-seventh reorganized. It had only 70 men and formed two companies. H. F. Price, former Captain of Company H, became First Sergeant of one company; R. W. Joyner, Company E, became First Lieutenant; McG. Ernul became Second Sergeant from First Lieutenant, Company E. Near Rice's Station the Twenty-seventh and Forty-eighth regiments, both just ninety-four muskets strong, drove the Federals from the rear of the main line and had a skirmish with a brigade of cavalry, in which they lost some of their provision wagons, which made rations short that night, there being just one quart of corn per man. Fried corn became a luxury.

At home, General Johnston was retreating before Sherman, and there was little fighting. The Seventy-first Regiment was with him. On the 6th was a day of rest and parade. The Seventy-first was the largest in the parade.

Appomattox was reached on the evening of April 8th, and the next morning General Lee found his 10,000 weary, hungry and worn-out soldiers with 40,000 Federals in his front and 25,000 in his rear. Yet Major-General Grimes did not want to surrender. That morning with his small division he had driven the Federals from General Lee's front and opened the road to Lynchburg for the wagons. To his surprise he received orders to retire, which he for some time refused to obey, until they came from General Lee. Then he withdrew, without any disorder. Once more the Federals rushed as if to overwhelm him, when Brigadier-General Cox's brigade of his division, with a deadly volley, drove them back. This was the last shot fired at Appomattox. In Cox's Brigade was the Third Regiment in which eighty-one men from Pitt County went to the front. Only four were paroled at Appomattox. General Lee surrendered. The sun of the Confederacy had gone down.

In North Carolina General Sherman was in pursuit of General Johnston, and on the 18th General Johnston surrendered near Durham, but the terms were not finally determined till the 26th. May 2d, the Seventy-first Regiment (Juniors) were paroled and left for their homes.

Appomattox showed terrible losses during the war. Something may be seen of them by seeing the list of those paroled who were from Pitt:

Company E, Twenty-seventh, left home with 112 officers and men; only 16 were there to be paroled. H left with about 100; only 4 were there.

Company B, Thirty-third, had 26 men from Pitt. Only 5 were there.

In the Forty-fourth, Company C left with 111, only 8 were there. D left with 93, only 10 were there. I left with 114, only 1 was there.

Company E, Fifty-fifth, left with 85, only 9 were there.

The losses in other companies in other regiments in other fields, were equally as great. The loss in property was equally as alarming.

By the Census of 1860 Pitt County had a male white population between twenty and sixty years of age, of 1,521. It furnished more than that many men for the Confederate armies and military duties. An incomplete roster shows:

Second Regiment .... 20 men.
Third, D, 61; E, 19; others 1).............................. 81 men.

Eighth, (G 131, surrendered 3 men at Greensboro) 131 men.
Ninth . ... 15 men.
Tenth, (H 14, others 10) .... 24 men.
Seventeenth, (B 15, K 118, others 2) .... 135 men.
Twenty-seventh, (E 112, only four fit for duty after Sharpsburg, 16 at Appomattox; H 100, 14 at Appomattox) .... 212 men.
Thirty-third, (B) .... 26 men.
Fortieth .... 14 men.
Forty-first .... 22 men.
Forty-fourth, (C 111, D 93, I 98, others 6) .... 308 men.
Fifty-fifth, (E) .... 88 men.
Sixty-first .... 19 men.
Sixty-seventh, (D 22, E 72, G 40, K 19, others 9).. 162 men.
Seventy-first, (H 19, others 1)—(Junior Reserves) 20 men
Seventy-fifth, (H 17, I 5) .... 22 men.
Other regiments .... 23 men.
Others .... 27 men.
Fifth Battalion .... 6 men.
Eleventh Battalion, (I 13, others 8) .... 21 men.

Total .... 1,376 men.

These do not include any enlistments and recruiting and conscripting for the fall of 1863, or later. Pitt must have furnished near 2,000 men.

Strange to say, the man who rose highest was a man who was in command of a regiment, the Fourth, that did not have a Pitt County man in it. Bryan Grimes entered the service as Major of that regiment, preferring it to Major of the Second Cavalry, or Lieutenant-Colonel of the Eighth, because of his lack of military training, and the superiority of its Colonel, who was a West Point graduate. By skill and bravery he won his promotions to Lieutenant-Colonel, Colonel, Brigadier-General and Major-General.

Other regimental officers were:

E. C. Yellowly, promoted from Captain of Company G, to Major of Eighth; and later Lieutenant-Colonel of Sixty-eighth.

C. J. O'Hagan, Assistant Surgeon Ninth to Surgeon Thirty-fifth.

G. W. Johnson, from Captain of Tar River Boys to Lieutenant-Colonel of Seventh Volunteers.

J. S. Dancy, Assistant Quartermaster Seventh Volunteers.

G. B. Singeltary, from Captain of Company H, Twenty-seventh, to Colonel. Later he was Colonel of the Forty-fourth.

R. W. Singeltary, from Lieutenant of H, Twenty-seventh, to Captain and Lieutenant-Colonel.

T. C. Singeltary, from Major to Lieutenant-Colonel of Twenty-seventh.

Dr. Wyatt M. Brown, Surgeon Seventh Volunteers, to chairman State Board of Examining Surgeons.

J. A. Jackson, Adjutant; W. L. Cherry, Assistant Quartermaster; Abram Cox, Commissary; D. F. Whitehead, Commissary; Dr. J. N. Bynum, Surgeon, and J. H. Johnson, Major, all of the Forty-fourth.

J. T. Whitehead, Major of the Fifty-fifth.

W. C. Jordan, Assistant Quartermaster of the Sixty-sixth.

There were others who held promotions without commissions, among them being L. R. Anderson, Captain of Company D, Forty-fourth, who was in command of the regiment when he was killed.

SKETCHES OF PITT COUNTY.   161

CHAPTER THIRTY-FOUR.

"Wheelers" — Dupree Kills Federal — Amnesty— Holden Provisional Governor—Delegates to Convention—Acts—Worth Elected Governor—School Matters—War-time School Books—Curious Lessons.

Following the surrender of General Lee, the assassination of President Lincoln spread consternation over the South.

GENERAL BRYAN GRIMES.

Four years of war and its evils and hardships had demoralized the country, and in the wake of the great armies of General Sherman and General Johnston were following a band of marauders. As those two great armies turned from Bentonville northwestward, some of these, calling themselves Wheeler's Cavalry because, perhaps, a few of them may have at some time claimed the honor of belonging to that division of cavalry, in General Johnston's army, under Gen. Joe Wheeler, invaded some eastern counties. The Falkland and Farmville sections suffered from their raid, many horses, much provisions and some other property being taken by them.

They were followed by a similar class from the Federal army. These "blue coats" were looked upon as having some authority, but the people could not submit to robbery. One of them went to the home of Thomas Dupree, near Falkland, and was trying to get a horse. Dupree warned him under penalty of his shot-gun to let his horse alone. The "blue coat" paid no heed to that warning. Dupree drew his gun; the other his pistol. The pistol snapped, but the gun fired, and the 'blue coat' lost an ear. The second shot killed him on the spot. Dupree had him buried where it was convenient. A few days later others came, among them a brother of the one killed. They were looking for Mr. Dupree, who could not be found. They took the body of their dead one away with them. Mr. Dupree was never punished for defending his property. It is claimed that others were treated somewhat in like manner before such robbery ceased. But for some time yet there was little semblance of law and order or protection to life and property.

May 29th President Johnson issued his Proclamation of Amnesty, granting pardon, principally, to the citizens of the South who had occupied no conspicuous position or high rank, in the war, on condition that they take the prescribed oath of loyalty to the Union. W. W. Holden was appointed Provisional Governor of North Carolina. Some kind of a reorganization of the State government followed, and an election for a convention to meet in October was called. Pitt sent to that convention Churchill Perkins and W. S. Hanrahan. This convention repudiated secession, the great debt caused by the war, and also slavery.

The election held November 7th resulted in the election of Jonathan Worth, Governor, over Provisional Governor Holden, by a vote of 32,529 to 25,807. North Carolina was virtually back in the Union and elected John Pool and W. A. Graham, Senators, to represent it in the United States Senate. But they were not admitted. Other indignities were also in store for its people, though there was now a semblance of rest and law.

During the war education had not been neglected in Pitt. In most communities were to be found young ladies who had had the advantages of a high school or college education, and such taught the neighborhood schools, while the men were in the field. During the last year of the war many boys left these "old field" schools and became soldiers. With the close of the war educational matters again received attention. In March, 1865, the superintendents authorized their chairman, James Murray, to collect "such drafts and at such times as he may need the funds," and an educational interest again awakened.

Some of the school-books of the later war period are curiosities to-day. Such a one is "The Dixie Elementary Speller," printed on home-made, dingy brown paper, with a few antiquated cuts, by Mrs. M. B. Moore. Its reading lessons are worthy of notice. Here is the temperance lesson:

"A boy must not drink a dram. Drams will make a boy's face red. The boy who drinks drams is apt to make a sot. A sot is a bad man, who drinks all the drams he can get. A sot is apt to be bad to his wife and babes. No one loves a man who gets drunk and beats his wife and babes. Girls must not fall in love with boys who drink drams. But some girls drink drams too. For shame! I hope I may not see so sad a sight. Now, if a sot gets a wife who loves drams they will both get drunk, and a sad pair they will be." This is a lesson of patriotism: "This sad war is a bad thing. My papa went and died in the army. My big brother went too, and he got shot. A bombshell took his head off. My aunt had three sons and all have died in the army. Now she and the girls have to work for bread. I will work for mamma and sisters. * * * But if I were a man and the law said I must go to war I would not run away like some do. * * * I would sooner die at my post than desert. And if my papa had run away, and been shot for it, how sad I must have felt all my life."

"The Geographical Reader for the Dixie Children" is interesting. It treats of America only, with the Confederate States as the principal country. After the usual introductory of latitude, longitude, zones, races, etc., it proceeds to a description of countries. After scoring the North on slavery, it proceeds: "In the year 1860 the abolitionists became strong enough to elect one of their men for President. Abraham Lincoln was a weak man, and the South believed he would allow laws to be made which would deprive them of their rights. So the Southern States seceded. * * * * Thousands of lives have been lost, and the earth drenched with blood; but still Abraham has been unable to conquer the 'Rebels' as he calls the South."

CHAPTER THIRTY-FIVE.

War-time School Books—Geographical Reader for Dixie Children—Description of the State—Its People—Patriotic — South Carolina — Review—Questions and Answers—Confederate Prowess Taught.

Of the Southern Confederacy this "Geographical Reader for Dixie Children," says, in part: "This is a great country. The Yankees thought to starve us out when they sent their ships to our seaport towns. But we have learned to make many things, and to do without many others, and above all to trust in the smiles of the God of battles. We had few guns, little ammunition, and not much of anything but food, cotton and tobacco; but the people helped themselves and God helped the people. We were considered an indolent, weak people, but our enemies have found us strong, because we have justice on our side.

"The Southern Confederacy is at present a sad country; but President Davis is a good and wise man, and many of the generals and other officers in the army are pious. Then there are many good, praying people in the land; so we may hope that our cause will prosper. 'When the righteous are in authority, the nation rejoiceth; but when the wicked bear rule the nation mourneth.' Then remember, little boys, when you are men, never to vote for a bad man to govern the country."

Its map of North Carolina and South Carolina gives very little information. Tar River is put down as "Taw" River. Neither Greenville, Tarboro, Washington, Wilson, nor Williamston appear. Kinston is spelled "Kingston". The following are extracts from what it says of the State: "South of Virginia, we find another large State, called North Carolina. * * * The soil of about half the State is good, but much of the other is so thin that those who live on it are very poor. The swamp lands in the east are very fertile. The west is suited to grazing—we mean by this, grass grows well, and cattle are easily raised. * * * Newbern was a pleasant town, but the enemy have spoiled it, and driven away the people. * * * The city of Raleigh, near the middle of the State, is the capital. This is often called 'The City of Oaks.'

"The people of this State are noted for their honesty, and for being 'slow but sure.' No braver men fought in the war for independence than those from North Carolina. While some few cowards refused to fight for their country, it is a notable fact, that nearly all of them, were of the ignorant class, and many of them did not know what patriotism was. We should feel as much pity for them as contempt, because they had not been properly taught.

"Education was much neglected in the Old North State, until within a few years past. She now has as many good schools and colleges as any sister State. Good people are now building up schools to educate the children of poor soldiers who are killed in the war. Nearly every child can get an education here if he will be industrious. Who will be ignorant?"

Of South Carolina it says: "This was the first to secede. Many persons blamed the South Carolinians for leaving the Union too soon; but it may have been best; it is impossible for us to decide. The war would have come, sooner or later. God usually punishes wicked nations by war. I mean by this that when people become too wicked He gives them over to hardness of heart to work out their own punishment, and sometimes destruction. How much better for all to be good."

The "Second Part" is a "Review" with questions and answers. After many of the usual common geography questions are found others, of which the following are specimens:

If the people of the United States had always elected good men for rulers what would have been the result?

A. We should have had no war.

Q. Why?

A. Because every man would have been willing to treat others justly, and there would have been no cause for war.

Q. Are these judgments for our sins alone?

A. They are partly for our sins and partly for the sins of our forefathers.

Q. Then how shall we expect peace, since sin has brought war?

A. We must repent of our sins, and ask God to bless our efforts to defend our country.

Q. Why?

A. Because if God be for us who shall be against us?

Perhaps the "War Time" arithmetic was the queerest book of all when the nature of its examples is considered. They were patriotic and intended to show the superiority of the Confederate soldier in battle and inspire the learner with enthusiasm and pride for his countrymen. Among them such as the following were common:

"If twelve Confederates kill sixteen Yankees and the Yankees kill three Confederates, how many were killed in all?"

"If a squad of twenty-three Confederates capture forty-nine Yankees and another squad of thirty-eight Confederates capture sixty-seven Yankees, how many Yankees did both squads capture?"

"If nine Confederates attack twenty-five Yankees and kill seventeen of them, how many of the Yankees were not killed?"

"If one Confederate can whip three Yankees, how many Yankees can eleven Confederates whip?"

"If one Confederate can guard seven Yankee prisoners, how many Confederates will it take to guard eighty-four Yankee prisoners?"

"If two companies of Confederates can whip six companies of Yankees, how many companies of Confederates will it take to whip thirty-six companies of Yankees?"

Such examples and teachings filled the boys' hearts with patriotic pride and made that longing to emulate the prowess of their countrymen in battle, which rushed many a schoolboy to the army, and too often to an unknown grave in a strange land.

CHAPTER THIRTY-SIX.

CARPETBAGGERS—LEGISLATURE OF 1866—PENSIONS—THIR-
TEENTH AMENDMENT — RECONSTRUCTION — MILITARY
GOVERNMENT—COTTON PLANTER—EDUCATION—WILLIS
BRILEY MURDERED—TWO OF THE MURDERERS HANGED
—NEGRO MILITIA—LAFLIN AND RICH—MISGUIDED MIS-
SIONARIES.

With the new government in force, there was some prospects of better times, but considering the South their legitimate prey, carpet-baggers and other adventurers began com-

WILLIS ROBERT WILLIAMS.

ing. At first their influence was little felt, but it was later to become worse than a nightmare. Pitt was receiving them.

In the legislature of 1866, were Churchill Perkins, in the Senate, and W. R. Williams and John Galloway, in the House. It is a fact not to be forgotten, that in this legislature W. R. Williams introduced a bill to pension the North

Carolina Confederate soldiers. The bill, however failed to pass. It was the first effort of its kind in the South.

The Thirteenth Amendment had been ratified by all the Southern States except Texas, but the Fourteenth was rejected by several and early in 1867 the woes of the conqueror began to be visited upon the South. Congress, over President Johnson's veto, passed a bill for "reconstructing" the South. By it our State government was abolished and a military government established, with General Canby at its head. In October an election was held for members of a convention. Under General Canby's orders and the Fourteenth Amendment, many of the best white people were disfranchised and the negroes allowed to vote. Under this government Pitt sent to that convention Byron Laflin and D. J. Rich, two carpet-baggers.

Even under these conditions Pitt was progressing. In July of 1867 a patent for a cotton-planter was granted Capt. Bryant Smith, of Falkland Township. It was a revolution in cotton planting.

This cotton-planter was a great invention, and revolutionized cotton planting in Captain Smith's section. Several years later J. C. Cox secured patents for some improvements and in a few years the Cox planter was sold over the entire South.

The superintendents of education met in September. It seems to have been the first meeting since March, 1865. The members were James Murray, chairman; Jesse Nobles, Henry Stancill, W. R. Williams, John Daniel, Caleb Cannon, and James W. May. The chairman's bond was fixed at $100. There were thirty-nine districts and the committees were appointed.

The presence of many carpet-baggers, and their fondness for the negro, and their exaltation of him, had bad effect on the negroes. They were making themselves odious to the white people and were also becoming common criminals.

Such must in part account for the murder of Willis Briley on the night of December 23d, 1867.

On that night a lot of negroes went first to the home of William McArthur, near Ballard's Cross-Roads, went into the house and took him prisoner. While they were pillaging the house he escaped. Without doing harm to the family or taking anything they left and went to Willis Briley's, at the Cross-Roads. There they went in, made him a prisoner, and

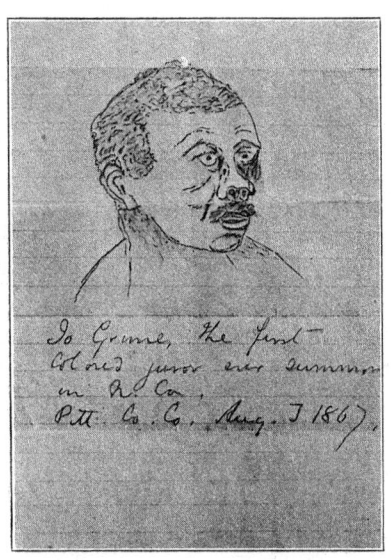

NORTH CAROLINA'S FIRST NEGRO JUROR

(Sketched by the late Judge W. B. Rodman, when holding the August 1867, Pitt County Superior Court.

proceeded to pillage the house. During this he escaped, being shot at. Later he was found under his buggy shelter, where he was shot, dying instantly. In the meantime McArthur had gone to a neighbor's, got a gun and returned. Finding the negroes at Briley's, he fired on them, when they ran, leaving a lot of things they were preparing to take away. Their object was robbery, as it was thought that McArthur and Briley had much money.

Richard Jackson, Needham Evans, Toney Kittrell and John Miller, were soon thereafter arrested, charged with being of the party that did the murder. Governor Worth ordered a special term of court for their trial January 4th, Monday, 1868. Judge E. J. Warren presided. True bills were found against them and also Curtis Cogsdell and Ned Blount, Curtis for the murder and the others for aiding and abetting. Curtis and Ned were never caught. Miller turned State's evidence and got twelve months in jail for robbery. Toney was not convicted. Richard Jackson and Needham Evans were convicted and hanged February 14th. Some years later John Miller was found hanging by his neck from the Snow Hill Bridge.

1868 saw many changes for the worse. New laws were made that changed many old customs. All able-bodied men between the ages of twenty-one and forty years were liable to military duty, and under this law a negro militia was organnzed. H. L. Smith was colonel of the Pitt militia. Byron Laflin was aide to Governor Holden with the title of Colonel. In the legislature were D. J. Rich, in the Senate, and Byron Laflin and Richard Short in the House. Dr. C. J. O'Hagan, Democrat, was beaten for Congress this year by Joseph Dixon, Republican, of Greene County, by a vote of 12,333 to 14,076.

The years 1868-9 were years of corruption and plundering of the State's treasury. The "Report of the Fraud Commission" reveals that all parties had a hand in the plundering, but the carpet-baggers stole everything they could. General Estes admitted that he paid Deweese $2,500 to be divided between Deweese and Laflin, for securing Laflin's vote and influence on a bill providing for the issue of $1,000,000 of bonds to the Wilmington, Charlotte and Rutherford Railroad. Laflin was one of Pitt's carpet-bagger members. There were many negroes in these legislatures and many sold out, with their carpet-bagger friends, on all occasions.

The enfranchised negroes were everywhere feeling their

importance and, aided and abetted by their new friends, were giving much trouble. On all occasions of big gatherings they were conspicuous and often insulting. Clashes and fights were not as frequent as they might have been, the forbearance of the whites preventing such when possible. Negro officers and soldiers were thick over the country, and justice was a farce. Many of the citizens were frequently charged with some offense and had to go before such courts for trial. No people ever submitted to more and worse government than did many of the Southern States, some counties of North Carolina and sometimes in Pitt. Among those who did perhaps the most harm were those so-called missionaries, male and female Northerners, who taught the negroes that they were the equals in every respect of their former masters. Their motives might have been better than the results.

CHAPTER THIRTY-SEVEN.

Riddick Carney—Attempt to Capture—Federal Lieutenant Killed—Second Attempt to Capture—Major Lyman and Negro Militia—Two Negroes Killed—Both Carneys Die—Horrible Tragedy—Ku Klux—Negro Officers—Specimens.

Like Jefferson Davis, some men were never reconstructed, and yet, unlike him, died with their boots on. Such a man was Riddick Carney, who lived about eight miles northeast of Greenville, just across Grindle Creek. His oldest son, James H. Carney, was killed in the war. This was his favorite son and the loss seemed to have had great effect upon him, embittering him against all Federals and their authority. He was charged with defying the new order of things and cruelty to negroes. For a long time the Federal authorities could not arrest him.

Some time early in 1866 a Federal lieutenant, with a squad of soldiers, from Washington, went out one night to arrest him and some others implicated with him. Arriving there, the house was surrounded and then entered. Only the women folks were found. They insisted that the soldiers should not go upstairs. The lieutenant took a torch from the fireplace and started upstairs. He was met by a load of buckshot and fell back mortally wounded. With Carney upstairs at this time were Enoch Moore, a neighbor, and J. T. Renfrow, recently from Georgia, and one or two others, all of whom were wanted by the Federals. No other attempt was made to go upstairs or get those up there, but taking their leader, the soldiers started for Washington. The lieutenant died at Pactolus, after having his wound dressed. His whole right breast was shot away. The soldiers returned to Washington with their leader a corpse.

On one occasion some Federal officers from Washington, on their way to arrest Carney, stopped at Pactolus and told their business. Church Perkins, a wealthy and prominent citizen, requested the officers to get supper with him on their return. They accepted the invitation and went on after Carney. This time Carney, Renfrew and Moore were arrested. Returning, the officers, with their prisoners, stopped at Perkins' for supper. Just before going out to supper, all again partook of liquid refreshments, which had been served freely. The officers were feeling good, took another drink and walked out for the dining room, as Carney and the others were taking theirs. Arriving at the table, Carney and the other prisoners did not show up. Returning to the parlor, the officers found an open window, but no Carney, Renfrew and Moore. They had escaped, and the officers had supper without them and also returned to Washington without them.

It was some time before another attempt was made to arrest Carney. Information being had that Carney was at home, the next attempt was made on the night before the fourth Sunday (26th) of April, 1868. Major Lyman had been superintending the Pitt election, with his negro militia, and determined to take the Carneys before returning to Goldsboro. Major Lyman, with ten negro militia and Sheriff Foley, went out a short time before day on the night mentioned. After surrounding the house, their presence was made known and Carney ordered to come out and surrender. In the house at this time were Carney, his wife, his son George, his son-in-law, Alonzo Whitehurst and his (Whitehurst's) wife. Another daughter, Mary, and her governess, were away, visiting in the neighborhood. George wanted his father to give up, but he said he would die first. Whitehurst reported that Carney was not there.

The house was then attacked and broken into. Major Lyman repeated the experiment of the lieutenant on the former occasion, tried to go upstairs, and was badly wounded in his left arm. The house was now set afire all around. George came downstairs to find a negro soldier in the parlor and shot him dead. Another negro soldier, standing in the door, raised his gun and shot George. George shot him at the same time and both fell dead. George fell in the fire and his body was right much burned before his sister was allowed or helped to drag it away. Whitehurst, who had taken no part in the fight, was badly wounded twice. He was gotten from the house, which soon burned down, the women having been allowed to come out some time before.

ONE OF THE FIRST TOBACCO BARNS IN PITT COUNTY.

The last seen of Carney alive was at an upper window, where he was apparently trying to get a shot at his besiegers.

There are so many conflicting tales of that fearful tragedy that the facts will never be known. Among the many statements are that Riddick Carney killed a negro, shooting from a window upstairs—that the shot that wounded Major Lyman also killed a negro who was behind him—that George Carney killed one negro and was shot while in the act of jumping out of doors, by the negroes outside, etc.

The house was a complete loss, with all its contents, nothing being saved except the clothes those who escaped wore at the time.

Major Lyman, with his surviving negro militia and Sheriff Foley, returned to Greenville that bright Sunday morning, bringing his two dead negro militiamen and Whitehurst and his wife. Whitehurst was left with the people of Greenville, who attended to his needs and wants, and his wife nursed him to recovery. No inquest was held over the Carneys, and no other legal proceedings were ever had in the matter, and it all became a thing of the past, though not forgotten. It is said that Major Lyman died soon thereafter of his wounds.

The Ku Klux Klan had spread to eastern North Carolina at this time and there was an organization in Pitt County. There were a number in the Carney neighborhood, and but for being slow in receiving notice of Major Lyman's visit, they would have wiped out his whole crowd. The leader in Greenville found out that the attempt would be made to arrest Carney, and sent out notice to those of that section, but the messengers were too late, as at the same time they were giving the notice to protect the Carneys, the news of the awful tragedy was heard. Major Lyman was perhaps already on his way there when the leader heard of it. Under a big persimmon tree, about a hundred yards east of the road, less than half a mile from the Carney place, on the south side of Grindle Creek, the members of the Ku Klux Klan of that section took that iron-clad oath, which, but for the lack of little more time, would have made a different tale of the Lyman-Carney tragedy.

This and a few succeeding years were years of negro officeholders. There were negro Justices of the Peace, negro constables, negro tax-listers and various offices filled with negroes.

But the carpet-baggers generally reserved those that paid best for themselves.

Negro justice was rather strange and often amusing. Two illustrations will be interesting: Dennis Atkinson was a Justice of the Peace, duly elected at the polls, by a majority of those voting. He had many cases. Among them he had a white man up for whipping a negro. A big crowd was always on hand, though such fights were not uncommon. After hearing the evidence, he gave his judgment that the white man should pay a fine of fifty dollars and costs, supplementing the judgment with a wink at the white man that was not misunderstood. Court was promptly dismissed and the white man called back. Atkinson then told the white man that he need not pay the fine or costs, that he had to do that way to fool the negroes. And the cost and fine were never paid.

Chance Bernard was a negro constable. Thinking the dignity of his office demanded that in executing papers he should carry some weapon, and being unable to get anything else, when he went out to serve a warrant, he armed himself with his grubbing-hoe. And thus he upheld the dignity of his office.

Another negro, elected a Justice of the Peace, went to the proper officer to take the prescribed oath, stating that he wanted him to "qualify" him. He was told that he could be sworn in, but that "all h—l couldn't qualify" him.

CHAPTER THIRTY-EIGHT.

NINTH CENSUS—THINGS IMPROVING—CONVENTION OF 1875—DELEGATES—VANCE AND JARVIS ELECTED—JARVIS BECOMES GOVERNOR—NEWSPAPERS—JARVIS ELECTED GOVERNOR—LATHAM ELECTED TO CONGRESS—GENERAL GRIMES ASSASSINATED—A LYNCHING.

The year 1869 saw carpet-bag rule in its full glory, and Pitt County felt its curse. But it was working out its own salvation, the people adapting themselves to existing conditions as best they could. The County was growing in population and the soil was rewarding its tillers with plenty. Though harassed by many reconstruction ills and evils, yet they did not suffer persecution and prosecution like some of the central and western counties. The Fourteenth Amendment had been forced upon the South and now the Fifteenth was proposed. As it only gave the negroes the rights that a military government had already given them, it was speedily ratified, and the negro became a constitutional voter, which only added to his woes.

The Census of 1870 gave Pitt a population of 17,276, as follows:

Township.	White.	Colored.	Total.
Belvoir	1,178	973	2,151
California	1,582	2,044	3,626
Chicod	939	744	1,683
Contentnea	1,413	705	2,118
Greenville	1,828	2,010	3,838
Pactolus	911	1,149	2,060
Swift Creek	1,011	789	1,800
Total	8,862	8,414	17,276

Greenville lost heavily of its population as compared with that of 1860. It was now only 601, a loss of 227 in ten

NOTE.—Before the next census California was divided into Falkland and Farmville townships.

years. There was yet no other incorporated town in the County.

Military domination still existed and the rumblings of a threatened volcanic outburst, though still heard, were growing less ominous. The white people were slowly regaining their power, and the hopes, so brightened in the expectation of the election of Horatio Seymour, as President, in 1868, were revived in the nomination of Horace Greeley, in 1872. Greeley had been one of the bondsmen of Jefferson Davis and

COL. W. M. KING.

had thus made strong friends of the Southern people. His defeat was another blow that increased the determination of the people to reconstruct themselves and conditions. It was a peace plan and its first victory was the calling of the Constitutional Convention of 1875. Pitt County sent to that Convention W. M. King and T. J. Jarvis. King had been prominent in local affairs and held several minor offices, among them that of County Commissioner. Jarvis had come to Pitt from Tyrrell County. He had been a soldier in the

Confederate Army, having been Captain of Company B, Eighth Regiment; had represented Currituck in the Convention of 1865; had been a member of the House from Tyrrell in 1868, 1870 and 1872, being Speaker at the latter term.

Louis Hilliard, formerly of Nash, living at Greenville, was elected a Superior Court Judge in 1874, but on a contest, W. A. Moore was declared still Judge. Hilliard held several courts.

The campaign of 1876 was a notable one. That year T. J. Jarvis was the Democratic candidate for Lieutenant Governor, on the ticket headed by Z. B. Vance, and with the whole ticket was elected. The Legislature of January, 1879, elected Governor Vance to the United States Senate and Lieutenant Governor Jarvis became Governor.

During the past few years there had been many newspaper ventures in Greenville. The *Express,* established by L. Thomas and Company, in 1877, and bought in February of the next year by J. R. and D. J. Whichard, was the only one so far with prospects of long life.

In 1880 Governor Jarvis was the Democratic candidate for Governor, and elected. L. C. Latham was the Democratic candidate for Congress from this, the First Congressional district, and elected. He was from Plymouth. He had served in the Confederate army, being promoted from Captain of Company G, First Regiment, to Major of that regiment. In 1864 he represented Washington County in the House, and in 1870 was elected to the Senate from that district. At that session he was President pro tem. He came to Greenville in 1875 and was a Tilden presidential elector in 1876.

August 14th, 1880, General Bryan Grimes was assassinated, at Bear Creek, very near the Pitt and Beaufort line. He was returning from Washington, with Bryan Satterthwaite, a boy about twelve years old, when he was shot from ambush, one shot taking effect, severing an artery. Several others lodged on the wood work of the top of his buggy, but none hit Bryan. He died almost instantly. Efforts were at once made to track and catch the assassin, but they were not then successful. It was found that the assassin stood behind a tree in the creek, had cut out an opening to the road, through the bush tops, and by this means got a good aim. Later William Parker was arrested and tried at Williamston for the crime, and after a long trial acquitted. Afterwards he practically boasted of the crime, and one morning in 1888, when the Washington bridge tender went down early to open the draw, for a boat to go on its trip up the river, he found a man hanging from the draw. It was William Parker. He had been lynched.

General Grimes was one of the most skillful, brave and successful fighters produced by the Civil War. Without military experience, he entered the service and successively rose from Major of the Fourth Regiment to Major General. Of him it has been said that "in devotion to duty, in faithfulness to every trust, in sincerity of purpose, in dauntless courage, in unselfish patriotism—in everything that constitutes a noble, generous, true man—North Carolina has never honored a son superior to Bryan Grimes." He was less than fifty-two years of age and lies buried in the family cemetery at Grimesland.

CHAPTER THIRTY-NINE.

Tenth Census—County Towns—Education—Evolutions of the Old Male Academy—Prominent Teachers—Latham Defeated—Yellowly Dead—Jarvis Minister to Brazil—Fine Babies—Earthquake—Latham Elected—Railroad.

The Census of 1880 gave Pitt a population of 21,794, 10,704 being whites and 11,088 being colored. By townships the population was:

Belvoir (including Bethel, 127; Penny Hill, 36)	2,593
Chicod	2,523
Contentnea	2,069
Falkland	1,937
Farmville (including Farmville, 111; Marlboro, 79)	2,497
Greenville (including Greenville, 912)	4,647
Pactolus	2,898
Swift Creek	2,630

Bethel had been incorporated about seven years before. It had been a post-office long before the war, there being two stores at Old Bethel, or the cross-roads, and having once-a-week mail to Greenville. On the completion of the Albemarle and Raleigh Railroad to Williamston from Tarboro, in 1882, it began to grow and the business moved nearer the depot, and since almost entirely to Railroad street.

Penny Hill, an important landing on Tar River, was also an important business point and recently incorporated.

Farmville was a new town, between Marlboro and Joyner's Cross-Roads, on the south side of Contentnea Creek. Joyner's had long been a post-office. There was a store and blacksmith shop. Marlboro was just a mile south. Antioch church had been built between these places in 1854 and was followed by a nice school building three years later. As the

---

Note.—Before the next census Belvoir was divided and Bethel formed; Farmville divided and Beaver Dam formed and Pactolus divided and Carolina formed.

other two places were not as progressive as the spirit of their communities, and the war having had its effect upon them, a store was built near the school-house. Soon two others were built and a prosperous little village resulted by the seventies, early in which it was incorporated, and Farmville became a town, too. Its progress was steady, and now it is one of the best towns in the State.

Marlboro, which has already been mentioned, was now losing its importance, and its plankroad was a thing of the past.

Greenville had made good growth from 1870, but was yet a small country town, the boats on the river giving it communication with the outside world.

Educational matters were now improving in the county. The public schools, which had at first been looked upon with so much disfavor, were now growing in number, favor and attendance. The school-houses were generally good frame houses, though not ceiled or plastered, there being but few of the old log houses remaining. The old Male Academy, that had such a long and honorable career, was under Professor W. H. Ragsdale, who came from Granville County and was destined to do much for the educational interests of the County. This was the school chartered in 1786, and which had, up to the war, educated young men and women from all sections of the country, and ranked with other schools of a like and higher grade. Its first home was on the southwest corner of Second and Greene streets. Much of the time a school for young ladies was taught in connection with it, but later became a separate school. The boys were taught in a two-story building that had a chimney at each end. The girls were taught in a separate building. Besides the great "Three Rs" of those days, many of the arts and sciences were taught. Among its teachers were many well known to the profession and others, who afterwards filled other positions. Among them were Professor Lovejoy, James Murray, Dr. C. J. O'Hagan, Dr. David R. Wallace, E. J. Warren (after-

EX-GOVERNOR T. J. JARVIS.

wards Judge) and others. Among the lady teachers were Mrs. Dockery, Mrs. Saffre, Mrs. Dimoch, Miss Sallie Ann Jones and others. The war interferred with its progress, and for several years after it was not well patronized, but under Professor Ragsdale it began to take on new life. There were other good schools in the county, among them being those of Farmville and Bethel and others, all of which were doing good work.

In 1882 Maj. L. C. Latham was again a candidate for Congress, but was defeated by W. F. Pool.

Col. E. C. Yellowly died at Asheville September 23, 1883. He had gone there for his health. He was a brave soldier, an able lawyer and an old-school gentleman.

After buying the *Express,* J. R. Whichard changed its name to the *Reflector,* which his brother, D. J. Whichard, bought from him in 1885.

Ex-Governor T. J. Jarvis was appointed Minister to Brazil by President Cleveland in March, 1885, and soon sailed for that country. He was there four years.

These were prosperous and good times in Pitt, and an observant tourist declared that "the county is remarkable for its fine babies, both white and colored, and the coming generation will undoubtedly be a marked one in the history of the county."

The year 1886 is still remembered as the earthquake year. The first shock was felt about nine o'clock on the night of the 31st of August. It was quickly followed by two other shocks. No damage was done, but it greatly frightened a great many people. For some time afterwards shocks were felt, but no damage was done. Charleston, S. C., was the center of the disturbance, and much damage was done there.

Maj. L. C. Latham was again a candidate for and elected to Congress in 1886.

The railroad from Scotland Neck to Kinston was finished as far as Greenville in 1889, and a regular schedule of trains put on. At first they stopped on the north side of the river, as the railroad bridge was not completed.

The temporary depot was on the Wilson place, a little south of the house, and was called Riverton. The work of extending the road on to Kinston was nearing completion, and soon after the bridge across Tar River was finished and trains were running into the present depot, they began a regular schedule to Kinston. The train left in the morning and came in at night, and large crowds were always on hand when it came in, and many would often go over early in the mornings to see it leave.

This marked a new era in the history of Greenville, and new life and growth took its hold on the town and its people.

188 SKETCHES OF PITT COUNTY.

CHAPTER FORTY.

Eleventh Census—Growth in Country and Towns—More Towns—Education—County Superintendents—Tobacco—Market Opened—Farmer Governor—Daily Reflector—King's Weekly—Jarvis Appointed U. S. Senator—Harry Skinner Elected to Congress—Great Fire—Telephones—Skinner Re-elected—Latham Dead—Records for Postmasters.

Pitt County made much progress and development from 1880 to 1890. Its population showed a good increase and also its industries and farming. Its population was now 25,519. By townships it was as follows:

Beaver Dam	1,068
Belvoir	1,340
Bethel (including Bethel town, 377)	2,068
Contentnea (including part of Grifton, 107)	2,812
Carolina	1,324
Chicod	3,089
Falkland (including Falkland town, 61)	1,759
Farmville (including Farmville town, 140; Marlboro, 92)	1,981
Greenville (including Greenville town, 1,937)	5,679
Pactolus (including Pactolus town, 105)	1,768
Swift Creek (including part of Grifton, 14)	2,631

By races the population was: white, 13,192; colored, 12,327.

Grifton was a new town, recently incorporated. The first mention of Grifton is that of "Petter's Ferry" about 1755, the land thereabout having been "patented" by one Petters. Later it was known as Blount's Ford or Ferry, then Bell's Ferry, and later incorporated under the name of Grifton. It has the distinction of being in two counties and three townships; also two congressional and two judicial districts, namely, in Contentnea and Swift Creek townships, Pitt County, and in Contentnea Neck township, Lenoir. It is in the Third and Fifth judicial districts. It is also in two

State senatorial districts, the Sixth and Eighth. Two sheriffs and three township constables, within their respective jurisdictions, as well as the town police, exercise legal authority in the town. This year the Scotland Neck and Kinston Railroad was completed to Kinston and a regular train service began. This gave a boom to Grifton.

This railroad ran through a fine section of country and other little towns sprang up along its route. Among them were Ayden and Winterville, both of which were destined to become of importance in the near future.

Falkland was a post-office with a daily mail many years before the war of 1861-5, with a good business. It is sup-

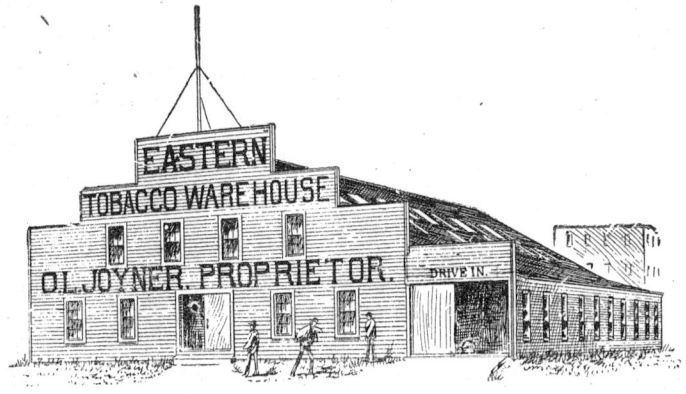

GREENVILLE'S FIRST TOBACCO WAREHOUSE.
(Burned some years ago.)

posed to have taken its name from Falkland, of Scotland, long the home of Scottish kings. It is ten miles northwest of Greenville, one mile from Tar River. It was incorporated about 1887.

There had been steady advancement along educational lines for some time, and Pitt's educational advantages offered by its public schools were good. There was more system about the work and more attention to the details. Most of the schoolhouses were now a single room frame building, with heater instead of chimney, home-made desks and benches, glass windows, blackboards and other helps, and many were painted.

Taken altogether, it was at that time a great improvement. G. B. King was now superintendent, having succeeded Major Henry Harding, who had devoted several years to the work. His predecessor was the late Elder Josephus Latham. Professor W. H. Ragsdale was elected superintendent in 1891.

For several years Pitt County had now been making tobacco and many of its farmers had taken prizes on the Henderson, Oxford, Durham, and other markets. A market was needed nearer home, and 1891 saw the beginning of the market at Greenville. A large crop had been made in 1890 and a larger crop planted this year. So a stock company was organized and the Greenville warehouse built. It was a success, and was followed by other warehouses, till the Greenville market is among the best and largest in the State.

In 1892 the Washington Branch Railroad was built. It extends from Parmele to Washington, nearly all its length being in Pitt. Pactolus is on this road.

Pactolus was quite an old place, but only recently incorporated. It is one mile from Tar River. In 1790 a Greek, by the name of Lincoln, settled near there. He was a school teacher. About 1810 he named the place Pactolus because the land was so fertile and the promise of reward so great, after the river Pactolus, in Asia Minor, whose sand was mixed with gold, and the country very productive. The first store was built about 1840 by Churchill Perkins. Yankee Hall was then, as long before, an important shipping point, and Pactolus profited and grew on this and its own business. The building of the railroad in 1892 gave it new life.

Oakley, Stokes and Whichard are towns on the Washington Branch that have sprung into existence since the building of that road. Oakley and Stokes are incorporated. Stokes is the largest and does the most business, though none has over 100 population.

The Farmers' Alliance was now an important factor in business and in politics, and Elias Carr, of Edgecombe, was nominated and elected Governor. He was a strong Allianceman, and one of the largest and best farmers in the State, being the first farmer elected to that office in many years.

In 1894 D. J. Whichard began the publication of the *Daily Reflector,* and Andrew Joyner began the publication of

HARRY SKINNER

the *Index,* a weekly paper. The *Index* was bought by Henry T. King, the next year, and the name changed to *King's Weekly.*

April 19th, 1894, Governor Carr appointed Ex-Governor T. J. Jarvis, a United States Senator to succeed the late Senator Z. B. Vance, who had died on the 14th. On the 26th Senator Jarvis was in his seat in the Senate.

In the fall Harry Skinner was a candidate for Congress on the Populist ticket, against W. A. B. Branch, who had served two terms. Skinner was elected. He came to Greenville from Perquimans, a young man, in 1875. He was a member of the Legislature of 1891.

Maj. L. C. Latham died October 16th, 1895. He was born September 11th, 1840. He was one of the ablest lawyears of the State and a powerful debater on the stump.

On the night of February 15th (Saturday), 1896, Greenville suffered a disastrous fire. It started in Edmunds' barber shop, late that night, and is supposed to have been caused by a lamp explosion or incendiary. All buildings on both sides of Main street between Third and Fourth streets, except Cherry's and Brown and Hooker's stores and the old Dancy building were a total loss. Several buildings on the south side of Third street were also burned. The loss was near $100,000.

A system of telephones having been put in Greenville, in July the exchange was put in operation. W. S. Atkins and D. E. House were the owners. It opened with less than one hundred 'phones.

At the fall election Harry Skinner was re-elected to Congress by a vote of 20,875 to 14,831 for W. H. Lucas, Democrat.

In 1897 J. R. Tingle was elected Superintendent of Public Instruction for the County.

Early in 1898 two post-office changes were made in the county that broke records of long time in two families. The Pactolus office had been filled by J. J. Rollins and his family for over sixty years. On the death of Rollins, T. J. Mobley was appointed postmaster. The Falkland post-office had been filled by Dr. P. H. Mayo and some of his family for more than forty years. This year J. F. Parker was appointed postmaster. Falkland had a daily mail from Tarboro to Greenville long before the Civil War.

CHAPTER FORTY-ONE.

SPANISH-AMERICAN WAR—GREENVILLE GUARDS—OFFICERS—MUSTERED IN AT RALEIGH—GO TO TYBEE—STORM—MUSTERED OUT—SKINNER DEFEATED—GREENVILLE FAIR—SECOND GREAT FIRE—TINGLE SUCCEEDED BY RAGSDALE—BRYAN GRIMES ELECTED SECRETARY OF STATE — RAILROAD — TELEPHONE MATTERS — AMENDMENT—TWELFTH CENSUS—TOWNS—DR. O'HAGAN DEAD.

The people of the United States, and especially those of the South, have always sympathized with Cuba in its struggles for independence. Therefore, when on the night of the 15th of February, 1898, the United States battleship Maine was blown up in Havana harbor, while on a friendly visit, there was an almost universal cry for war, to avenge the death of 264 of her officers and men by that catastrophe. War was declared the last of April, and in response to the call of President McKinley for 125,000 men, the Greenville Guards, Pitt's military company, offered its service. However, less than half the men actually enlisted and were mustered into service, but with other enlistment the company had a strength of 106 officers and men. It became Company E of the Second North Carolina Regiment. Among its officers were J. T. Smith, Captain; J. C. Albritton, First, and E. V. Cox, Second Lieutenants; J. V. Johnston, J. McD. Windham and A. D. Johnston, Sergeants; H. H. Blackley, H. C. Fornes, D. S. Moore, W. W. Perkins and J. T. Robey, Corporals; H. A. Blow and J. H. Cheek, Musicians; all from Pitt. Captain Smith and Musician Blow were veterans of the Confederate army of 1861-5; the others were young men.

The company was mustered in at Raleigh and after six weeks of camp instruction the regiment was divided into squads and sent on duty to various points south. Two companies, A and E, were sent to Tybee Island, Georgia, under command of Maj. W. T. Wilder. While at Tybee Island they had no greater experience than that of one of the severest storms known on the coast, which blew many tents down and away, and caused the loss of much property, but no lives. They never reached Cuba, nor were they ever blood-bathed in the battle's fury, for theirs was the misfortune to never be allowed to conquer the valiant foe, their services not being

J. BRYAN GRIMES.

needed in Cuba. So they were finally given a thirty days furlough, at the end of which they assembled at Tarboro and were mustered out the latter part of November.

At the fall election Harry Skinner was again a candidate (for a third term) for Congress, but was beaten by J. H. Small, by a vote of 19,732 to 18,263.

This was also the year of Greenville's first fair. An association had been formed and ground secured from J. L. Moore for the purpose. A race course was laid off and buildings erected. The fair was well advertised and well attended. The racing was very good and the exhibits would have done credit to a greater occasion. It was a success, but was not repeated, though the grounds were used for races several years afterwards.

Greenville suffered another great fire in May, 1899. It started in an upper room, over Cheek's bar, the origin being unknown. South of Fourth street all buildings on the east side of Main street were burned as far as the James Long store; on the west side all were burned as far as the Bank of Greenville; several others on Fourth street were also burned. The loss was about $100,000.

In July the commissioners elected Prof. W. H. Ragsdale County Superintendent to succeed J. R. Tingle.

In 1900 J. Bryan Grimes was nominated by the Democrats for the office of Secretary of State and elected by a vote of .... to .... for Dr. C. Thompson. He is the first native Pitt County son to occupy so high a position in our State government.

The East Carolina Railroad, from Tarboro, was completed to Farmville in 1900. It was originally a lumber road, running out south from Tarboro, but its president, H. C. Bridgers, concluded to make a freight and passenger road and extended it.

The Carolina and Virginia Telephone Company bought out the Greenville Telephone Company, from Atkins and House, this year and greatly increased its facilities for business, and extended it by building more country lines.

This year was known as the Amendment Year, the last legislature having passed an act to submit an amendment, for the purpose of disfranchising the negroes, to the people at an August election. It was a warm campaign and the matter was agitating the people in every county. The summer was a season of speech-making all over the State. It was ratified by a large majority, the vote in Pitt being 3,414 for 2,042 against.

The Census of 1900 gave Pitt a population of 30,889. By races it was: white, 15,397; colored, 15,492.

By townships it was:

Beaver Dam	1,312
Belvoir	1,342
Bethel (including Bethel town, 457)	2,279
Carolina	1,604
Chicod (including Grimesland, 277)	3,721
Contentnea (including Ayden, 557; part of Grifton, 200; and Winterville, 229)	4,047
Falkland (including Falkland town, 139)	2,139
Farmville (including Farmville town, 262)	2,361
Greenville (including Greenville town, 2,565)	7,323
Pactolus (including Pactolus town, 52)	1,679
Swift Creek (including part of Grifton, 29)	3,082

Grimesland was first known as Nelsonville and became a post-office under that name in 1885, when it was only a cross-roads, with one or two small stores. In 1887 the name was changed to Grimesland, in honor of General Bryan Grimes. In 1893 it was incorporated, and since has had a remarkable growth in business and population.

Ayden was laid out and named in 1890, on the lands of W. H. Harris. It became a place of importance, being on the railroad and in the midst of a fine farming section. In addition to business growth it soon became the seat of two good schools, the Carolina Christian College and the Free Will Baptist Theological Seminary.

Grindool, Statons and House are stations on the Scotland Neck and Kinston road between Parmele and Greenville; and Littlefield and Hanrahan are stations between Ayden and Grifton.

Shelmerdine is a thriving little town on the Beaufort County Lumber Company's road, which extends from Greenville to near Vanceboro. It has about 250 people.

Fountain is a new town on the East Carolina Road. It was incorporated in 1903 and has grown rapidly. It is now estimated to have near 400 population.

Tugwell is a station between Fountain and Farmville.

In 1877 John C. Cox obtained a patent for improvements in a cotton-planter and began manufacturing them at his place, half a mile west of the present Winterville. This business made others, and soon it was a business center. The railroad came in 1890, and four years later the business was all moved to the railroad and soon Winterville became the

DR. CHARLES J. O'HAGAN.

manufacturing town of the County, with various industries. In 1899 the Winterville High School opened in a two-room house with twenty-two pupils.

Dr. C. J. O'Hagan died December 18th, 1900. He was born in Ireland September 16th, 1821. He was an educated and talented man, stood high in the esteem of all and attained a national reputation in his profession.

CHAPTER FORTY-TWO.

FIRST FOUR-WEEKS TEACHERS' INSTITUTE IN STATE—RURAL FREE DELIVERY—HARRY SKINNER APPOINTED UNITED STATES DISTRICT ATTORNEY—SPECIAL TAXES FOR SCHOOLS—TEACHERS ORGANIZE—COUNTY BOARD OF EDUCATION—FULL-TIME SUPERINTENDENT — HOUSES — MEDALS—GRIMES RE-ELECTED—SKINNER RE-APPOINTED—RAILROADS—PUBLIC BUILDING—STEEL BRIDGES—GRIMES ELECTED THIRD TIME—TRAINING SCHOOL—PITT DRY.

At Winterville, in the summer of 1901, was held the first four weeks Institute for Teachers held in the State. It was held for the benefit of the teachers of Pitt and Greene counties, and Professor Ragsdale, Superintendent for Pitt, and Rev. M. P. Davis, Superintendent for Greene, were in charge. Professors C. L. Coon, of Salisbury; F. L. Carr, of Snow Hill; G. E. Lineberry, of Winterville, and Z. D. McWhorter, of Bethel, were the instructors. There were 127 teachers in attendance.

In September, 1901, the first Rural Free Delivery of mail was put in operation in Pitt. Three routes were established and the carriers began with little mail to distribute. Its growth since has been phenomenal.

In 1902 Harry Skinner was appointed United States District Attorney by President Roosevelt, for the Eastern District of North Carolina.

The people were now becoming more interested in educational matters, and Bethel was the first town in the County to vote a special tax and establish a graded school. The Bethel school had previously had only two teachers, but they were now increased to five and the school term lengthened from three months to eight, and a good library was established. This was in 1902. On the 8th of November there was a teachers' meeting in the court-house and a Teachers' Association organized.

Greenville voted a graded school tax in 1903 and its school opened in November in a large brick building on the site of the old Academy. It began with a large attendance, and besides the Superintendent had six teachers. A graded school for the negroes was also opened at the same time.

At Ayden a special tax was voted, the Christian College property bought and a graded school begun.

These were followed by Grifton, Centreville and Standard in 1904. The next year saw still other places doing likewise, and it continues.

PROF. W. H. RAGSDALE.

In 1904 J. Bryan Grimes was again the Democratic candidate for Secretary of State and again elected.

Under an act of the legislature of 1897 school matters were put in the hands of three men, constituting the Board of Education for the County. A. G. Cox, W. F. Harding and S. M. Jones were the first Board. They elected Professor Ragsdale, County Superintendent. He was again elected in 1903, and was to give his whole time to the work.

Many school districts have been consolidated or extended, better houses built and better teachers employed. In 1890 there was not a public school with more than one teacher. Now there are fifteen employing two teachers, one employing three, and five employing five or more, Greenville being the largest, with eleven, in addition to the Superintendent.

A Teachers' Betterment Association was organized in the fall of 1906. It is to encourage better conditions for both school-houses and grounds. Miss Bettie Wright was its first president.

Among the school-houses now in the country districts are many with two rooms, some with three, and some have a separate music room. These buildings are nice, modern houses, nicely finished, painted and inviting. They are furnished with patented desks, have maps and pictures on their walls, are well lighted and heated and have valuable libraries. The music rooms are even better furnished and have oil stoves and upright pianos. Much progress has been made educationally and the people are interested in keeping in touch with it.

Another stimulus to educational interests was the offering by Secretary of State J. Bryan Grimes a medal to be known as the Mary Octavia Grimes Medal, for the best essay on local history, by a Pitt County school girl or boy, in the public schools. This medal has been the source of keen emulation and much research. This offer was followed by A. G. Cox offering one for the second best essay. These offers have been followed by other medal offers, all of which stimulate the boys and girls in a profitable rivalry.

In 1906 President Roosevelt reappointed Harry Skinner United States District Attorney.

The Norfolk and Southern Railroad, from Raleigh to Washington, by Greenville, was completed in 1907, and it carried its first passengers to the State Fair to hear William Jennings Bryan speak. This road runs through Farmville and Grimesland and opens up a fine section. Two new stations are Arthur, between Farmville and Greenville, and Simpson, between Greenville and Grimesland. This road was begun several years before and finally bought by the Norfolk and Southern, which completed it, giving another direct line to the Northern markets.

Shortly before adjourning, in the spring, 1908, Congress passed a bill appropriating $10,000 for purchasing a site for a public building for Greenville. Offers for sites have been advertised for, an inspector has considered the sites offered, and bought the Harrington lot in front of the court-house.

The East Carolina Railroad has been extended to Hookerton, in Greene County, from Farmville. Grading for the extension of the Norfolk and Southern from Farmville to Snow Hill was finished in the summer.

During the summer the old wood bridge across the river at Greenville was replaced by a handsome steel one, costing near $50,000. Another steel bridge has been built across Big Contentnea Creek (or Moccasin River), at Grifton, to replace the old wood bridge there. Another work of the county commissioners was the building of a mile of experimental road, in conjunction with the Federal Government. The road begins on Dickinson avenue at the Atlantic Coast crossing and extends one mile up the old plankroad.

J. Bryan Grimes, Secretary of State, was again renominated this year, and again reelected.

A State election, upon the question of State-wide prohibition, was held in 1908, and the State went dry, or for prohibition, by a very large majority. Pitt gave a large majority for prohibition. Under the Watts bill much of the County had been dry and some other places had voted for the dispensary. Thus the legal sale of liquor had been considerably restricted. State prohibition went into operation January 1st, 1909.

CHAPTER FORTY-THREE.

Laughinghouse Superintendent of Penitentiary—Post-office Site—Training School Opened—Its History—Senator Fleming Dead—Big Fire—Court-house Burned—Records Saved—Greenville Post-office Advanced to Second Class.

In the spring of 1909, Governor Kitchin appointed Captain J. J. Laughinghouse Superintendent of the State penitentiary and farms, to succeed J. S. Mann. Captain Laughinghouse had been very prominent in the County and had twice represented the County in the lower house of the legislature.

The Federal government having made an appropriation of $10,000 for a public building for post-office purposes for Greenville, several sites were offered for it. In the summer of this year, the site was selected and bought. It is the Harrington lot, in front of the court-house, at the corner of Evans and Third streets.

October 5th, 1909, the East Carolina Teachers' Training School, at Greenville, was opened for the reception of students. Provision was made for the establishment of this school by the legislature of 1907, an appropriation of $15,000 being made for buildings, and the State offering it to that place which would do the most to get it and offer the greatest inducements to secure its location. Quite a number of places contended for it, but Greenville's offer was best, the County offering the same amount that Greenville did. Greenville voted $50,000 and the County $50,000, all in bonds. Work was soon begun on the buildings, an Administration building, two dormitories and a dining hall. The legislature of 1909 gave $50,000 more for buildings, $13,000 for maintenance the first year and $15,000 a year thereafter.

The main buildings were completed by the opening and

the others near completion. The buildings completed are the Administration building, two dormitories, dining hall, power and electric plant and infirmary. The school is for the training of teachers for the public schools. About two hundred and fifty boarding pupils can be accommodated in the buildings.

James L. Fleming, County Senator in 1907, was the author of the Training School bill, and worked unceasingly for its passage through the legislature. After the passage of his bill, he worked as unceasingly for Greenville as its location. His efforts were ably seconded by others. But he did not live to see the success of the school. He met an untimely death in an automobile accident, November 5th, 1909. With three friends he was in an automobile ride on the new sand-clay road near Greenville. He was one of the occupants of the rear seat. In endeavoring to pass a wagon the automobile, which was going at a terrific speed, left the track and plunged against an oak, at the E. B. Higgs' place. He was thrown out some distance, and falling on the hard road, on his head, met instant death. Harry Skinner, Jr., another one of the occupants, was thrown out and received injuries that resulted in his death in a few hours. The automobile was wrecked, and the other occupants received injuries that were very serious.

On the night of the 23d of February, 1910, Greenville, and the County, suffered heavy losses by fire. About one o'clock that night the old John Flanagan buggy shops were discovered to be on fire. A very stiff northeast wind was blowing and the fire spread rapidly. Every building except one dwelling, on the square in front of the court-house, was burned. Most of the buildings were wood and burned rapidly. Across Evans street, the fire spread to the Pitt County buggy shops. From there to the court-house and jail was a short leap for the flames, and from there to the Masonic temple the fire followed. The property loss was over $100,-000, with about half that amount of insurance.

The court-house was built about 1860 and was a splendid building of its kind. Some years ago vaults were put in and these saved the records of clerk's office and of the register of deeds' office, with scarcely any damage. The only loss by

NEW STEEL BRIDGE ACROSS TAR RIVER AT GREENVILLE.

any office were the court papers of the clerk's office. There was but little insurance on the court-house and jail.

The Masonic temple was a new building. In it the Masons, Odd Fellows and Pythians met. Most of their property and records, except some of the Masons, were lost. The Board of Education had an office on the ground floor and lost all but the records and some furniture.

Owing to the increase in the receipts at the Greenville post-office, this office was advanced to second class in 1909.

The steady increase to 1910 indicate that this year will show an increase that will reach $10,000, which will entitle Greenville to free delivery of mail.

ADDENDA.

In July, 1910, Harry W. Whedbee was nominated for Judge for this district. Judge D. L. Ward, of New Bern, was also a candidate for the nomination, having been appointed a few months previous to succeed Judge Guion, resigned. On the nomination of Judge Whedbee, Judge Ward sent in his resignation, nominee Whedbee was appointed to succeed him, and at once entered upon the duties of the office.

Judge Whedbee is a native of Perquimans County, but has lived in Greenville since boyhood. He has been Mayor and held other important positions. He is a lawyer of ability and stands high in the profession.

The census of 1910 gave Pitt County a population of 36,340, a gain of 5,451 over that of 1900.

CONCLUSION

Pitt County is centrally located in the Eastern part of the State. It is naturally an agricultural County. The soil is well adapted to various crops and with intelligent cultivation produces abundantly, richly rewarding the cultivator. Its three most valuable crops are cotton, tobacco and corn. It produces annually an average each of cotton and tobacco, of $1,000,000, sometimes more, and sometimes a little less. It produces a big crop of corn, but not so large in value. Besides grain, potatoes, peanuts and other crops, it is a fine County for trucking. Truck can be grown in all parts and is a very valuable early money crop. Any truck grown in Eastern Carolina can be grown profitably in Pitt. Fruits, grapes and nuts are also a very valuable and profitable crop. Many species of game are abundant and many northern hunters have been attracted here for the winter.

The climate is far superior to many "Ideal Climates." The winters are short and seldom severe. Cold waves and the tails of blizzards sometimes reach Pitt, but have been tempered by our Sunny South and seldom last more than a few days, a temperature of several degrees below freezing being often followed in a day or two, by almost spring weather. The summers are long but not excessively hot, due to a stiff southern breeze. The rainfall is abundant, but seldom such as to do damage to crops.

In transportation the County is unsurpassed by almost any county in the State. The Atlantic Coast Line Railroad passes through the County from north to south and the Norfolk and Southern from east to west, intersecting each other at Greenville. Another branch of the Atlantic Coast Line, from Parmele to Washington, passes through the northeastern part of the County for a distance of about eighteen miles, the East Carolina, from Tarboro to Hookerton, passes through the western part of the County for a distance of

EAST CAROLINA TEACHERS TRAINING SCHOOL

nearly ten miles, and the Beaufort County Lumber Company has a road from Greenville to near Vanceboro that does considerable freight business and takes passengers. Tar River enters the county from the northwest and taking a southeast course, runs through the centre, and is navigable nine-tenths of the year, and on the south are the Neuse and Moccasin rivers, both navigable streams. These give ample and quick transportation.

The history of Pitt County is a history of progress and along no lines has progress been greater than in the matter of education. There are over 6,000 white and 5,900 colored children in the County. Ninety per cent of the whites are enrolled and the average attendance is eighty per cent. The enrollment and attendance of the colored is not so good. Nearly every town has a white graded school and many white districts in the country employ more than one teacher. There are 132 white teachers and only four of these hold second grade certificates. Forty-five districts have libraries, containing more than 5,000 volumes. There are fifty-seven colored teachers. The value of school property is near $100,000, and this does not include the E. C. T. Training School, which would run the amount up to fully $300,000. Last year's school fund was $33,000 and this does not include near $15,000 local school taxes collected. Private donations to public schools amounted to $3,810 last year. All school buildings are modern, many of them being after the plans approved by the State.

A Woman's Betterment Association, for improving and beautifying school grounds, is doing a great work. For this work last year, the Association collected and spent $2,260.

Perhaps one-third of the population of Pitt County claims church membership, and there are denominations enough to give every one a chance to attend services. A great improvement has been made in church buildings in late years and now there are many fine church edifices in the County.

Labor conditions are good and few landowners fail to get good tenants. Tenants often make good crops that give them surplus money at the end of the year. The man who works makes money. The principal labor is colored. The County needs more white farmers, more white labor, and offers them rich returns for their labor.

Prior to the emancipation of the negro, all American history was practically a history of the white race. With emancipation the negro became a citizen with an increased interest in himself and country. His sudden advancement without previous preparation did not make him a better citizen and his attempts to wield powers not within his grasp retarded his advancement. However much the racial antagonism, the whites at once began to help him, by inaugurating an educational era for him. For quite a time his little education was dangerous, but time has made him see that his interest is the interest of all. Therefore, he has been making progress educationally, industrially, mentally and morally. Many now have fair education, some have fairly well equipped themselves for teachers and are uplifting their fellows, many by industry and economy have acquired homes and are doing well, some few have tried the professions with but indifferent success, and some few still have raised themselves above their surroundings and made names for themselves.

The tax returns for 1909 show the total valuation for taxation of all property of every kind was $8,395,206. There were returned 3,120 white polls and 2,593 colored. The property listed was as follows:

	Acres of Land	Real Estate	Personal Property	Total
By whites	375,244	$3,718,048	$2,331,435	$6,049,483
By colored	16,743	236,284	116,668	352,952
Total	391,987	$3,954,332	$2,448,103	$6,402,335

Real and personal property............................ $6,402,335
Railroad and telegraph and telephone 1,992,871

Total $8,395,206

SKETCHES

OF

PROMINENT PITT COUNTY MEN AND WOMEN

1704--1910

ILLUSTRATED

SKETCHES OF PITT COUNTY

TYSON, GENERAL LAWRENCE DAVIS, was born on the old Tyson homestead on the north side of Contentnea Creek, about ten miles west of Greenville and three miles east of Farmville, July 4th, 1861. His father, Richard Lawrence Tyson, a planter and merchant, and his grandfather, Sherrod Tyson, also a large planter and extensive land-owner, were born on the same farm. His father was a Confederate soldier, enlisting April 4th, 1862, in Company K, Seventeenth North Carolina Regiment. He was a non-commissioned officer, 3d Sergeant of his company. His great-grandfather was a soldier of the Revolution. His father died at Raleigh, N. C., June 30th, 1879. His mother, Mrs. Margaret Louise Tyson, born September 20th, 1840, is a daughter of the late Moses and Martha (Briley) Turnage. Her father was a large planter and in the war of 1812-15, was a Corporal in Captain Samuel Vines' Company. Her grandfather, Benjamin Briley, was a private in the same Company.

His father was very desirous that his son should have the best educational advantages, but the impossibility of securing good teachers so soon after the civil was, led him to move to Greenville about 1873, where there were some better schools. Afterwards his father moved to the western part of the state and in the Summer of 1879 Lawrence secured an appointment as Cadet to the United States Military Academy, at West Point, New York, having won the appointment in competition with eleven others. He became a Cadet at the Academy July 1st, 1879, and four years later, June 1st, 1883, was graduated and appointed a Second Lieutenant in the 9th United States Infantry and sent west. He was in the frontier service in Kansas, Wyoming, Arizona and New Mexico and was in two active campaigns against hostile indians before being transferred to New York in 1887. He was again transferred, to Arizona in 1889.

In 1890 he was appointed Professor of Military Science and Tactics at the University of Tennessee, at Knoxville. While discharging this duty, he found time to study law and after two years graduated from this University, a Bachelor of Laws. Three years later in 1895 he resigned from the United States Army and gave his time to the practice of law at Knoxville, Tennessee.

On the outbreak of the Spanish-American war in 1898, he offered his services to President McKinley, who appointed him Colonel of the Sixth U. S. Volunteer Infantry, known as the Sixth Immunes. After serving at Knoxville, Tennessee, and Chicamauga Park, Georgia, he was sent to Porto Rico. For several months he was in active service there and in command of a large portion of the Island. Returning to the United States he was mustered out in the Spring of 1899, and recommended for Brevent Brigadier General, for meritorious services during the war.

In 1902 he was elected a Representative from his county, Knox, to the General Assembly of Tennessee, defeating his opponent by a handsome majority. When the Assembly met in January, 1903, he was elected Speaker of the House of Representatives, defeating some very popular opponents. In 1908 he was a Delegate at-Large from Tennessee to the National Democratic Convention at Denver, Colorado. He was for six years Inspector General of the State of Tennessee with the rank of Brig. General. He is at present engaged largely in manufacturing and is the President of several large Textile plants and coal and land companies. At the North Carolina Home Coming week, at Greensboro, North Carolina, in October, 1903, he was a Guest of Honor and one of the principal speakers for that occasion. He has for several years been prominent in the politics of Tennessee and has been prominently put forward for the Democratic Nomination for Governor of the State.

He is a member of the Protestant Episcopal Church, being now a vestryman of the Church.

He is a member of the Benevolent Protective Order of Elks.

February 10th, 1886, he married Miss Bettie McGhee, daughter of the late Col. Charles M. McGhee and Cornelia H. (White) McGhee of Knoxville, Tennessee. Her father was a very prominent railroad man and capitalist of Tennessee. Her mother's family have been very prominent in Knoxville and one of her ancestors, General James White, founded the City of Knoxville. Their children are Charles McGhee Tyson, now a Sophomore at Princeton University, and Isabella McGhee Tyson, now at Miss Spencer's Boarding School for Young Ladies, in New York City.

GRIMES, GENERAL BRYAN, was born on the Grimesland farm, November 2nd, 1828. About 1760 Demsie Grimes, a son of William Grimes of Norfolk County, Virginia, came to North Carolina, married Penelope Coffield, of Bertie, and settled in Edgecombe on Fishing Creek. Not long thereafter he bought much land on Tar River in Pitt and moved to it, calling it Avon. William Grimes, the only son of Demsie Grimes, married Ann Bryan, daughter of Colonel Joseph Bryan and granddaughter of John Porter the first great leader of the people in the Colony of North Carolina. In 1786 he bought much land lower down the river and named it Grimesland. His son, Bryan Grimes, married twice, his first wife being Nancy Grist, daughter of General Richard Grist and grandaughter of Col. John Bryan of Craven County. One of their sons, Bryan Grimes, is the subject of this sketch.

Bryan Grimes was educated at Bingham School and the University of North Carolina, graduating from the latter institution in June, 1848. Soon thereafter his father gave him Grimesland and he became a planter. Returning from a visit to Europe in 1860, he found the country agitated over secession. Hearing of the bombardment of Fort Sumter, he hastened to Charleston and continued his trip further South, going as far as New Orleans. He returned in May to find himself already a candidate with F. B. Satterthwaite for the State Convention just called by Governor Ellis. As a member of that Convention, he voted for Secession, May 20th, 1861, and a few days later resigned, as he accepted the appointment by Governor Ellis as Major of the Fourth Regiment, preferring it to that of Major of the Second or Lieutenant-Colonel of the Eighth, both of which were also offered him. Having no military training his choice was influenced by the fact that George B. Anderson, a West Pointer, was Colonel of the Fourth.

Major Grimes joined his regiment at Garysburg. It soon went to Richmond, then to Manassas, arriving there two days after the battle. Colonel Anderson being made Commandant at Manassas, Major Grimes was then in command of the regiment, the Lieutenant-Colonel being absent. Returning to Richmond he was appointed Lieutenant Colonel, May 5th. His regiment did conspicuous duty at the evacuation of Yorktown. At Williamsburg, Colonel Anderson was in command of the brigade and the command of the regiment devolved upon Lieutenant Colonel Grimes. At Seven Pines, May 31st, he commanded the regiment and out of twenty-five officers and 520 men, every officer, except himself, and 462 men were killed or wounded. In this battle a cannon ball took off the head of his horse, and in falling one leg was caught under the horse. The regiment wavered, but waving his sword he shouted "Forward! Forward." Being freed from his dead horse, he seized the flag then lying on the ground, all the bearers and guards being killed or wounded, led the charge and captured the works.

June 19th, 1862, Lieutenant Colonel Grimes was appointed Colonel. At Mechanicsville, June 26th, he had a horse killed under him. Over the protest of General Anderson who declared that "although small in numbers, Colonel Grimes and his regiment is the keystone of my Brigade," he was detailed by General D. H. Hill to take the prisoners and stores to Richmond. In July, while suffering from typhoid fever he returned to Raleigh, but was with his regiment in time for the Maryland campaign, taking part in the fights before crossing the Potomac. Although unfit for duty on account of injury from a horse's kick, he took part in the battle of South Mountain, September 14th, where he had a horse killed under him. He was unfit for duty for some time on account of the horse kick. General Anderson was mortally wounded at Sharpsburg, and Colonel Grimes was placed in command of the brigade, which he commanded at Fredericksburg and until relieved by General Ramseur in February, 1863.

At Chancellorsville, May 1st, 1863, Colonel Grimes commanded his regiment, which with a Mississippi regiment, successfully charged up to the main body of General Hooker's army. When hard fighting was at hand General (Stonewall) Jackson would say, "Press them, Colonel." On the second day he took an active part in routing General Seigel's Corps. On the third day a brigade refused to make a charge when so ordered. Colonel Grimes and General Ramseur volunteered to make the charge, climbed the breastworks, formed, charged bayonets and captured the works. Thus an inferior force, without firing a gun captured a greatly superior. In this charge, Colonel Grimes and his regiment trampled on the Brigade that had refused to charge, Colonel Grimes trampling upon the commanding officer, putting one foot on his back and the other on his head, grinding his face in the dirt. In this fight Colonel Grimes' sword was broken by a ball, his clothing perforated by bullets, one lodging in his belt, and he was wounded in the foot. Out of 327 officers and men of this regiment, forty-six were killed and 157 wounded.

In the Gettysburg campaign, about eight miles from Harrisburg his regiment completely routed about 500 Pennsylvania sugar loaf hat militia, capturing many hats, but no militia. On the first day at Gettysburg, his regiment was the first to enter the town, driving the Federals to the heights beyond, capturing more prisoners than it had men, and would have taken the heights beyond, but was recalled. On the second and third days, his regiment did important service and on the return, he commanded the rearguard.

Declining to become a candidate for the Confederate Congress, he continued in active service and in November, 1863, was again given command of General Ramseur's Brigade, while he, General Ramseur, was home. He was again in command of his regiment in the Wilderness campaign. On May 12th, 1864, at a critical moment without authority, Ramseur being wounded, he led a second charge of Ramseur's Brigade and captured more Federals that the brigade he commanded had men. General Junius Daniel had been mortally wounded and Colonel Grimes was placed in command of his brigade. Throughout the Wilderness campaign and at Spottsylvania his division was in the thickest of the battle and did great execution. On the 19th General Rodes complimented him saying, he had "saved Ewell's Corps and shall be promoted, and your commission shall bear date from to-day." He received his commission as Brigadier General, June 5th it bearing date of May 19th. In July he went home on a sick furlough.

At Winchester, September 29th his brigade did severe fighting, he had his horse killed under him and but few of his staff escaped severe wounds. At Cedar Creek, when General Sheridan rallied his men to the return attack General Grimes made desperate efforts to save the day, but without avail. He exposed himself recklessly and had two horses shot under him. In this battle General Ramseur was mortally wounded and General Grimes was placed in command of his division. November 23rd his division routed 4,000 of General Sheridan's cavalry. During the winter 1864-5 his division was on duty about Richmond and vicinity. In February, 1865, he was commissioned Major General.

In March, 1865, General Grimes' Division relieved General Bushrod Johnson's Division in the trenches in front of Petersburg, defending a line of three and a half miles with only 2,200 men. March 25th was made the last attempt to break through General Grant's lines. Just before dawn, 300 sharpshooters, of General Grimes' Division, with empty rifles left their works, dashed across an open space of about 100 yards, surprised and captured the Federal pickets, mounted the Federal works and captured 500 Federals. The remainder of his division and other troops followed, but by the failure of General Pickett's Division to support them, they had to fall back after two hours of fighting against ten to one, and a victory was lost.

On the night of April 1st Petersburg was evacuated. On the retreat General Grimes, then in command of his own division and that of General Bushrod Johnson and General Wise's Brigade was the rear guard of General Lee's army. At Appomattox he also had under him the divisions of Generals Evans and Walker, and commanded all the infantry actually engaged on the 9th. That morning General Gordon and General Fitz Lee were undecided which should make the attack on the Federals. General Grimes became worried at such indecision and delay and volunteered to lead the attack. Given that privilege, he had placed under him in addition to the troops he then commanded the Divisions of Generals Walker and Evans and made the attack, soon reporting the way open to Lynchburg for General Lee's army. He was astonished when ordered by General Gordon to withdraw. This he refused to do until so ordered by General Lee. While withdrawing a superior force attacked when he ordered General Cox to meet it. This General Cox did and repulsed the attack. That was the last shot at Appomattox.

Being informed that General Lee had surrendered, he was greatly mortified, wanted to cut his way through the Federal lines and join General J. E. Johnston in North Carolina. Being convinced by the protests of other general officers that such action, though successful, would be violating the truce and a reflection upon himself and also General Lee, he shared the fate of General Lee's army in the surrender. Accepting his parole, he returned to his family and home, to help in the rebuilding of the fortunes of his country.

After living in Raleigh in 1866 and '67, he returned to his Grimesland farm where he lived the life of a successful farmer and useful and honored citizen, till his death, August 14th, 1880. That day when returning from Washington with twelve-year-old Fenner Bryan Satterthwaite—the son of a friend—he was assassinated from ambush as he was crossing Bear Creek. Only one shot took effect, but that severed an artery and death resulted at once. He was buried in the family cemetery at Grimesland.

William Parker was soon arrested and after some delay, tried and acquitted at Williamston for the murder of General Grimes. In a few years Parker practically confessed or boasted of the killing of General Grimes, and one morning in May, 1888, he was found hanging from the draw of the Washington bridge. He had been lynched.

General Grimes was twice married. April 9th, 1851, he married Elizabeth Davis, daughter of Dr. Thomas Davis, of Franklin County. She died November, 1857, leaving one daughter now the wife of Samuel F. Mordecai. September 5th, 1863, he married Charlotte Bryan, daughter of John H. Bryan, of Raleigh. She, with eight children, survive General Grimes.

SHEPPARD, HENRY, SR., was born in Snow Hill, January 10th, 1813. His father, James Glascow Sheppard, was a son of Benjamin Sheppard. His mother was Mary J. Harper, who married James Glascow Sheppard after the death of W. H. Armstrong, her first husband. She died when Henry was only three years old. He attended the Snow Hill school until his father moved to Nashville, Tennessee, in 1827, and put him into a printing office. An only brother, Harper Sheppard, became a very prominent lawyer and newspaper man in Tennessee.

Henry was very anxious to return to North Carolina and the day he was twenty-one, began the journey on horseback, through the snows of a severe winter. Arriving at Greenville he accepted a position in the store of Sherrod Tyson, sr. Two years later became a partner with his employer in a business at the Tyson place about ten miles west of Greenville. Marrying a daughter of his partner in 1841, he quit merchandising and went to farming.

In 1849 he was elected Clerk of the County Court, being the first democrat elected in many years. He was four times reelected, but had to resign in 1861 on account of ill health, but was soon thereafter a war candidate for the legislature, being defeated by Dr. E. J. Blount, a Union man. Having several times refused to become a candidate for any office, in 1874 he accepted the nomination for Clerk of the Superior Court. He was elected and also the entire democratic ticket, it being the first elected since the war. In 1878, owing to confusion in the convention, a later convention nominated B. W. Brown for Clerk. Sheppard claimed the nomination by the first convention, went before the people and was elected. He died October 30th, 1881, lacking one year of completing the term, and one year of having served in the same office twenty years. He was buried at the old homestead.

"As an officer he was always courteous, obliging and efficient. As a public man, he was of a retiring honest nature. * * * "He was conservative in politics. * * * "In his private life he was a devoted husband and father, a true friend and a generous open-handed, affectionate man. He was devoted to his county and State."

He was married three times. January 21st, 1841, he married Margaret Ann, daughter of Sherrod Tyson, sr. They had twelve children. The first died young. Elizabeth (married J. T. Williams), James G., B. S., Mary, Alice, Pattie, Henry, Margaret, Susan E., William, Alexander. Mrs. Sheppard died in 1863 and in 1865 he married Mrs. Ann E. Turnage, widow of Benjamin Turnage and a daughter of Dr. Neal. They had two children, Lawrence B. and Harper D. She died in 1870 and in 1875 he married Ella Williams, daughter of Richard Williams. They had two children, Annie W. and Hernie.

WILLIAMS, DR. ROBERT, Surgeon in the Revolution, was a son of Robert Williams, a Welshman, who settled in Pennsylvania in 1720 and came to North Carolina in 1727, settling on Tar River, near the Falkland landing, on what is now known as the Hughes land, buying several thousand acres of land from the Earl of Granville. He was married four times, lived to be one hundred and five years old, and left many descendants.

There near Falkland, Robert, the subject of this sketch, was born August 25th, 1758. He received the best educational advantages of the times and completed his medical studies in Richmond and Philadelphia. In March, 1779, before he was twenty-one years old, he became surgeon in the American army, at Camp Liberty Town. He at once made requisition for all the medicines to be had and this no doubt brought him to the notice of the State authorities, for in the following October he was appointed surgeon. This brought out the fact that he had been acting since the previous March and therefore he was ordered paid from that date. Little is known of his services, but he was with the militia at Guilford Court House March 15th, 1781, when General Greene practically defeated Lord Cornwallis. After the Revolution he retired to his farm and the practice of his profession. He was a representative in the General Assembly in 1786 and 1787. He was a member of the Convention at Hillsboro, July 21st, 1788, that rejected the Constitution of the United States. After this he was a representative in the General Assembly in 1791; and Senator in 1793-4-5, 1802-3,4, 5-6-8-13-14. He was also a member of the Constitutional convention which met at Raleigh June 4th, 1835.

During all this period he did an extensive practice, his home being practically a hospital or sanitarium, patronized by the people of the eastern part of the State. And too he found time for other duties, taking interest in his farm and educational matters, being a trustee of Pitt Academy from its charter in 1786.

He died October 12th, 1840, "loved for his virtues and respected for his services."

He was married three times. His first wife, whom he married in 1781, was Fannie Randolph, of Virginia.

His second wife, whom he married in 1792, was Nancy Haywood, of Edgecombe County.

His third wife, whom he married in 1804, was Elizabeth Ellis, also of Edgecombe County.

He was the father of fourteen children, two by his first wife, three by his second and nine by his third.

SALTER, EDWARD. There were three Edwards in the Salter family and one or more was conspicuous in Colonial and Revolutionary times. Edward sr., settled at Tuscarora, now the Mrs. F. C. Saunders farm, where Edward jr. was born. Edward jr. had three sons, Edward, John and Robert.

It is very probable that Edward jr. was a "Commissioner of Peace" for Beaufort and also a member of the Assembly in 1731; was a River and Road Commissioner, 1745; Salter's landing made place of inspection of tobacco, with warehouse 1752; remonstrated against conduct of certain Justices of the Peace 1764; Clerk of the Court 1772.

Edward jr. and his son Edward were no doubt both members of the Committee of Safety, and it is probable that the last Edward was the member of the County Committee recommended by the Continental Congress; clerk to the Committee of Safety 1774; delegate to New Berne August 25th, 1774, and member of committee to notify Standing Committee of the Province that Pitt had organized committee, &c.; delegate to Provincial meeting at New Berne April 3rd, 1774, and member of Assembly that met regularly next day; was at Tarboro when learned of negro insurrection and sent timely warnings, July, 1775; member Provincial Congress and on District Committee of Safety; member Halifax convention that instructed for Independence, April, 1776; member Halifax convention November, 1776, that formed State Constitution; member Senate 1779-80-81-82; Lieutenant Colonel of Pitt regiment 1779 in place of George Evans; captured Tory supplies in Edgecombe intended for Lord Cornwallis' army 1781.

The date of the birth and death of all are unknown.

MAY, MAJOR BENJAMIN, was a native of Scotland and born in 1736; came to North Carolina and settled in Pitt County, on south side of Contentnea creek, about two miles west of the present town of Farmville; was "Saddler to the County and Province" in 1767; member of Committee of Safety 1774, and also member of the County Committee agreeable to the recommendation of the Continental Congress; was one of the committee to build the court house and jail at

Martinborough 1774; Captain of Company of Patrollers 1775; was one of those appointed by the Halifax Provincial Congress to receive arms, ammunition, &c.; member of the Halifax Convention, November 1776, that formed the State Constitution; July, 1779, appointed 1st Major of Pitt regiment; said to have been in the battle of Guilford Court House, February 15th, 1781, commanding militia; after long service resigned as Justice of the Peace 1784; trustee of Pitt Academy 1786; member House of Commons from 1804 to his death 1809.

Major May was married three times and left a large family. His first wife was Mary Tyson, daughter of Cornelius Tyson, an early Pitt county settler and very large land owner. They had three sons; Benjamin, jr. (married Mary or Penelope Grimes or perhaps both) William, (married Susan Forbes) James, (married Harriett Williams) and several daughters, one of whom, Mary, married Colonel Samuel Vines. He had no children by his other wives.

SALTER, COLONEL ROBERT, was second son of Edward Salter jr. and early prominent in local affairs. In 1770 reported from Tarboro that Regulators were going to New Berne to interfere with the Assembly; raised a company of infantry against Regulators 1771; joined Governor Tryon's army at Colonel Bryan's, 100 miles west of New Berne and was in review at Smith Ferry next day, May 3rd; did picket duty with his company May 7th, and as baggage guard May 8th; at Alamance May 16th; appointed sheriff same year, 1771; reported delinquent, as sheriff in the sum of 498 £ 2s 3d in 1773; member Committee of Safety 1774 and on committee to receive donations for help of Boston; member Provincial Congress at Hillsboro, appointed Commissary for New Berne District and Lieutenant Colonel of Pitt militia, member committee of "Secrecy, Intelligence and Observation," 1775; was near Wilmington with his company and probably in Battle of Moore's Creek; resigned as commissary and succeeded by James Salter 1776; was at Tarboro when he learned of plot of Tories to murder prominent men and officials; member of Senate, recruiting officer 1777; commanded militia escort of commissioners to run the line between North Carolina and Virginia 1779; died May, 1779.

ARMSTRONG, GENERAL JAMES, was member of Pitt County Committee of Safety and one of those named to solicit donations for the relief of the people of Boston; December 9th, 1774, was member of the County Committee which was elected "agreeable to the directions of the Continental Congress"; elected Second Major of Pitt militia, 1775; was one of the Committee of "Secrecy, Intelligence and Observation"; was promoted Colonel, 1777, and in active service about Philadelphia, where the losses of his regiment were so great that it was consolidated with Colonel Patton's regiment, and he returned home.

He was soon again in active service; was in command of a regiment at Stono Ferry, S. C., June 20th, 1779, and severely wounded; presided at a Court of Inquiry, that acquitted Gideon Lamb, with honor, of charges against his conduct at Brandywine; allowed the use of $50,000.00 by the Assembly for recruiting purposes, about Cross Creek; resigned from army June 1781, allowed half pay and put in charge of recruiting at home.

On resignation of Brigadier General William Caswell, was elected Brigadier General by the Assembly for New Berne district, but General Caswell was reinstated; was member of State Council 1784; was elected by the Assembly of 1786, Brigadier General for New Berne district; Trustee Pitt Academy, 1786; member of House of Commons 1789; member of Fayetteville Convention 1789, voting for ratification of Federal Constitution; was one of the committee for building court house, under Blount bill, 1789; member Senate 1790.

Died late in 1794 or early in 1795.

Family name has disappeared from Pitt County and most descendants are to be found further South.

BLOUNT, WILLIAM, became a citizen of Pitt County, when a part of Craven County was added to Pitt in 1786. He was probably born in Beaufort county; was member of House of Commons from Craven 1780; member Continental Congress 1782-83; member House Commons 1783-84; member of Continental Congress 1786-87; appointed by Governor Richard Caswell his substitute to the Convention at Philadelphia in 1787 that formed the Federal Constitution; member State Senate from Pitt 1788-89; at session of 1788 seconded motion for a second Convention to consider the Federal Constitution; introduced bill for new court house for Pitt at 1789 session and was on committee for building same; member of Fayetteville Convention of 1789, that ratified the Federal Constitution.

In 1790, when the Territory South of the Ohio, (Kentucky and Tennessee) was organized President Washington appointed him Governor. He was President of the Convention of Tennessee in 1796 and on the admission of Tennessee, was one of its first (two) United States Senators; September 8th 1797 was expelled from the Senate, for alleged instigation of the Creek and Cherokee Indians to assist the British in conquering Spanish territories near the United States; elected member of the Tennessee Senate, and made President thereof, while the United States Senate was impeaching him.

He died at Knoxville March 10th, 1810, aged fifty-six years. Time has vindicated his action that led to his impeachment and added more honor to his memory. He married a Miss Granger of Wilmington and one son was highly honored by the people of Tennessee.

EVANS, RICHARD, on whose land the town of Martinborough was laid off under an act of the Assembly of 1771, was a member of the Assembly 1768-69-71. He introduced the bill, which failed to pass the first session, but did pass at the next.

In the supplementary Act of 1774 for removing the court house to Martinborough, he was one of the committee named for that purpose. He died in 1784 or 1785.

EVANS, MAJOR GEORGE, was member of Committee of Safety and other special committees; member of Assembly 1773; member of County Committee directed by Continental Congress 1774; member committee for moving court-house 1774; 1st Major Pitt Militia 1776; member Halifax Convention, November 1776, that formed State Constitution; declined election as Lieutenant Colonel, which was accepted by Edward Salter; member House of Commons 1781; date of death unknown.

GORHAM, GENERAL JAMES, and two brothers came from England. Arriving in Pamlico river, he sold his ship and cargo, and bought land about Strawberry Hill. He also bought much land higher up the river, among which was that now known as the Charles Vines, Swain and Gorham places.

He was a member of the Committee of Safety and of other important committees; was a delegate to New Berne April 3rd 1775; member of the Hillsboro Provincial Congress 1775; and was made Major of the District Minute Men; petitioned for the discharge of Mr. Clawson from teaching dancing, March 23rd 1776; appointed to receive arms, ammunition, &c; member Halifax Convention November 12th 1776; reduced to ranks and without command, 1777; member House of Commons 1779; was with General Sumner's Brigade at Ramsey's Mills on Deep River, in command of volunteers—61 infantry and 19 light horse; commanded 400 militia, with rank of General, at Peacock's Bridge 1781, in skirmish with Tarleton and 800 British; member House Commons 1781-82; trustee Pitt Academy 1786. Died at Strawberry Hill.

SIMPSON, GENERAL JOHN, a native of Massachusetts, was born March 1st 1728, and early in life settled in Pitt County (then Beaufort) on Tar river, about six miles below what is now Greenville, naming his place Chatham. He took an active part in the public affairs of his day and was a lieutenant of Militia in Captain John Hardee's Company in 1757. He was a member of the Assembly of 1760 and took a prominent part in having Beaufort County divided, the upper part becoming Pitt County. Petitions for a new county were presented to the Assembly at the first session of that year, but the matter was postponed to the November session, when Simpson presented a bill for the purpose of creating Pitt County. It passed and he was named as one of the committee for building the court house, prison, pillory and stocks. He was its first sheriff and one of the commissioners to run the line between Pitt and Dobbs counties in 1763. He was a member of the Assembly for the years 1764-5-6-7-8-9, though he must have been Register of Deeds for part of the time as Governor Tryon so appointed him November 20th, 1766. His place on Tar river was made a place for the inspection of Tobacco in 1764. In 1768 he and some others, he being the leader, prevented the Justices of the Peace doing any business and therefore prevented the regular levy of taxes. For this complaint was made to the Assembly by William Moore and probably others. He was then a member of the Assembly and for this action he was called to the Bar of the Assembly and censured by the Speaker. Soon thereafter he was granted leave of absence and remained away for the Session. But when it was known that some Regulators were about to march to New Berne to interfere with the proceedings of the Assembly of 1770, he offered his services, with 358 militia, of which he was Colonel, to Governor Tryon, to oppose them.

March 13th, 1771, Governor Tryon appointed him sheriff and he was active in raising a company against the Regulators, which was at Alamance under Captain Robert Salter. November 13th, same year, Governor Martin appointed him Register of Deeds. His schooner, John and Elizabeth was captured by the Spanish at Vera Cruz and nothing heard from it in some time and when the facts became known he wanted the government to get him pay for his losses. The government did not do so, so he lost much by it. This was in 1772. He was in the Assembly of 1773 and a delegate appointed by the Committee of Safety, to New Berne August 25th, 1774. There he was a member of the Committee to notify the Standing Committee of the Province that the County Committee had organized and was also a member of the Committee recommended by the Continental Congress, and made its chairman.

He was sent by the County Committee of Safety to the meeting at New Berne April 3rd, 1775, and was also a regularly elected representative in the Assembly that met at same place April 4th, (next day). He took an active part in suppressing the negro insurrection of July same year and was a member of the Hillsboro Provincial Congress August 20th, 1775. He had long been Colonel of the County Militia and he was now continued in that position by the new authorities, and also made chairman of the County Committee and member of the Committee of "Secrecy, Intelligence and Observation." He was a member of the second Provincial Congress of 1775; of the Halifax convention, April 1776 and appointed a Justice of the Peace; was elected a member of the District Committee of Safety, vice Roger Ormond, deceased. He complained to the Congress of 1777 of the lack of arms and ammunition. He was a member of the House in 1778, vice William Robeson, resigned; member of House 1779, but resigned on being elected member of the

State Council; was elected Brigadier General in 1780; member of State Senate in 1781 and of House in 1782. When Pitt Academy was incorporated in 1786, he was one of the Trustees; was member of State Senate in 1786; having never had pay for his services in the Assembly of 1782, the Assembly of 1787 paid him for the same. He died March 1st, 1788, aged sixty years less some days.

He married a daughter, Elizabeth, of John Hardee. Their children were Mary Randall, Susannah, Elizabeth, Samuel, Alice, John Hardee, Ann, Joseph, and Sarah. Susannah married Lawrence O'Bryan, Ann married John Eason and Sarah married Dr. Joseph Brickell. The others never married.

HARDEE, COLONEL JOHN, is first mentioned as a member of the River and Road Commission in 1745, the powers of which Commission were enlarged in 1752 to include the making navigable other streams, creeks, &c. He was Captain of a Company of Militia in 1754 and also a member of the Assembly. When the County was formed in 1760 the court house, prison, pillory and stocks were to be built on his lands and he was one of the commissioners for that work. Court was held in his house until the court house could be built, and the freeholders met at his house to elect vestrymen for the newly erected Parish to be known as St. Michael's Parish. He was a member of the Assembly of 1762 and a Justice of the Peace in 1764. That year Edward Salter found complaint against him and some others as Justices and complained to the Assembly. This was met by a counter complaint against Salter and no more was heard of the matter.

He was chairman of the first meeting of the freeholders in opposition to British oppression and a member of the committee to notify the Provincial Standing Committee that a county Committee had been organized and also a member of the Committee recommended by the Continental Congress. In the Minutes of the meetings of the County Committee of July 17th, 1775, is the following: "Captain John Hardees Comp'y meat & Choose Different Officers as under Mentioned in too Companies—Viz,

    Wm. Burney, Capt.
    Isaac Hardee, Lewtenant,
    Isaac Hardee, Ensign.
    Wm. Tillghman, Capt,
    Samuel Cherrie, Lieutenant,
    Nathan Cannon, Ensign."

On the divison of his company under different Captains, he was no doubt then promoted Colonel.

He died December 12th, 1784, aged 77 years, 8 months and 25 days. He married Susannah Tyson.

BROWN, JULIUS, a member of the Greenville Bar, is a son of Fernando Brown, who married Miss Ann M., daughter of the late H. W. Martin, sr. His father is a son of the late Rev. Samuel Brown. Julius was born November 18th, 1880, near Bethel. He was reared on the farm. He received his education at the Bethel High School and the University of North Carolina.

In the Fall of 1902 he received license to practice law and located at Bethel. After three years of successful practice there he removed to Greenville, in 1905. Since locating at Greenville he has devoted himself strictly to his profession and is enjoying a lucrative and growing business. In politics he is a democrat and though he has never sought office his friends put him forward for the nomination for representative in the General Assembly in 1906, and he received a most flattering vote in the convention.

He comes of a Methodist family. He is a Mason, an Odd Fellow and a Pythian. He has held many important lodge positions.

He is a good lawyer, a strong advocate, a man that makes friends.

BROWN, REVEREND SAMUEL, was born in Martin county, September 20th, 1818. He was a son of James and Millie Brown, who came from New Jersey to Martin county. James Brown was a son of Alexander and Rebecca Brown, who settled in New Jersey from England. While Alexander was English, Rebecca was of Scotch parentage. They came from England about 1760. Alexander was a soldier of the Revolution.

At the age of twenty-one years, Samuel came to Pitt county, locating near what is now Bethel. Soon thereafter he married Miss Mary Ann, a daughter of Samuel Little. She died in 1865, and a few years after her death, he married Miss Rillie Hopkins.

He lived and died on his farm, though for many years he held the position of County Surveyor. For more than forty years he was an active Methodist minister, though he had retired several years previous to his death. He was a strong and enthusiastic Mason. He was well and favorably known in Pitt and adjoining counties. Though he did not enlist in the army he was a strong supporter of the "Lost Cause." He died December 17th, 1907, leaving many descendants among whom were five great-great grand children.

His children by his first wife were Fannie who married Robert Ward and after his death married Warren Andrews, F. L. who married Sallie Ward, John E. who married Mary E. Martin, Fernando, who married Ann M. Martin, and Arcenia, who married W. W. Andrews, and two girls, who died young; by his second wife there were two children one dying young, the other, Bettie, who married John Keel.

F. L. and John E. were in the Confederate army. Fernando was too young for the service.

HARDING, FORDYCE CUNNINGHAM, son of Major Henry and Susan Harding, was born at Aurora, Beaufort County, February 12th, 1879. He finished his education at the University of North Carolina, graduating in 1898. In the meantime he had taught several schools. He then read law at the University and was licensed in ...... He then began practice in Greenville (his parents had lived there since 1885) ....years later his brother, W. F. Harding, having finished his education and law course, was associated with him in the practice of law. In ...... his brother located at Charlotte, since which he has practiced alone. Although he had never been very active politically, recognizing his worth in 1906, after having been a member of the Democratic County Executive Committee, he was elected county chairman, which position he still holds. He is Chairman of the Board of Trustees of the Greenville Graded Schools. He is a member of the Methodist church, a Royal Arch Mason, a Pythian and an Odd Fellow, in all of which he is a prominent and useful man.

In .... he married Mary Harding, daughter of the late Fred Harding. They have one child—a girl.

LAUGHINGHOUSE, CHARLES O'HAGAN, son of J. J. and Eliza Laughinghouse, was born in Greenville, February 25th, 1871. His father is a large farmer and prominent in public affairs, having held a number of positions, been a member of the Legislature (House), and is now Superintendent of the State Penitentiary. His mother is a daughter of the late Dr. C. J. O'Hagan, a Greenville physician of national reputation. He grew up on his father's farm, near Grimesland, and was educated at Chocowinity, Horner's and the University of North Carolina. He began reading medicine under his grandfather, and then attended the University of Pennsylvania, graduating in 1893. He then came to Greenville and began practice with his grandfather. A member of the North Carolina Medical Society, he was chairman of the Section of Anatomy and Surgery in 1895. He was essayist of the Society in 1897; a member of the State Board of Medical Examiners from 1902 to 1908, being President of the Board from 1904 to 1906; chairman of the Section of Medical Jurisprudence and State Medicine in 1910, and also a delegate to the meeting of the American Medical Association in 1910. He has been a member of the Seaboard Medical Association since 1903.

Dr. Laughinghouse is a democrat and has served both his town and county, at different periods, more than once as superintendent of health. He was elected county coroner in 1900, and has served as such four terms, and was (1910) elected for a fifth term, having no opponent. Though devoting his time almost exclusively to medicine, he is interested in several important enterprises. He was one of the organizers of the Greenville Banking and Trust Company; is interested in the National Bank, in the Pitt Lumber and Manufacturing Company and in the Reflector Publishing Company. He is a Mason, an Odd Fellow and a Pythian.

In 1896, he married Carrie, daughter of W. H. Dail, a prominent business man and farmer of Snow Hill. They have three children.

FLANAGAN, ROY CHETWYND, son of John and Mary Wise Flanagan, was born in Greenville, N. C., June 12th, 1873. His father was a Confederate soldier, was Treasurer of Pitt County for a number of terms, and founded the John Flanagan Buggy Company. His grandfather, Thomas Flanagan, was a farmer and a private in Capt. Samuel Vines' company in the War of 1812-15. His great-grandfather, Edward Flanagan, was a soldier of the Revolution. His mother is a daughter of the late Captain John Stanley Gaskill, master and owner of the three-masted brig "Samuel L. Mitchell," and was lost at sea with all the crew August 24th, 1848, between New York and the Bahama Islands.

Mr. Flanagan received his preparatory education at the common schools of Greenville and at the Greenville Academy. In 1891 he went to Washington, D. C.

Two years later he was appointed to a position in the Government Printing Office. While filling this position he attended Georgetown University, reading law at night, graduating with the class of 1903 with the degree of LL.B. The Summer of 1903 attended University of North Carolina, and was admitted to practice in Fall of 1903 upon examination by the Supreme Court of North Carolina. On receipt of his license to practice law he located at his old home, Greenville. The next year, 1904, he was appointed Postmaster at Greenville, N. C., by President Roosevelt, and was reappointed in 1908. He is a Republican in politics. In 1904 he was elected chairman of the Republican Executive Committee and has been unanimously chosen each year since to this position. In 1902 there were 33 Republican votes cast in the county, in 1908 there were 889. He is a Royal Arch Mason, an Odd Fellow, a Pythian and a Red Man, being now a member of the Great Board of Appeals of the Great Council of Red Men of North Carolina. He is a member of the Episcopal Church, and is now a vestryman of St. Paul's Church, Greenville, N. C. He is President of the Home Building and Loan Association and a bank director. In 1904 he was married to Miss Helen Perkins, daughter of J. J. Perkins, of Greenville, N. C. They have two children.

O'HAGAN, CHARLES JAMES, was born in Londonberry, Ireland, September 16th, 1821. His father, John P. O'Hagan, was a newspaper man of that city.

He was educated at Belfast, Ireland, and came to America in 1842. He soon came to North Carolina and made Greenville his home, though he taught school in the country several years. He began the study of medicine in 1845, and two years later entered the New York Medical College, from which he graduated in 1855, having worked his way through the college by studying, spending one year in college and practicing in Greenville the next, and thus rotating till graduation. Then he devoted himself to the practice, making Greenville his home. He became a member of the State Medical Society in 1858, and later was its president. In the war of 1861-5 he was first surgeon of the Ninth Cavalry and later of the Thirty-fifth Infantry, General M. W. Ransom's Brigade, and surrendered at Appomattox.

After the war he returned to his practice at Greenville. He was a prominent figure in reconstruction times and braved many dangers, personal and otherwise. Once he, with several others, were arrested and taken to Goldsboro before a reconstruction tribunal, charged with various crimes (?), but nothing detrimental resulted therefrom.

In 1868 he was a candidate for Congress against Joseph Dixon, of Greene County. It was a time of bitterness and strife, and he made a most wonderful and bold campaign, though he had little hope of election. He served Greenville both as mayor and commissioner at different times. He rendered services to his people and country, both as a private citizen and public official. He did a very large practice, but his liberality and charity was a great tax upon his resources. He was an honored member of his profession, serving as president of the State Medical Society, member of the Board of Censors, member of the American Medical Association and six years president of the State Board of Medical Examiners. He was twice married. His first wife was Eliza Forrest, of Greene County. His second was Elvira Clark, of Pitt County. Both preceded him to the grave. There were two children by his first wife, Eliza, wife of J. J. Laughinghouse and Martha, and one, Charles James, Jr., by the last. He died December 18th, 1900, and was buried in Cherry Hill Cemetery. An imposing granite monument, surmounted by a tall shaft, erected by the family, marks his grave.

He enjoyed a national reputation as a physician and surgeon, and had been highly honored by the National American Medical Association.

MOYE, DR. ELBERT ALFRED, son of Elbert A. and Mary Moye, was born near Farmville, July 7th, 1869. His father was a farmer, served through the war of 1861-5 (Lieutenant Co. G. Eighth Regiment), member of the Legislature (House 1877, Senate 1879), and Clerk of the Superior Court from 1885 to 1898. His mother was a daughter of Newit Edwards, a farmer of Greene County. His grandfather, Alfred Moye, was a very prominent whig of ante-bellum days, and served many times in both branches of the legislature.

Dr. Moye was prepared for college at Davis's Military Institute, La-Grange, and graduated from the University of North Carolina in 1893. Having taken up the study of medicine, he then entered Jefferson Medical College, Philadelphia. He graduated in 1896, and then remained one year as resident physician in the Jefferson Medical College Hospital. He came to Greenville in 1897 and since has enjoyed a large and lucrative practice, to which in 1909 he added the drug business, having one of the most modern and best-equipped drug stores in the State.

Dr. Moye has always been interested in the progress of his town. He was one of the organizers of the Greenville Banking and Trust Company and later of the National Bank, of which he is a director. He was one of the organizers of the Pitt Lumber and Manufacturing Company, and is a director. He was also prominent in the reorganization of the John Flanagan Buggy Company, which resulted in the erection of its present large factory and extension of business. In addition to his practice, drug business and interest in several enterprises, he is a large farmer, practical and successful. He is a member of the North Carolina Medical Society, the Pitt County Medical Society and a Knight of Pythias.

In 1897, he married Hortense, a daughter of the late Alfred Forbes, a large merchant and farmer. They have two children living.

COTTEN, MRS. SALLIE SOUTHALL, daughter of Col. Thomas James and Susan Sims Southall, was born in Lawrenceville, Va., but her girlhood was spent in Murfreesboro, N. C., and she has always been identified with the Old North State. She was educated at Greensboro Female College, and in 1866 married Mr. Robert Randolph Cotten, and in 1868 moved with him to Pitt County. She rendered efficient service to North Carolina as a Lady Manager, both on National and State Boards at the Chicago World's Fair. Was also appointed Lady Manager for her State at the expositions of Atlanta and Charleston. She is an enthusiastic believer in organized womanhood, and for years was associated with the Congress of Mothers, in which she held many offices, and remains now an Honorary Vice-President of that organization. She is active in the work of the N. C. Federation of Woman's Clubs, and for many years has been President of the End-of-Century Club of Greenville. She is also a member of the King's Daughters and the Daughters of the Confederacy.

She is the author of The White Doe—a poem of some length, founded on the early history of North Carolina. She has also written many other poems and short stories, which were published in various magazines, but her time has been given principally to rearing her children and conducting her domestic affairs, and dispensing the hospitality of her home, Cottendale.

CHERRY, MRS. SALLIE ANN, was born in Beaufort County, North Carolina, January ...., 1829. Her father, ... Johnston, came from England and settled at Wade's Point, then Hyde County. He was a merchant and was lost at sea, being bound for New York to buy merchandise. She was then about two years old. Her mother, then twice a widow, married again and moved to Greenville.

At Greenville she began attending school and was long a pupil of Miss Sallie Ann Jones, a noted educator of those times. She then attended the Warrenton (N. C.) Female Seminary, graduating in 1846, at the age of seventeen. Her diploma testified that she passed "a thorough public examination and acquitted herself in a highly commendatory manner, in the following branches, viz.: Orthography, Reading, Chirography, Geography, Grammar, Arithmetic, Composition, Botany, Algebra, Rhetoric, Natural, Mental and Moral Philosophy, Logic, Geometry, Chemistry, Astronomy, Nat. Theology and Mythology. She has acquired much taste and skill in Needlework, Drawing, Painting, and in the execution of Instrumental and Vocal Music," etc. This was signed by N. L. Graves, A. M., and Mrs. E. B. W. Graves, Principals, and two assistant teachers. Through school, she became one of the popular and brilliant young ladies of Greenville. She also found time to cultivate that love and talent for literature which, but for her apparent isolation, might have won her fame.

November 1, 1853, she married T. R. Cherry, a prominent young business man of Greenville. In her writings, just thirty years later, she said: "Just thirty years ago I was married. * * * An only child, a quiet life, a devoted Christian mother, I had as happy a heart as ever beat in the bosom of a bride: never giving a thought that was not connected with something pleasant." Marriage meant the cares of the wife and mother, and, devoted to those duties, she yet found time for literary work. She became a contributor to *Godey's Lady Book* and to the local press. She was the first Greenville subscriber to *Demorest's Magazine*. Failing eyes did not deter her in her work, and though totally blind the last sixteen years of her life, she continued to write and left much verse and reminiscence, prized by her children.

The following are a few extracts from her various writings contained in "blank" books:

"I live in Greenville, Pitt County, North Carolina; if you will take the trouble to look on the map you will find the town is just 25 miles from Tarboro, which was at the time I speak of our nearest point on the railroad."

"This (Greenville) is a beautiful town, but no attention is paid by the au——."

"There was only two Pianos in the town and I don't remember a single young lady that could play a tune on either of them. They were so small they would only be valued now as curiosities."

"I had the first sewing machine—Wheeler and Wilson—that ever was in Greenville."

> "Jewels and grain, rich shining ores,
> Are trophies from our State's deep stores—
> Resplendent shineth every gem—
> Victoria's glittering diadem
> In all its setting, hath no light
> So rare as thine, strange Hiddenite."

"It is impossible even to sit out at night on some of the porches without having the olfactories grievously offended."

In 1889 she was left a widow. She died December 30th, 1908, leaving three children.

The publication of her verse and reminiscenses would be a valuable acquisition to our literature.

YELLOWLY, COLONEL EDWARD C., was born in Martin County, N. C. He came to Greenville as a boy to attend the Greenville Academy, then taught by Professor J. M. Lovejoy. When Professor Lovejoy went to Pittsboro he continued under him until prepared for the University of North Carolina, which he then entered. Taking up the study of law, he was licensed to practice in 1843. Locating at Greenville, he was soon appointed County Attorney. Prominence and rivalry led to a challenge to fight a duel by by H. F. Harris, which resulted in the death of Harris, October 1st, 1847. (See Sketches of Pitt County, page 110.) He was averse to fighting and this sad affair seemed to affect him through life.

May 16th, 1861, he was commissioned Captain to raise a company for the war, which became Company G, Eighth Regiment, and went to Hatteras, where it saw hard service. In 1863 he was a candidate for the Confederate Congress, his opponent being R. R. Bridgers. His friends claimed he was elected, but cheated out of it and wanted him to contest, but preferring field duty, he would not contest. August 3d, 1863, he was promoted Major of the regiment. October 1st, 1863, he was promoted Lieutenant-Colonel of the Sixty-eighth Regiment. He saw much service and had to contend with a dissatisfaction among some troops while stationed in the north of the Albemarle section that almost resulted in open mutiny. He was a member of the Legislature (House) in 1865.

After the war he devoted himself to his practice and farm interests, which were large. In his latter years his health failed, and at Asheville, North Carolina, where he had gone to recuperate, he died September 23d, 1885, aged about 70 years. His remains were brought to Greenville and buried in Cherry Hill Cemetery.

He never married.

WILLIAMS, JOHN, was a son of Robert Williams, who settled near Falkland in 1727. He was early prominent in local affairs and a member of the Pitt County Committee of Safety in 1774. He also served on other important committees and as early as 1777 was a Justice of the Peace. He was a member of the first State Legislature, being in the Commons, and also in 1778-9-80 and 81. He was in the Senate in 1784-5 and again in 1787. (Date of birth and death not accessible.)

ROBERSON, WILLIAM, was a member of the Pitt County Committee of Safety in 1774, and also a member of the Committee recommended by the Continental Congress— one of the committee on building courthouse, prison and stocks at Martinborough, 1774—was a delegate to New Berne, April 3d, 1775—member of the Provincial Congress and a member of the "County Committee of Safety, Intelligence and Observation"—member of the Halifax Congress, April 4th, 1776, and November 12th, 1776—member first State Legislature, 1777, being in the Commons—again in 1778, but resigned on being elected entry taker. (Date of birth and death not accessible.)

COX, DR. BERIAH THADDEUS, son of Josiah and Sallie Ann Cox, was born July 30th, 1863, near Handcock's Church, in Pitt County, N. C.

His father was a farmer, and was also a Confederate soldier in Company "I," Sixty-seventh Regiment. In 1864 he was transferred to Kinston, N. C., where he served as guard over captured Confederate deserters.

His grandfather was Joseph Cox, and his great-grandfather was Abraham Cox, both of whom were farmers. His father's mother was Nancy Handcock, daughter of Eld. James Handcock, son of General Handcock, who, in the settlement of this section of the State, participated in many conflicts with the Indians; having been killed near Snow Hill, N. C., while leading his men in battle, driving back the Indians.

His mother was a daughter of Noah Tyson, who was the son of Eld. Noah Tyson, a Baptist minister. The latter was long pastor of Great Swamp Church, near Greenville. In the year 1792 he preached 189 funerals, and 84 in 1793.

Dr. Cox was prepared for college in Mrs. Mary Smith's school, near Coxville, N. C., and matriculated at the University of North Carolina in the fall of 1884, pursuing his college course there for two years. While at the University he began reading medicine under Dr. T. W. Harris.

In October, 1886, he entered the University of Maryland to continue his course in medicine. During the vacation of 1887 he read under Drs. C. J. O'Hagan and F. W. Brown, at Greenville. The fall of that year he returned to the University of Maryland, where he graduated in April, 1888. He went before the State Board of Medical Examiners for North Carolina the following May. Successfully passing his examinations, he returned to his father's homestead and begun the practice of his profession, continuing there until 1899, when he located at Winterville. In the year 1901 he added the drug business to his practice. On February 12, 1904, his drug store and office, with contents, were totally destroyed by fire.

He served as County Superintendent of Health for three years—September 1st, 1890-September 1st, 1893.

He has taken little active interest in politics, but in 1908 he received the Democratic nomination for the Legislature (House) and was elected over his opponent by 1,785 majority, leading all candidates for the Legislature for that year. He declined to again be a candidate in 1910. While in the Legislature he served on several very important committees. Among the bills he introduced was the one creating vital statistics for cities and towns of North Carolina containing one thousand or more inhabitants.

He is a farmer and is interested in many of Winterville's industries, being an officer and stockholder in several. He gave liberally in the building of Winterville High School, being elected president of the first board of trustees.

He is a member of the North Carolina Medical Society, and also the Pitt County Medical Society, having served as both president and vice-president of the latter.

In 1891 he married Mary V. Smith, a daughter of W. H. and Mrs. Mary Smith. They have four children, all daughters. The oldest, Miss Venetia, is attending the Salem (N. C.) Female College, and the second, Miss Jeannette, is attending the State Normal and Industrial College at Greensboro.

WHICHARD, DAVID JORDAN, son of David F. and Violetta (Jordan) Whichard, was born in Greenville, August 8th, 1862. His father entered the Confederate army as a private in Company C, Forty-fourth regiment, and was promoted Commissary Sergeant. After the war he served as deputy sheriff, deputy Register and Register of Deeds. His mother was a daughter of A. G. Jordan, a farmer and school teacher, of Pactolus.

Mr. Whichard secured a good common school education, mostly under his mother, who was one of Greenville's pioneer teachers, and entered a print shop, becoming part owner of a newspaper, before he was sixteen years old. After a partnership of several years, he bought the interest of his brother. Their first paper was the *Greenville Express*, which became the *Eastern Reflector* in 1882, and also the *Daily Reflector* in 1894, both of which were merged into a stock company in 1910. He has served two terms as Clerk to the Board of Aldermen, one term President of the Chamber of Commerce and also has been President of the North Carolina Press Association. He is a member of the Baptist church, has been Superintendent of the Sunday School and for twenty-six years one of its deacons. He is a Royal Arch Mason. Soon after the building of a telegraph line from Tarboro, he became operator, and has continued with the Western Union since it bought the line, and for some time was express agent.

In 1888, he married Hennie, daughter of the late H. A. Sutton, and they have four children. His oldest son, David J., Sr., has served two terms as Page in the General Assembly.

COX, AMOS GRAVES, son of John C. and Elizabeth Cox, was born July 12th, 1855. His father was a farmer and mechanic, with an inventive turn of mind. He invented and manufactured the first wheat threshers ever sold in Pitt County. Another invention was a machine that beat out wheat, without cutting it from the field, and also sacked it. He sold this patent to Western people. His last and most successful invention was improvements in cotton planters, and the fame of Cox's planter is known all over the South. He was a Confederate soldier, in Company G, Eighth Regiment. He also served the county as surveyor. His grandfather, Amos Cox, was also a farmer. His mother was a daughter of Graves Gardner, a farmer.

Mr. Cox's early life was spent on the farm, attending the country school and working around the shop and farm. When grown he worked as a carpenter for some time, but marrying he settled down on the farm, began making cotton planters and selling them through the country. In 1885 he began merchandising in a little store 12 x 16 feet. Succeeding to his father's business, he enlarged and extended it and it grew. A post-office was established at his place of business in 1889 and the place named Winterville. He was postmaster and so continued for many years. The railroad was extended from Greenville to Kinston in 1890. A siding was given him for shipping purposes, there being nothing there but a woodrack. About 1894 he moved his business to the railroad, organized the A. G. Cox Manufacturing Company, for the manufacture of planters, carts, wagons and other farm implements. Soon a buggy manufactory followed. Having patented a fertilizer distributor, that was manufactured there. A small school had been kept for some years, but in 1899 it was succeeded by the Winterville High School, which is now a large and successful school under the direction of the Neuse Baptist Association. About this time or before a flour mill had been erected, being the only one in the county. A cigar factory had also been organized and was in successful operation, but the tobacco trust soon made it unprofitable and work was discontinued. In 1906 an oil mill was built, and it was the first one in the county. The same year a bank was organized. In the inauguration of all these enterprises he was the moving spirit, a large stockholder, an officer and a prime promoter of their success. He has seen Winterville grow from a woodrack fifteen years ago to a town, now with perhaps 500 people, with a number of creditable and successful enterprises, in all of which he is greatly interested. He has never sought political honors, but in 1898 he was elected a member of the County Board of Education, which position he has held since and has been chairman since 1899. He has served his people in other minor capacities.

He has been a deacon in the Baptist church twenty years. He is a Master Mason, was a Granger and Alliance-man and is a member of the Farmers' Union. He married Susan A. Jackson, daughter of Allen Jackson, a farmer. They have five children. Fountain F., the oldest son, is completing his education at Wake Forest College; his second, Roy, is Superintendent of the A. G. Cox Manufacturing Company.

KING, HENRY THOMAS, fourth son of Thomas and Martha A. (Turnage) King, was born near what is now Farmville, November 9th, 1861. He received a common school education and began life in a country store. After eight years of clerking and merchandising, he went to Tarboro, in January, 1889, and established *The Carolina Banner*, a weekly newspaper, which was discontinued after two years. In 1892 he was appointed deputy sheriff by his brother, R. W. King, who had been elected sheriff of Pitt County. He held this position two terms, or four years. January, 1895, he bought *The Index*, a weekly paper at Greenville, from Andrew Joyner, changed the name to *King's Weekly*, and published it as a weekly, semi-weekly, tri-weekly or daily until the fall of 1907, when it was discontinued. In 1900 he was appointed a State fertilizer inspector and served two years. In 1901, to fill a vacancy, he was elected a member of the Board of Aldermen of Greenville and served one year. In 1902 he was elected a member of the Legislature (House)—was an independent candidate for the same in 1904 and the Republican candidate for the State Senate in 1906. He is now a United States Commissioner, appointed by the late Judge Thomas R. Purnell. He is a member of the Christian (Disciple) church, and in 1906-7 published *The Watch Tower* as a church paper.

He is now (1910) the Republican candidate for Congress in the First District.

June 27th, 1901, he married Blanche, daughter of William F. and Eunice L. (Latham) Draughon. They have two children—daughters—living.

MOORE, LARRY I., was born near Wilson, March 14th, 1870. His father, Elder Andrew J. Moore, was a native of Pitt County, having been born near Falkland and lived there many years. His grandfather, Ichabod Moore, was many years a Primitive Baptist minister, serving churches in the county. His father was a Confederate soldier, Captain of Company F, Sixty-first North Carolina Regiment. He was severely wounded near Charleston and was retired from active service. Later he was recruiting officer in Pitt and adjoining counties. After the war he became a minister of the Primitive Baptist Church and has been serving churches in Eastern Carolina forty years or more. His mother, Mrs. Elizabeth Moore, is a daughter of the late Larry D. Farmer, of Wilson.

When Mr. Moore was about eight years old his parents moved to Whitaker's, N. C., where they still reside. His father taught a high school at Whitaker's many years, and there he got his education. When sixteen years old he entered the railroad service at Whitaker's as telegraph operator and agent, was later promoted to the office at Wilmington, where he remained until he was twenty-one years old. He then took up the study of law, and after taking the course at Chapel Hill was licensed to practice.

He located at Greenville and soon entered upon a successful practice. He always took great interest in politics, and in 1898 was the Democratic nominee for Solicitor in the Third (Pitt) Judicial District. He was elected, and again elected in 1902, and again in 1906. From 1904 to 1906 he was Chairman of the Democratic Executive Committee of Pitt county. He had taken an active part in advocating and helping get the Norfolk and Southern railroad to pass through Greenville and was its local attorney. Being offered a general attorneyship, requiring him to locate at New Berne, he resigned the Solicitorship in 1907, accepted the attorneyship offered and soon thereafter moved to New Berne.

He is very prominent in fraternal orders and has been highly honored by them. He is a member of the Independent Order of Odd Fellows, Knights of Pythias, Masons, belonging to the Blue Lodge and Chapter at Greenville, Knights Templars Mount Lebanon Lodge at Wilson and the Shrine Oasis Temple at Charlotte, and is a 32d degree Mason, Scottish Rite.

Besides his large law practice, he has many other interests and is a stockholder and director in several important enterprises. He was one of the organizers of the Greenville Banking and Trust Company and its first President. He was also interested in the organization of the National Bank of Greenville.

He married Miss Ella, youngest daughter of Colonel and Mrs. W. M. King, of Greenville, and has an interesting family of three children, two boys and a girl.

RAGSDALE, WILLIAM HENRY, son of Smith G. and Amanda H. Ragsdale, was born in Granville County, North Carolina, March 3d, 1855. His father was a farmer, and in the Civil War was a member of the Senior Reserves. His mother was a daughter of Captain W. H. Royster.

Professor Ragsdale was raised on the farm, working and attending the common schools until he entered Wake Forest, from which he graduated in 1880. He then accepted the principalship of Vine Hill Academy, at Scotland Neck, which position he held three years. He then came to Greenville and accepted the principalship of the old Male Academy, which he held two years. In 1885 he married and returned to Granville County, where he taught until he came back to Greenville in 1891, again taking charge of the old Male Academy. The same year he was elected County Superintendent of Education. He continued to teach and hold the position of County Superintendent except the years 1898-9, until 1903, when the Board of Education required him to give all his time to the work, which he has since then. He has now been Superintendent seventeen years.

He has always been active in educational work. In 1899 he was President of the North Carolina Teachers' Assembly, which met that year at Morehead City. The first four weeks' Teachers' Institute in the State was instituted and held by him at Winterville in the summer of 1901. In 1906 he was elected Chairman of the State Text-book Commission for five years. He was one of the strongest supporters of the movement that led to the establishment of the East Carolina Teachers' Training School at Greenville, and last year was selected to teach in that department of the Summer School, known as School Management.

Professor Ragsdale is a member of the Baptist church, is one of its deacons, and has been one of its Sunday School teachers twenty-five years. He is an Odd Fellow and a Blue Lodge and Royal Arch Mason. He is widely and well known in school circles and in much demand as a speaker on any educational topic, having made many addresses for the advancement of educational work in many counties. He has held and assisted in many teachers' institutes.

September 16th, 1885, he married Bettie, a daughter of the late H. A. and Elizabeth Sutton, of Greenville. She died June 2d, 1902. They had five children, all living.

COBB, ROBERT JOHN, son of James C. and Mary E. Cobb, was born on the farm in what is now Beaver Dam township, June 10th, 1855. His father was a farmer and merchant, who rose to competency and prominence in his community by industry and integrity.

Mr. Cobb's educational advantages were very limited. He worked on the farm and attended the country schools. In 1871, his father began business building a store on his farm. In 1876, Robert was clerk in the store and there began his business career. This business was successful and he became a partner with his father, the firm being J. C. Cobb & Son. In 1890 they opened business in Greenville with Robert as manager as he had been of the business in the country. The next year he was one of the prime movers in the establishment of a tobacco market in Greenville. He was not only a large stockholder in the old Greenville Warehouse Company, but was active in promoting its success. In 1900 he retired from the mercantile business. The same year he was elected a member of the Board of Aldermen, and was one of the principal stockholders and organizers of the Greenville Banking and Trust Company. He was made a director and elected its first cashier, which position he held until elected its president in 1906, which position he held two years, and then retired. In 1902 the Building and Lumber Company was organized with him as president. This firm sold out its business in 1909. In 1903 he did a great help towards the graded school. When those bonds were not finding buyers he came forward and took them, thus relieving the directors of much embarrassment. He is a director of the school and has been since its organization. He is also a director, stockholder and treasurer of the Farmers Consolidated Tobacco Company, an organization for the purpose of conducting warehouses for the sale of farmers' tobacco. In 1908 he took large stock in the Cabinet Veneer Company, was prominent in its organization and was elected vice-president. All these enterprises have been very successful and add much to progress and prosperity of Greenville. He is a member of the firm of York & Cobb, contractors and builders, which does a large business. Prominent among the work of this firm are the entire buildings of the East Carolina Teachers

Training School and the white graded school building at Tarboro. He is also interested in large farming operations and stock raising.

In 1887 he married Mollie A., daughter of Charles D. Rountree, a well-known citizen of Greenville. They have four children, Cecil R. Cobb being the head clerk at the Cabinet Veneer Company.

KING, ALLIE (VINES), daughter of Colonel Samuel and Polly (May) Vines, was born in Pitt County (now Falkland Township), April, 1803. Colonel Vines was a large planter and slave-owner, a man of prominence and influence. He was a captain in the war of 1812-15, and afterwards long colonel of militia. He was born in 1781 and died in January, 1863, aged over 82 years. Her mother was a daughter of Major Benjamin May.

Allie Vines' education was that afforded by the best schools of her times and community. She was the oldest of a family of thirteen daughters and two sons. Thus her early life and training was such as to greatly fit her for the duties and cares that were later to fall upon her. February 13th, 1823, she married John King, the only child of Thomas and Polly (Truss) King. Thomas King was a planter, succeeding to his father's estates. His father, Abram King, was one of the early settlers on Tyson's creek, a large planter and a man of prominence. John King died June 15th, 1845, leaving his widow with nine children, the only one grown dying the following January. He was studying medicine at Cincinnati and filled an unknown grave. The task of rearing and educating the others was no small responsibility. Another sorrow was added to her already great burden, when in 1853, Warren, her fourth son, died too from home. After years of cares, sorrows and trials, she saw her other children grown, and prospects for a bright future. But war now was over the land and in October, 1864, claimed another son, Thomas, as one of its prey. And again in less than two short years (June, 1866), death claimed Mary, one of her married daughters. The next few succeeding years that cast the blight of reconstruction over the South were years of anxiety for her, for she yet had three sons and they were prominent actors in the drama of those times. But her years of cares and sacrifices were partially rewarded in seeing these sons honored by their fellow-men. That was glory for her. Few mothers have been rewarded more in the lives they built, and in their fruits. (See sketches of Thomas King, Captain John King, Colonel William M. King and Dr. Robert W. King.) Her daughters were Mary (married G. W. Parker), Nancy W. (married B. F. Moore), and Allie V. (married Colonel Walter Newton).

In 187.., when attempting to get into her buggy, she had a fall and suffered a fracture of the thigh. She had stopped on the roadside to gather some shrubs and, being by herself, it was some little while before help came. The fracture never healed and after much suffering she died February, 1883, and was buried in the family cemetery beside her husband.

Early in life she became a member of the Christian (Disciple) church and ever lived a consistent and consecrated Christian. Her virtues were many—a ministering angel to the suffering, a helping hand to the needy, obedient to every call of duty. Of a strong cultured mind, tender heart and great goodness, hers was a life of duty—of duty performed, of cares not unmixed with sorrow and suffering—rewarded with children, and children's children, to rise up and call her blessed, and with the great promise of life eternal.

KING, COLONEL WILLIAM MAY, the sixth child of John and Allie (V.) King, was born at the old King homestead, November 18th, 1833. He received a good common school education and began life as an overseer. After marrying he settled down as a farmer. In the war of 1861-5 he was assigned to home duty but for a short while was at Camp Mangum at Raleigh. He was afterwards colonel of the militia. In 1866 Governor Holden appointed him a Justice of the Peace and by appointment and election he held this position many years. In 1870 he was elected a County Commissioner and was reelected in 1872. In 1874 he was elected one of Pitt's representatives in the Constitutional Convention, which met the next year. As an independent candidate for sheriff he was defeated in 1880, but was elected in 1882 and again in 1884 and again in 1886. In 1892 he was voted for for the State Senate, but was not an active candidate. In 1894 he was elected on the populist ticket register of deeds for the county and in 1896 was elected a county commissioner. Since then he has not been active in politics. Until elected sheriff he had always lived on his farm and devoted his time to farming, with the addition of merchandising a few years at home. After being elected sheriff he moved to Greenville and has since lived there. He has always taken an active interest in public affairs and those pertaining to farmers. He was a prominent Granger, and later an Allianceman. He is a Royal Arch Mason and a member of the Universalist church.

November 18th, 1856, he married Almeta, daughter of Howell and Delphia (Newton) Peebles. November 17th, 1906, they celebrated their Golden Wedding, with children, grandchildren and great-grandchildren present. They have had eight children, four of whom are living.

Colonel King is a very large man, weighing near 275 pounds. Mrs. King is also large and has weighed over 200. Their children are all of large stature and the family would average 200 pounds each. He is 6 feet 2 inches tall and so well proportioned that he does not appear to be a big man, unless at close distance.

WHITE, SAMUEL TILDEN, ex-treasurer of Pitt County, was born near Greenville, December 30th, 1873. He comes of old English and Revolutionary stock. His great-great-grandfather was a resident of Craven county long before the Revolution and fought for Independence; his great-grandfather, James A. White, was a soldier of the war of 1812-15 and for a time did duty at Beacon Island; his grandfather was James S. White, and his father, Captain Charles A. White, of Company E, Sixty-seventh Regiment, North Carolina Confederate troops. Captain White was a Craven county man, but came to Pitt county after the war. He married Miss Louisa A. Corey. On his farm near Greenville, Samuel was born, being the third son.

Mr. White's educational advantages were limited, and at the age of fourteen he entered his father's store, in Greenville, where he clerked until he succeeded to the business. This business he conducted with marked success until he sold out and devoted his time to his other interests.

After a hard fight in 1904, the democratic county convention nominated him for treasurer. At the following election he was elected, and has been twice re-elected—in 1906 and 1908. At each convention he won his nomination over some of the best and most popular men in the county.

As a member of fraternal orders, he is prominent and has been highly honored. He is a member of the Independent Order of Odd Fellows, Knights of Pythias and the Independent Order of Red Men. He now occupies the exalted position of Great Sachem of the State Council of Red Men of North Carolina.

In 1900 he married Miss Annie W. Sheppard, daughter of the late Henry Sheppard. She died in 1906, leaving two children.

KING, DR. ROBERT WILLIAMS, the seventh child of John and Allie (V.) King, was born at the old King homestead, November 15th, 1835. He read medicine and graduated from the best colleges of the times. He located at Wilson, North Carolina, and was a surgeon in the war of 1861-5. He took much interest in public affairs, was very popular and a good speaker. He was twice chairman of the county democratic executive committee and was later twice elected to the State Senate. In 1890 he was prominently mentioned for the democratic nomination for Representative in Congress, from the second district. He enjoyed a large practice, and while visiting one of his patients in 1890 he suffered a fall and fractured his collarbone. From this injury, and complications, he died, January 19th, 1891. He was buried in the Wilson cemetery. He was a member of the Christian (Disciple) church and took great interest in its progress. He was a prominent Mason.

In 1855 he married Carrie M. Buyum, who died a few years since. They had two children—daughters, both living.

KING, THOMAS, the third child of John and Allie (V.) King, was born at the old King homestead, April 28th, 1828. He received a good common school education and began life as a farmer, a few years later adding merchandising. Taking great interest in all affairs of his country he never sought office, but was content to serve his people in humble capacities, and among such was that of school committeeman. He was a whig and strong Union man, but when the inevitable came, he readily volunteered, May 15th, 1862, as a private in Company D, Forty-fourth Regiment. After a short stay at Camp Mangum, Raleigh, his regiment went to Tarboro, and while doing duty in that section was at Tranters creek, when Colonel George B. Singletary was killed. The regiment soon went to Virginia and did duty about Richmond and vicinity, being in many of the hard-fought and bloody battles of the war. On the death of General Stonewall Jackson, Company D, Forty-fourth Regiment was the Guard of Honor while his body lay in state in the Capitol at Richmond. In a skirmish on Squirrel Level road, near Petersburg, October 8th, 1864, he was mortally wounded, dying October 24th, 1864. Though that was his first wound, he had many narrow escapes, shots through his clothes and once a ball pierced a Testament in his upper left vest pocket and lodged against his flesh. Enlisting as a private he soon became lieutenant and later often commanded the company. While in the army he came within a few votes of the whig nomination for sheriff of his county, by his friends at home. He was a Mason and a member of the Christian (Disciple) Church.

May 11th, 1848, he married Martha A., daughter of Moses and Martha A. (Briley) Turnage. Moses Turnage was a planter, of Welsh descent and a soldier in the war of 1812-15 (in Captain Samuel Vines' Company). They had four children, all sons.

MOORING, GUILFORD MORTIMER, son of William L. and Catherine Mooring, was born February 1st, 1847. His father and his grandfather, John Mooring, were large and prosperous farmers.

Mr. Mooring received a common school education, working on the farm until the spring of 1864, when seventeen years old he enlisted in Company G, Eighteenth Regiment. He went through the last year of the war and was never wounded, though while on picket duty a ball so closely grazed his face that he felt its force. He was in twenty-two battles and one of the color-bearers of his regiment. The regiment had ten color-bearers, only two of whom lived to surrender with General Johnston. Of Company G, there were only three men present. He then returned home and went back to farming. He soon thereafter began his public career as a justice of the peace, which position he held several years. He was elected a county commissioner in 1876 and in September, 1877, he was appointed sheriff to fill the unexpired term of Sheriff E. A. Wilson. In the democratic convention that year there was some trouble over the nomination for sheriff, and he refused to let his name go before the second convention. He was not long out of the sheriff's office before he was again elected a county commissioner, which position he held many years. In 1898 he was elected sheriff, but declined a renomination in 1900. He then returned to his farm where he remained out of politics until 1910, when he was elected a representative in the Legislature. For a number of years he has been a member of the Pension Board of the county, which board passes upon the eligibility of Confederate soldiers for pensions from the State.

In 1873 he married Josephine Moore, daughter of the late Samuel Moore, a farmer. She died in December, 1907. They had eight children, all of whom are living.

KING, JOHN, third son of John and Allie V. King, was born February 6th, 1830. He received a common school education and after a short experience as clerk in a store at Falkland began business for himself. After a few years he sold out that business to devote his time to his farming interests. He was Captain of militia in 1860, and during the war, 1861-5, he was assessor of taxes "in kind." For several years after the war he was in the mercantile business, moving to Tarboro about 1867. On the death of his wife he returned to his farm near Falkland. He was Associate Justice of the Pitt County Inferior Court several years. In 1882 he was elected to the State Senate as an independent, serving one term, after which he did not take an active interest in political affairs. During his life he performed many minor public duties, and was many years a Justice of the Peace. He was a member of the Christian (Disciple) church and a Mason. He took great interest in the Grange and its work, was Master of his local and also of the County Grange and was for some time County Lecturer. He was primarily a farmer and loved his farm, and often interested in other business, practically lived and died a farmer. His was an ideal farm life. Never considered wealthy, his life was one of comfort and plenty and the respect and esteem of all.

He was thrice married. His first wife was Martha Joyner, daughter of Abram Joyner, his second was Bettie Cobb, of Edgecombe, and his third was Fannie Bynum, daughter of Allen Bynum, all of whom preceded him to the grave. He died June 25th, 1910, leaving one daughter by his first wife, two sons and a daughter by his second and three sons by his last.

One of his sons, George B. King, is a lawyer, was County Superintendent of Schools, member of the legislature (House) of 1899, Private Secretary to W. A. B. Branch in Congress from 1891 to 1895, postmaster at Greenville from 1895 to 1899 and now holds a government position at Washington, D. C.

FLEMING, JAMES LEONIDAS, son of Leonidas and Harriet E. Fleming, was born November 1st, 1867. His father was a farmer, a Confederate soldier, in Company H, Twenty-seventh Regiment, and a county commissioner several years. His mother was a daughter of Major Jones, a farmer. Mr. Fleming was raised on the farm and attended school at Greenville. He graduated from Wake Forest College and then taught school a year. He then studied law at the University of North Carolina and was licensed in 1892. He located at Greenville, and was soon elected mayor. He served more than one term. When the Inferior Court was practically re-established, he was elected solicitor, but the court never sat. He was twice a member of the Board of Education. In 1904, he was the democratic nominee for the State Senate and elected. He was re-elected in 1906, but declined a renomination in 1908. After being elected to the Senate in 1906, he began the work of getting the bill for the establishment of a State school in the east. He prepared the bill, fought for it in season and out of season, before the committees and in the Senate. The result was a bill providing for the establishment of The East Carolina Teachers' Training School. His next work was to get it for Greenville. In this he was ably seconded and zealously supported and it was won. The East Carolina Teachers' Training School was built at Greenville. It was his crowning achievement and he saw the fulfillment of his faith and works. But only for a short while. In the prime of life and usefulness his life went out. He was killed in an automobile accident, November 5th, 1909, about a mile from Greenville, on the old plank road. He died instantly, being thrown some distance, breaking his neck. Two other deaths resulted from that accident, and the fourth escaped almost miraculously.

He was a Mason, a Pythian and an Odd Fellow. He was a good lawyer, a forceful and pleasant speaker and a staunch friend.

In 1899 he married Lula White, daughter of Captain C. A. White. They had three children, two girls and a boy.

SMITH, MARY, daughter of Edward and Sarah Nelson, was born in Craven County, North Carolina, October 27, 1825. Her father was a descendant of the Nelsons, of Kent, England, and her mother was a daughter of Charles Reach. Though her education was limited she began the work of teaching in 1845. The next year, 1846, she married William H. Smith, of Pitt county, and of course became a Pitt county woman. She continued to teach and having never studied grammar, mastered it by teaching it. Family duties made her give up teaching herself, but she employed a teacher and continued the school until 1869, when circumstances forced the school to discontinue. Three children had married, but there were still seven at home, four of whom had never attended school. Determined they should know something, in 1870, she fitted up an upstairs room for school purposes, but with room for her spinning wheel. With no servant and all the household work, including preparing the three meals each day, she found time for three hours in the forenoon and three in the afternoon for teaching and carding and spinning when not hearing recitations. The secret that she was teaching a school was soon out and neighbors' children began to come. Soon she had no time for carding and spinning nor place for her wheel, for the room was full of children. She had to occupy the old schoolhouse and on the first day the attendance was over forty. About this time an old gentleman, John G. Elliot, a good Latin scholar and fine mathematician, too old for active work, visited her and made it his home. Under him, she studied Latin, algebra, geometry and surveying. She was soon able to teach them and prepared her children for college. For eighteen years she taught, and six of her children and two of her grandchildren were teachers. At some time afterwards she again taught her last school being in 1891, she then being sixty-six years old.

In her late years she conceived the idea of building a church at Winterville. A strong and earnest church woman and worker, she saw that church completed and dedicated, an enduring monument to her zeal and energy. Monday, October 2d, 1905, she saw the dedication and consecration of that church. One of her sons, Reverend Claudius Smith, of Washington, D. C., and one of her grandsons, Reverend William E. Cox, whose ordination to the priesthood, her son preaching the sermon, she had witnessed the day before at Greenville, and Bishop Strange, took part in these services. After these services, a family reunion dinner, with a number of friends and relatives was had on the grounds. Her work on earth was nearing its close. Many a great life had accomplished less. A more than fourscore life, filled with usefulness, service and blessings was ending. Ready to meet the Master, she obeyed his call, Monday, February, 18th, 1907.

She builded better than she knew.

JOYNER, OLTHUS LEELAND, son of Jacob and Mary Joyner, was born near Farmville, N. C., February 12th, 1869. His father, as was his grandfather, Aaron Joyner, was a planter. When the civil war came he was one of the early volunteers, joining the Tar River Boys, who went to Hatteras, were later captured and sent to Governor's Island then to Fort Warren near Boston. Being exchanged, he again volunteered and served throughout the war. His mother was a daughter of Benjamin H. and Nancy (Cunningham) Sugg, of Greene county.

Receiving a good common school education he early embarked into the tobacco business, being one of the pioneer tobacco men and warehousemen of Greenville, and the only man then connected with the market who is so connected today. In 1891 he with R. J. Coble and others organized a company for establishing a tobacco market, the old Greenville Warehouse being built. He was one of the first warehousemen. After many years on the market as a warehouseman, in 1903 he planned the organization of The Farmers Consolidated Tobacco Co., and that season it began business with one warehouse. The business has continued to grow and expand until it operates three warehouses in Greenville, one in Wilson, two in Kinston, one in Robersonville and one in Washington, and last season its total sales were 14 million pounds. From the beginning, he has been President and General Manager. He has also found time to engage in other enterprises. He is also a large farmer and stock raiser. One secret of his success has been advertising. He well knows and understands its value, and is a liberal, persistent and judicious advertiser. In June, 1892, he married Annie Lyon, daughter of A. A. and Anastia Forbes. Mrs. Joyner's father is a noted musician and served throughout the civil war.

CLARKE HENRY S., was born in Beaufort county, 18—. He received a fine college education, was a large farmer and a lawyer. He represented Beaufort county in the legislature (House) in 1832-4-5 and was solicitor for the State in 1842. He was a member of Congress (representative) 1845-7. He married A. M. Perkins, of Pitt county, and lived in Greenville many years. He died in Greenville .... 187.., and was taken to Beaufort county for burial. He was an able man and also wealthy. He was one man whom office did not flatter and one term in Congress gave him enough of politics. He would not accept a second term.

BLACKLEDGE, WILLIAM S., of Craven county, who was in Congress 1821-3, was a native of Pitt county. He was also a member of the legislature from Craven in 1820. His father, William Blackledge, was long a member of the legislature from Craven in 1797-8-9 and in Congress from 1803-9 and again 1811-13. He was for a while a resident of Pitt county. He died October 19th, 1828. His son died March 21st. 1857.

JAMES, COLONEL FERNANDO GODFREY, son of John G. and Mary R. James, was born at Hertford, Perquimans county, February 23d, 1857. His father was a native of Pitt county and a dentist. In those days dentists spent some time in each town of his circuit, and it was while at Hertford that this son was born. Later he (his father) made Greenville his home and in addition to his dentistry, long kept the old Hotel Macon and sales stables.

His grandfather, William James, came to Pitt county from the Eastern Shore of Virginia and was a Revolutionary soldier. His mother was a daughter of Godfrey Langley, who was a very prominent farmer and business man.

He was educated at the Pitt Academy and the University of North Carolina. He was studying law under Chief Justice R. M. Pearson when that able jurist died, and his law course was completed under Smith and Strong. He was licensed in 1880. He returned to Greenville and entered upon the practice of law as a partner with the late Colonel I. A. Sugg, whose former partner, T. J. Jarvis, had been elected governor. Later the firm became that of Rodman, Sugg & James, by the addition of Judge W. B. Rodman, of Washington. Judge Rodman having died some years before, the firm of Sugg & James dissolved in 1889, and he practiced alone. In 1882 he was elected mayor of Greenville and held the office continuously by re-election until 1892, then resigned, having been elected to the State Senate. He was defeated for the same office in 1894 but elected again in 1898 and 1900, thus serving three terms. In 1900 he was elected a member of the democratic State executive committee, which position he still occupies. That year he was also a delegate to the national democratic convention at Kansas City that nominated Bryan and Stevenson. In 1905, Governor Glenn appointed him an officer of his staff with the title of Colonel, and on the resignation of Solicitor Moore of his (third) judicial district Governor Glenn tendered him the appointment of solicitor, which he declined. He is both a Master and a Royal Arch Mason.

In 1882 he married Mangie Cherry, daughter of the late J. B. Cherry, one of Greenville's leading merchants and long county treasurer. Her mother was Pattie Sherrod, a granddaughter of John Simpson. They have six children. One son, James B. James, educated at Horner's and the University of North Carolina, and licensed to practice law in 1908, is now associated with him in his practice of law. Another son, Charlie James, is teller in the Greenville National Bank.

BARNHILL, MABEL, daughter of Julius H. and Melissa A. Barnhill, was born in Bethel township on the farm. Her father was a young Confederate in Company H, Tenth Regiment and when the war was over returned to the farm. Her mother was a daughter of the late B. L. T. Barnhill, an ordnance officer in the Confederate army. His grandfather (her great-grandfather) was an officer in the Revolutionary war.

After receiving a good high school education, she decided to study pharmacy and entered the drug store of Dr. F. C. James, in Bethel, March 19th, 1901.

Dr. James, being a graduate in pharmacy as well as medicine, took great care to instruct her in her chosen profession. She later took a course at Page's School of Pharmacy, Greensboro, North Carolina. She was the only woman in the class 1906. She was one of the ten of that class who passed a successful examination before the North Carolina State Board of Pharmacy in Raleigh, November 2d, 1906, and was granted license to practice pharmacy. She was the third licensed female pharmacist in North Carolina. She returned to Bethel after receiving her license and became a partner with Dr. F. C. James. She is still with him and a most valuable asset in his business and practice. She is business manager of the Matinee Drug Co.

She now ranks among the most skilled, efficient and popular in the profession. She became a member of the North Carolina Pharmaceutical Association on July the 8th, 1908.

HARDING, MAJOR HENRY, son of Nathaniel and Elizabeth Harding, was born at Chocowinity, Beaufort county, May 8th, 1836. His father was a farmer, captain of militia in 1812-15 and a Justice of the Peace near all his life. His grandfather was a major under General Greene in the Revolution. His ancestors were among the earliest settlers of New England. His mother was a daughter of Cornelius Patrick, a soldier of the Revolution, who was with Arnold on his expedition to Quebec in 1775.

Major Harding was raised on the farm, working and attending school, finishing from Trinity Parochial School, at Chocowinity, with a good academic education. He then began teaching and had been teaching five years, when he left the schoolhouse for the field of war, volunteering in Captain Swindell's company, which went to Hatteras, and at the expiration of twelve months, for which it had enlisted, disbanded. Governor Vance then commissioned him Captain to raise a company. This company went into the Sixty-first Regiment as Company B. He was later promoted Major of the regiment. The regiment saw much service in Virginia, the Carolinas and Georgia. In 1863 it was encamped on James Island, near Charleston. On another part of the island were a lot of negro soldiers. The United States gunboat Chippewa was lying in Stono river to protect them. Major Harding conceived a plan to capture it. Early one morning in July, 1863, his regiment made the charge, succeeding in getting to the boat but could not scale its sides. The guns of the boat could not be lowered enough to reach the Confederates and any appearance over the sides of the boat was an invitation for a ball. So the boat could do nothing but weigh anchor and float down the river. But not before several on the boat had been killed and the boat damaged. As the boat swung around the regiment had to seek shelter, as grape and canister were flying thick. However, only one Confederate, B. A. Davis, private in Company F, was wounded. He died in a few minutes. The regiment then charged on the negro soldiers, drove them from the island with great loss. Those negroes who did not run may be there yet. All their camp and supplies were captured without the loss of a man. Returning from the war, he went to work on the farm and in 1866 was elected to the legislature (House). In 1876 he was elected a county commissioner and was twice reelected. In 1885 he moved to Greenville. He had served four years on the Board of Education, when in 1889, on the death of Superintendent Josephus Latham, he was elected county superintendent to fill the vacancy He held this position four years. In 1892 he was elected register of deeds, and since the expiration of that term, with the exception of two years, he has been a Justice of the Peace. He is senior warden of the Episcopal church, was long a lay reader, teacher and superintendent of the Sunday School. He is a Past Master Mason and a democrat.

In 1867 he married Susan Sugg, daughter of Benjamin H. and Nancy Sugg, of Greene county. They have six children, four sons and two daughters. Their sons are F. C. Harding, a lawyer of Greenville; W. F. Harding, a lawyer of Charlotte; H P. Harding, superintendent of Charlotte graded schools, and J. B. Harding, engaged in railroad work in Mexico.

CHERRY, JAMES BURTON, son of William and .... Cherry, was born January, 1840. His father was a farmer and he was raised on the farm. He was educated at Pitt Academy, Asheville, and Horner's, and was merchandising before he was twenty-one years old. He was clerk of the County Court and Master in Equity during the war of 1861-5. In 1864 he was elected clerk of the Superior Court and held it four years. All this time he had continued his mercantile business. He had been associated with his brother, J. J. Cherry, but bought his interest and a few years thereafter, 1868, took T. R. Cherry as a partner, the firm being T. R. Cherry & Company. This partnership lasted until 1888, when T. R. Cherry retired. A few years later he associated with him in the business J. R. and J. G. Moye, the firm then being J. B. Cherry and Company. This partnership continued to his death. In 1874 he was elected treasurer of Pitt county and held the office continuously by re-election until 1890, when he declined a reelection. But in 1898 he was again elected treasurer and twice thereafter reelected, when he positively declined to be a candidate for reelection. Altogether he was clerk of the court eight years and treasurer twenty-two years, with a record of efficiency and popularity to be justly proud of.

He was a member of the Methodist church, and a Pythian. He was twice married. His first wife was Pattie Sherrod, a granddaughter of John Simpson; his second was Ada Pearce, daughter of B. C. Pearce. There is one child by the first wife, Mrs. F. G. James, and one by the second, J. B. Cherry, Jr.

He died March 13th, 1905.

SMITH, JOHN RICHARD, born May 18th, 1868, } Brothers.
SMITH, ROBERT WILLIAMS, born November 11th, 1869 }

The lives and work of these two brothers have been so closely blended that a sketch of one is almost a sketch of the other, therefore, it is best to give them together. From infancy to manhood and on, their career, their interests have been as one. Their father, Theophilus Smith, was a farmer, as was also their grandfather, William Smith. Their father was a Confederate soldier and died when they were quite young. In 1878 they went to Oxford, North Carolina, where they remained two years at the asylum, then under Dr. Mills. Ill health of their mother called them home and they again took up the work of her farm. She died in 1888 and the next year they went to Winterville, as clerks for A. G. Cox, who took more than a business interest in them and their future. He aided and encouraged them in the opening of a store in 1891, John having charge of that business, Robert remaining with Mr. Cox until 1893, when the business demanded the services of both, Robert also went to Ayden. Their business has had a phenomenal growth and they are interested in many of the most successful enterprises of their town. The Bank of Ayden, with $10,000 capital, was organized in 1903. They were the largest stockholders and John was elected cashier, which position he still holds. The business of the bank has grown and the capital stock is now $25,000. In May, 1902, a disastrous fire destroyed much of the business section of Ayden and their losses were very heavy. Again in January, 1906, they were severe losers by fire. This year they incorporated their business, under the firm name of The J. R. Smith Company, with a paid in capital of $25,000, the authorized capital being $100,000. Of the new firm, John is President and Robert is Vice-President. Their business is very extensive, reaching out to at least four counties. In 1908 this firm bought out the Ayden Milling and Manufacturing Company, a company with $15,000 capital stock. They had been interested in this concern since its organization. John is also president of the Ayden Loan and Insurance Company, another enterprise that is doing much for the upbuilding of the town and vicinity. They have recently bought out the East Carolina Land and Development Company, and will develop much property in and around Ayden. They own much real estate in Pitt, Craven and Greene counties. Both are members of the Christian (Disciple) church and prominent in church work. They are both Masons and Odd Fellows.

John married Mary, daughter of Elder Fred McGlohon, a Free Will Baptist minister and a farmer, who was a representative in the Legislature of 1893. They have two children, daughters, living. Robert married Cora, daughter of W. F. Hart, a farmer. They have four children, sons, living.

BLOW, ALEXANDER LILLINGTON, son of William J. and Dorcas S. Blow, was born in Greenville, June 29th, 1851. His father was a well-known physician and a representative in the legislature (House) from Pitt county ten years, from 1848 to 1858. In the war of 1861-5 he was a surgeon in the Twenty-seventh Regiment. His grandfather, James Blow, was a large farmer, in the western part of the county. His mother was a daughter of Joseph Masters, of Hyde county, who was a representative in the legislature (Senate) from Hyde in 1800.

Mr. Blow was attending the common schools when in the latter part of March, 1865, he enlisted in the Eighth Texas Regiment, then in General Johnston's army. After General Johnston's surrender near Durham, he returned home and entered Pitt Academy where he finished his education. He then became a clerk in a store. Later he studied law under Colonel Yellowly and was licensed in January, 1874. Shortly he became associated with J. T. Lyon, in the publication of *The Register*, a weekly paper, published in Greenville. In September of that year, he was elected register of deeds for the county and withdrew from the paper business. He held that office by reelection until 1881, when he was appointed clerk of the Superior court to succeed Henry Sheppard, deceased. He held that office to the end of that term, one year. He was solicitor of the Inferior court two years. He was a town alderman in 1881 and again in 1900, serving the two terms of two years each. In 1902 he was elected State Senator and again in 1908. He was elected a member of the democratic county executive committee in 1874 and held that position until 1904. From 1874 to 1883 he was secretary to the committee and from 1883 to 1904 he was chairman. For many years he was attorney for the Board of County Commissioners. He first began the practice of law in 1874.

He is a member of the Methodist church and is chairman of the Board of Trustees. He is a Master Mason and has been prominent in Masonic circles and work.

In 1874 he married Alice M. Monteiro, of Virginia. They have seven children, all living.

GRIMES, JOHN BRYAN, son of General Bryan Grimes and Charlotte Emily Bryan, daughter of the late Hon. John H. Bryan, was born at Raleigh, N. C., June 3, 1868, but he has lived since his infancy at Grimesland, Pitt County. Educated at private schools, Raleigh Male Academy, Trinity School (Chocowinity, N. C.), Lynch's High School (High Point, N. C.), University of North Carolina, Bryant & Stratton's Business College (Baltimore, Md.), Farmer and business man; member State Farmers' Alliance; aide-de-camp on staff Governor Elias Carr with rank of colonel; member State Board of Agriculture 1899 and 1900; President North Carolina Tobacco Growers Association 1900; Chairman North Carolina Historical Commission; member Executive Committee State Literary and Historical Association; Vice-President and member Board of Managers North Carolina Society Sons of the Revolution; member Executive Committee Trustees of University of North Carolina; Chairman Democratic Executive Committee Chicod Township 1890 to 1900. Always active in politics. Endorsed by Pitt County and several parts of the First Congressional District for Democratic nomination for Congress in 1898, but declined to become a candidate. Elected Secretary of State in 1900, again in 1904 and again in 1908. In 1908 leading the State ticket both in the majority and in the number of votes received. Belongs to following fraternal orders: A. F. & A. M.; Knights of Pythias; J. O. U. A. M. and Royal Arcanum.

Married November 14, 1904, Mary Octavia Laughinghouse, who died December 2, 1909, and on February 3, 1904, to Elizabeth Forrest Laughinghouse. Children by first wife, Helen Elise Grimes, and by last marriage, John Bryan Grimes, Jr., and Charles O'Hagan Grimes.

WILLIAMS, WILLIS ROBERT, was born near Falkland September 3d, 1826, in the house in which he lived and died. His father was Robert Williams, a son of John Williams, prominent in Revolutionary history of Pitt county. John was a son of Robert Williams, a Welshman, who first settled in Pennsylvania, but came to North Carolina in 1727, settling near Falkland where he bought several thousand acres of land.

Left an orphan when young, Mr. Williams was reared and educated by an uncle, who gave him a fine college education. As a young man, he was prominent in public affairs, serving as school committee, member of the County Board of Education and examiner of teachers. Some time in the latter 60's he was made a Justice of the Peace and at different periods held this office more than twenty years. He was prominent in the Grange movement, was master of the local and later of the State Grange. He was often a delegate to the National Grange. He served long on the State Board of Agriculture and director of State institutions. His legislative career began in 1866 when he was elected a member of the House. At that session he introduced a bill to pension the Confederate soldiers, it being the first effort of the kind in the South. However the bill failed to become a law. He was elected to the State Senate in 1884 and reelected in 1886, 1888 and 1890. He was a candidate for Superior Court Clerk in 1894. He was a member of the Greenville Lodge of Masons and a member of the Christian (Disciple) church.

Early in life he married Harriet P., daughter of Colonel Thomas H. Leary, of Edenton, who preceded him to the grave. They were the parents of eight children, five boys and three girls. After her death he led a retired life on his farm, where he died September 7th, 1910, being eighty-three years and four days old.

Though always feeble, he was an active man and interested in public affairs. He was one of the fathers of the Agricultural and Mechanical College at Raleigh. He always championed the cause of the farmer and was really the father of the six per cent interest law, though he did not secure its enactment. He was a member of the Christian church sixty or more years and perhaps attended more State conferences than any other layman; he was a Mason more than fifty years. He was a man of thorough education, extensive information, wide travel and broad views.

WOOTEN, FRANCIS MARION, son of Robert L. and Julia A. Wooten, was born at LaGrange, N. C., August 4th, 1875. His father was a farmer. His mother was a daughter of M. R. C. Loftin and Julia Parker Loftin.

He was educated at Columbia College, New York, and the University of North Carolina at Chapel Hill. Taking up pharmacy, he was licensed in 1897 and in 1904 he located at Greenville, where he had lived several years prior to 1897. While a pharmacist and engaged in the business he took up the study of law, was licensed to practice in 1905 and began practice at Greenville. In 190.. he was elected Mayor, which office he then held two terms. In 1910 he was again elected Mayor to fill an unexpired term. Thus he now combines pharmacy, law and executive duties. He is a member of the Episcopal church and a "lay reader." He is a Mason, with his membership with Unanimity Lodge at Edenton, North Carolina. He is also a member of Tar River Lodge, Knights of Pythias, Greenville, North Carolina. He is an active business man, a good lawyer and popular Mayor.

July 7th, 1909, he married Elizabeth Hampton Wade, a daughter of ...... Wade, of Farmville, Virginia.

JARVIS, THOMAS JORDAN, was born in Currituck county, North Carolina, January 18th, 1836. He began life as a school teacher, graduating from Randolph-Macon College, Virginia, in 1860. In 1861 he closed his school and enlisted in Company B, Eighth regiment, and was promoted from Lieutenant to Captain. At Drewry's Bluff in 1864 he was severely wounded, his right arm having been useless since. Returning home after the war he moved to Tyrrell county and was elected to the Andrew Johnson State Convention of 1865. He was licensed to practice law in 1866. In 1868 he was a Seymour and Blair candidate for elector as well as a candidate for the legislature, being elected to the latter. He was reelected in 1870 and elected Speaker of the House. In 1872 he moved to Pitt county and was a Greely and Brown candidate for elector. With W. M. King he was elected to Represent Pitt county in the Constitutional convention of 1875. In 1876 he was elected Lieutenant Governor on the ticket with Z. B. Vance, and on the election of Governor Vance to the United States Senate he became Governor February 5th, 1879. In 1880 he was elected Governor for the full term, thus serving six years. In March, 1885, President Cleveland appointed him Minister to Brazil, where he remained four years. On the death of Senator Vance Governor Carr appointed him United States Senator, April 19th, 1895, to fill the unexpired term. Since then he has devoted himself to his profession, though taking an active interest in public matters.

LATHAM, REVEREND JOSEPHUS, son of Thomas J. and Nancy C. Latham, was born at Pantego, Beaufort County, North Carolina, June 6th, 1828. His father was one of the pioneer ministers of the Christian (Disciple) church in North Carolina and was also a large landowner, with many slaves. He received a good common school education. At fifteen years of age he became a member of the Christian church at Pantego, being baptized by his father. Three years later, when he was only eighteen, he became a minister of that church and made that his life work, though he was also a farmer and gave much attention to educational work, teaching at various times and places. He taught the Farmville High School many years and many of the successful men of that section, and others, received their training under him. He was a member of the Pitt County Board of Education and County Superintendent from 1883 to 1889.

After many years itinerary, during which he served the Kinston church several years, he made his home on his farm near Greenville and was for many years pastor of Mount Pleasant. During his ministry, only sickness, the performance of some other sacred duty or unavoidable circumstances, made him miss preaching every Sunday in the year. And besides, he held many revival meetings and preached at other times. During his ministry he baptized about 3,000 persons and married near 500 couples. He died April 27th, 1889, aged 60 years, 10 months and 21 days, and was buried in Mount Pleasant cemetery near his home. A marble tomb marks his grave.

For many years he was a member of Covenant Lodge of Odd Fellows at Greenville and was also a Knight of Honor. He was a strong prohibitionist and all his life a total abstainer. He was utterly unselfish, and spent his life in the service of his Master and for his fellow man.

One cold day he met a Confederate soldier, who was barefooted and not too well clothed. After a short conversation with the soldier, he pulled off his shoes and socks and gave them to the soldier.

May 31st, 1852, he married Martha Brown, daughter of Alfred L. and Nancy E. Brown, Reverend John P. Dunn officiating. At the age of 81 years his widow, with two of their children, survive him.

(She died September, 1910.)

KING, RICHARD WARREN, third son of Thomas and Martha A. (Turnage) King, was born near what is now Farmville, September 11th, 1858. Receiving a common school education, he began clerking in a country store before he was grown. Later in other business he canvassed much of the eastern counties. In 1882 he was appointed deputy sheriff under Sheriff King, which position he held for the three terms of his uncle. In 1888 J. A. K. Tucker was elected sheriff and he was continued in office of deputy sheriff for the two terms of Sheriff Tucker. So acceptably and efficiently had he performed the duties of deputy for ten years that in 1892 he was nominated by the Democrats for the office of sheriff and elected at the following election. In 1894 the county commissioners refused to accept the bond of sheriff-elect, W. H. Harrington, and appointed him sheriff for the ensuing two years. Having served altogether fourteen years in the office he was not a candidate for renomination in 1896. In 1906 he was elected a county commissioner and under that administration, the steel bridges at Greenville and Grifton were built. He has always taken an active interest in politics and served on many committees, having been a member of the county, district and many other committees. He is a member of the Christian (Disciple) church and a Mason.

September 28th, 1891, he married Mattie E., daughter of W. B. and Mattie E. (Edwards) Moye. They have seven children living.

SKINNER, COLONEL HARRY, son of James C. and Elmira W. Skinner, was born in Perquimans county, May 25th, 1855. His father was a member of the legislature (House) several times from Chowan county and also clerk of the Court of Perquimans county near forty years. His grandfather, Henry Skinner, represented Chowan county a number of times in the legislature in both Houses and later represented Perquimans many terms in both houses of the legislature. He was also a member of the Governor's Council. His great-grandfather, William Skinner, represented Perquimans at the Halifax Convention of 1776, and on the organization of troops in 1776 was elected Lieutenant Colonel. He was later promoted Brigadier General. The Skinners were from England and among the early settlers of Albemarle, where they became large planters and slave owners and very influential. His mother was a daughter of Allen Ward, a large planter.

Colonel Skinner was prepared for college at Hertford Academy and graduated from Kentucky University at Lexington with degree of L. B in 1875. He had studied law and was sworn in as an attorney at Lexington, but coming to Greenville, he continued its study under Major L. C. Latham and was licensed in North Carolina in 1876. He at once formed a partnership with Major Latham. In 1878 he was elected a member of the democratic congressional committee. From 1880 to 1884 he was chairman of the Pitt county democratic executive committee and in 1883 also chairman of the congressional committee. In 1888 he was elected to the legislature (House), and being a strong Allianceman took a prominent part in matters pertaining to its cause. When it resulted in the formation of the populist party, he was one of its organizers and an active participant in its proceedings. He canvassed the State in 1892, and was the populist candidate for Congress in the first district in 1894. He was elected and reelected in 1896, but was defeated in 1898. He is now the only living ex-representative of the first district.

In 1901 he was appointed United States District Attorney for the Eastern District of North Carolina by President McKinley, and reappointed in 1905 by President Roosevelt. Since the expiration of his second term he has devoted himself to his large law practice in both the State and Federal Courts. He is a Mason and an Odd Fellow. He is public spirited and enterprising and principally through his efforts a building and really the public school for Greenville resulted, which grew into the graded school.

Colonel Skinner has been twice married. His first wife was Miss Monteiro, of Richmond, Virginia, by whom he had four children, one of whom, Harry Skinner, Jr., an able and bright young lawyer, with great promise of a useful and brilliant career, lost his life in an automobile accident near Greenville, November 3d, 1909. His second wife was Ella Montiero, of Greenville, by whom he has one son.

LAUGHINGHOUSE, CAPTAIN JOSEPH JOHN, son of Joseph H. and J. A. Laughinghouse, was born in Pitt county, October 4th, 1847. When Thomas Laughinghouse came to America about 1750 he left his brothers engaged in the wholesale grain business in Liverpool. Their descendants have continued the business to the present time. Thomas settled in Pitt (then Beaufort) county. John, a son of Thomas, was an officer in the Revolution, serving under General Washington and was with him at Yorktown. John had three sons, Thomas, who went to Arkansas: (Judge George Laughinghouse of that State was one of his descendants;) Joseph, who went to Alabama; and Edward L., who remained in Pitt and became a large planter. Edward L. had three children, William J., John H. and Annie. Annie married F. B. Satterthwaite. John H., who, like his father, was a large planter, was the father of Joseph J., the subject of this sketch.

Captain Laughinghouse's father died in November, 1862, and left him practically in charge of his mother's business. She died in March, 1863. He then went to Horner's Military school, where he remained until April, 1864, leaving school to join the Junior Reserves, composed of seventeen-year-old boys, Company H, Seventy-first Regiment, of which company he was elected First Lieutenant, and the following October (1st) four days before he was seventeen years old, he was promoted Captain. He is said to have been the youngest Captain of any North Carolina troops. The first four months after his enlistment he served as Adjutant of his regiment. The regiment was in General Hoke's Division of General Joseph E. Johnston's army the last four months of the war.

After the war Captain Laughinghouse taught school a year, clerked a year and at the age of twenty was engaged in the shingle business, making some money. His father's estate, somewhat encumbered, had suffered heavily by the war, necessitating the sale of the land in 1869. He became the purchaser, and went to work with a will to redeem it, and in time was successful. He has always been an active democrat and has served many years as committeeman, both of his township, county and State. He was almost a lifelong Justice of the Peace. He was four years an Associate Justice of the County Inferior Court.

In 1904 he was elected a member of the legislature (House) and reelected in 1906. In 1909 Governor Kitchin appointed him Superintendent of the State prison and farms. Under his management the earnings of the first year were more than doubled. He has been one of the county's largest and most successful farmers and at one time was said to be the largest tobacco grower in the State. He is a prominent Mason.

In 1870 he married Eliza, daughter of the late Dr. C. J. O'Hagan. They have three children living: Dr. C. O'H. Laughinghouse of Greenville, Mrs. J. Bryan Grimes of Raleigh, and Ned Laughinghouse of Greenville.

LATHAM, MAJOR LOUIS CHARLES, son of Charles Latham, was born at Plymouth, N. C., September 11th, 1840. His father was a prominent lawyer of Plymouth.

Major Latham was prepared for college in the Plymouth schools and graduated from the University of North Carolina in 1859. He read law under Judge Asa Biggs and then attended Harvard Law School.

The events of 1860-1 interrupted his studies. He returned home, volunteered, and May 20, 1861, was made Captain of Company G, First Regiment. He was wounded at Sharpsburg and soon thereafter promoted Major of the regiment. He commanded the regiment at Chancellorsville and was wounded at the Wilderness, May 5th, 1864. Recovering he again joined the army and surrendered with General Lee at Appomattox. While at home in 1864 he was elected to the legislature (House). At the close of the war he resumed his law studies and was soon licensed to practice. In 1870 he was elected to the State Senate and in the absence of Judge Warren, President of the Senate, he was always chosen to preside. He was a candidate for the democratic congressional nomination in 1872, 74 and 78, but defeated, and in 1880 was nominated by acclamation and also elected. He was again a candidate in 1882, but was defeated by W. F. Pool. He came to Greenville in 1875 and was a Tilden and Hendricks elector in 1876. In 1886 he was again a candidate and elected to Congress. After this term he devoted himself to his profession, being one of the ablest and most eloquent lawyers in the State. He died October 16th, 1895.

Major Latham was twice married. His first wife was a Miss Norcum, of Plymouth, by whom he had one child. His second wife was a Miss Montiero, of Richmond, Va., by whom he had four children, one of whom is now United States Consul.

MOORE, DAVID COLUMBUS, son of David and Arcenia Moore, was born September 18th, 1850. His father was a farmer and had two sons in the Confederate army.

Mr. Moore received a common school education and farmed a number of years. In 1877 he was elected a Justice of the Peace, which position he held twenty years. In 1878 he was elected a member of the legislature (House) and reelected in 1880. Having moved to Bethel he was first elected Mayor in 1876 and by reelection he was Mayor sixteen years. In 1885 he was elected member of the County Board of Education, serving two years. In 1891-92 he was deputy register of deeds under D. H. James, and also in 1893 under Major Harding. In 1898 he was elected clerk of the Superior Court and reelected in 1902, 1906 and 1910. He is an active democrat and has served as member of both his township and county executive committees. He is an Odd Fellow and a Red Man.

In 1875 he married Martha C. Andrews, daughter of Henry and Mary A. Andrews. They have four children: Andrew J., assistant cashier Greenville Banking and Trust Company; Thomas J., teller of the Murchison National Bank of Wilmington; A. Thurman, deputy clerk of Pitt Superior Court, and David C. Jr., attending school.

DAVIS, ROBERT LANG, oldest son of B. A. and Mary A. Davis, was born in Pitt County, March 3d, 1856. His father was a farmer, member of Company F, Sixty-first Regiment, war of 1861-5, and was killed near Charleston, S. C., July, 1863, in an infantry attack upon a Federal gunboat. His grandfather, Benjamin Davis, was a farmer. His mother was a daughter of Robert and Mariah Lang.

Mr. Davis was reared on the farm and his educational advantages were limited. When sixteen years old he began clerking in the store of his uncle, W. G. Lang. Seven years later, 1879, he began business himself in Farmville. Soon W. R. Horne was associated with him, the firm being Davis and Horne. Mr. Horne withdrew in 1886. In 1893 his brothers, Francis M. Davis, and John R. Davis were taken into the business, the firm becoming R. L. Davis and Brothers, which it has continued since.

The first bank in Pitt County, the Bank of Greenville, was organized in 1896, and R. L. Davis, of Farmville, a large stockholder, was its president, and is now, having served continuously. He was elected a county commissioner in 1900 and reelected in 1902. He has served his town both as mayor and alderman, and his people in many other capacities. He has ever been foremost in promoting the industry and enterprises of his town and section. Among such and in which he has been a prime mover, are, the Bank of Farmville, organized in 1904, of which he has been its only president; the Farmville tobacco market, opened in 1905; the Farmville district graded school; the Farmville oil mills, now about ready to begin operations, of which he is president; and a number of other enterprises.

When Mr. Davis began business in 1879 his capital was limited and competition almost deathdealing, but by close and strict attention to his business he surmounted many difficulties and built up a business that extends to several counties. He is a merchant farmer, manufacturer and capitalist. As a merchant his firm does the largest business in Pitt County; as a farmer, he is the largest landowner in the county and is practical and successful; as a manufacturer, he is interested in a number of enterprises and much of their success is due to his ability as a financier; as a capitalist, he is an extensive banker and does a large business. Thus he is Pitt County's largest merchant, largest farmer, largest banker, prominent in all affairs of the county, and a bachelor.

COTTEN, ROBERT RANDOLPH, son of John L. and Nancy A. Cotten, was born in upper Edgecombe county, June 20th, 1839. His father was a farmer. His grandfather, Roderick Cotten, was a planter also. His mother was a daughter of the late Aaron Johnson, a large and wealthy planter and slaveowner.

From the common schools, Mr. Cotten went to Baltimore, where he finished his education and for a while made Baltimore his home, engaging in the mercantile business as a traveling salesman. When the war of 1861-5 began he came back to Edgecombe and enlisted in Company G, Third North Carolina Cavalry. He went through the war and surrendered with General Lee at Appomattox. After the war he began business in Tarboro and came to Falkland, Pitt county, and opened business about 1868. He soon had a branch business in Wilson, and was one of the directors of the first bank organized in that town. He has held many positions of trust and honor. He was long a director of the State Hospital at Raleigh, of the State penitentiary and has been a member of the democratic State executive committee fifteen years. For several years after coming to Pitt he was a Justice of the Peace, and on the organization of the Pitt County Inferior Court, he was elected its chairman and held that position several years. In 1908 he was nominated and elected a member of the legislature (House) and is now a State Senator, having been elected at the election on November 8th, 1910. He is a large farmer, with his farms in a high state of cultivation, and also a merchant, supplying his farms and otherwise doing business. He is a member of the Episcopal church.

March 7th, 1866, he married Miss Sallie Southall, daughter of Colonel Thomas Southall, of Murfreesboro, N. C. They have six children, three sons and three daughters. Bruce Cotten, their oldest son, is a United States army officer, and married Mrs. Edith Johns Tyson, of Baltimore. Lyman A. Cotten is a United States naval officer and married Miss Bessie Henderson, of Salisbury, N. C. Preston S. Cotten is a lawyer of Norfolk, Virginia. Their daughters, all married, are Mrs. Julian Timberlake, of Raleigh, N. C.; Mrs. Russell B. Wiggin, of Boston, Mass., and Mrs. Douglass B. Wesson, of Springfield, Mass.

---- Abraham 164
---- earl of Granville 26
---- king of England 71
---- king of Scotland 189
---- sheriff of Pitt 82
ADAMS, Levin 104 Peter 104 Sumner,104 Thomas 104
ALBRITTON, B 133 J C 193 Richard,106 Samuel 104 William,106
ALDERSON, John 31
ALEXANDER, John 45
ALLAN, Colonel 100
ALLEN, Colonel 101 John 100 104 Mrs 100 Samuel 106 Shade 100 Shadrach 96 100
ANDERSON, Brigadier-General 133 Captain 145 152 Colonel 127 215 General 216 L R 126 127 149 160 Ruell 148 Watson W 104
ANDREWS, Arcenia 227 Edmund 108 Henry 261 Martha A 261 Mary A 261 W W 227 Warren 227 William W 104
ARCHDALE, Governor 17
ARMSTRONG,90 Brigadier-General,90 Colonel 82 James 93 96 98 99 102 221 W H 218
ARNOLD,251 Ambrose 104 Benedict 93
ASCUE, Josiah 83
ASHE, Brigadier-General 78 John 47
ATKINS, W S 192
ATKINSON,60 Amos 53 55 58 60 64 78 Dennis 178 James 60 Mrs S W 135 P A 120 122 123
BAKER, Abram 108
BALDWIN, John 104
BANKS, John 102 Red 33
BARNHILL, B L T 250 Henry 104

BARNHILL (continued) Julius H 250 Mabel 250 Melissa A 250
BARR, Robert 106
BARRETT, Captain 129 J B 120 142 W A 91
BARROW, Mr 33
BATES, Luke 78
BATH,33
BATTON, Major 74
BEARDSLEY, L P 120 123
BEAUFORT,31
BEAUREGARD, General 119
BEDDARD, Noah 104
BELL, Benjamin 96 104 James 96 Reading 105 Willie 105
BERNARD, Chance 178 J P 127 W A 120 William Sr 113
BIGGS, Asa 260
BLACKBEARD,23
BLACKLEDGE, William 248 William S 248
BLACKLEY, H H 193
BLAND,154 C C 154 J J 127
BLINN, Nath 66
BLOUNT,33 Coll 66 E J 218 Jacob 57 King 17 Mr 60 62 65 Mrs 222 Nathaniel 68 Ned 172 Reading 93 Thomas 101 William 90 93 99 115 222 Wm 61 96
BLOW, Alexander Lillington 254 Alice M 254 Dorcas S 254 H A 193 James 254 Musician 193 W J 112 William J 254
BLUNT, James 26 King 21 26 27 Tom 21 26
BONNER, Thomas 45
BOWERS, Benjamin 69 82 Captain 75 John 70 80 Sheriff 69

BOYD, John 31 McD 148
BRADY, Nathan 106 William 70
BRANCH, W A B 192 245
BRICKELL, Joseph 105 Sarah 225
BRIDGERS, H C 195 R R 130 233
BRILEY, Abednego 106 Benjamin 206 213 Jonathan 104 Martha 213 Martha A 244 Moses 213 Willis 171
BRITTON, Miles 104
BROOKS, James 57 William 105
BROWN, 192 Alexander 226 Alfred L 257 Ann M 226 227 Arcenia 227 B W 218 Bettie 227 F L 227 F W 234 Fannie 227 Fernando 226 227 First Lieutenant 127 H W 127 James 226 John 45 110 John E 227 Julius 226 Martha 257 Mary 227 Mary Ann 226 Millie 226 Nancy E 257 Printer 110 Rebecca 226 Rillie 226 Sallie 227 Samuel 226 Surgeon 122 123 W M B 120 123 126 Wyatt M 122 160
BRYAN, Ann 214 Charlotte 218 Charlotte Emily 254 Colonel 48 160 James A 100 John 215 John H 218 254 Joseph 214 William 67 84 104 William Jennings 200 Willaim 58 William 55 62 Wm 57
BUCK, 31 Isaac 42 Noah 104
BURGESS, 152
BURKE, Governor 89
BURNEY, John 29 Wm 225
BURRINGTON, Governor 27
BUSHROD, General 217
BUTLER, General 154
BUYUM, Carrie M 243
BYNUM, Allen 245 Fannie 245 J N 160 John 87
CALHOUN, Samuel 27
CAMMEL, William 105
CANBY, General 170
CANNON, Caleb 170 Nathan 225
CARENEY, Stephen 105
CARNEY, 174 175 176 George 175-177 James H 174 Mary 175

CARNEY (continued) Mary's Governess 175 Mrs 175 Richard 174 Riddick 174 176
CARR, Elias 104 254 F L 198 Governor 191 257
CARRUTHERS, William 31
CARSON, Mr 76
CASWELL, Colonel 74 99 General 89 94 98 Governor 80-84 95 98 Richard 39 45 59 67 76 80 93 William 84 88 222
CHANCE, Thomas E 108
CHEEK, J H 193
CHERRIE, Samuel 225
CHERRY, 150 192 Ada 252 J B 250 J B Jr 252 J H 150 J J 252 James Burton 252 John 108 M G 133 Mangie 250 Miss F G 252 Pattie 250 252 Sallie Ann 231 T R 232 252 W L 126 133 160 William 252
CHOCOWINITY, 33
CLAIBORNE, Colonel 139
CLARK, Elvira 230 H S 120 J E 152 Major 66 W 108
CLARKE, A M 248 Henry W 248
CLAWSON, Mr 223
CLEMENTS, Willie 104
CLEMMONS, William 108
CLEVELAND, President 257
CLINGMAN, T L 130
COBB, 133 Bettie 245 Cecil R 241 Howell 104 James C 240 Mary E 240 Mollie A 241 Robert John 240
COBLE, R J 248
COGDELL, Richard 65
COGGINS, 150
COGSDELL, David 145
CONGLETON, 33
COOKE, 151 John R 132
COON, C L 198
COOPER, John 69
COOR, James 76
COREY, Louisa A 243
CORNWALLIS, Lord 87-89 94 220
COTTEN, Bruce 152 John L 263 Lieutenant-Colonel 129 Lyman A 263 Nancy A 263 Preston S 263

COTTEN (continued)
  Robert Randolph 263 Roderick 263 Sallie 263 Sallie Southall 231
COTTON, Randolph 231
COX, A G 199 200 253 Aaron 106 Abraham 234 Abram 127 160 Amos 236 Amos Graves 236 Beriah Thadeus 234 Brigadier-General 158 E V 193 Elizabeth 236 Fountain F 237 G W 124 J C 170 Jeannette 235 John C 196 236 Joseph 234 Josiah 234 Mary V 235 Mrs 236 Roy 237 Sallie Ann 234 Susan A 237 Venetia 235 William E 247
CRAVEN, Colonel 74
CRAWFORD, William 105
CRISP, Charles 105
CUNNINGHAM, Nancy 248
DAIL, Carrie 228 W H 227
DANCY, 192 J S 133 160
DANIEL, Benjamin 223 G W 123 General 145 John 170 John S 116 Josiah 104 Junius 147 150 216
DAVIS, 150 B A 251 Benjamin 262 Elizabeth 218 Francis M 262 J R 132 Jefferson 174 180 John R 262 M P 198 Mary A 262 President 165 R L 262 Robert Lang 262 Thomas 89 218
DAYNOR, Mr 65
DEWEESE, 172
DIMOCH, Mrs 186
DINKINS, Frederick 105
DIXON, Joseph 172 229 Josiah 140
DOBBS, 41 Colonel 74 Governor 31
DOCKERY, Mrs 186
DOWD, Patrick 109
DOWNS, Isaac 104 William 105
DRAUGHON, Blanche 238 Eunice L 238 William F 238
DUDLEY, Jesse 105
DUNN, John P 257
DUPREE, James 139 Sterling 95 Thomas 139 162

DUVAL, Lewis 27
DUVALL, Lewis 23
EASON, Ann 225 George 104 J S 132 John 225 Lieutenant 155
EBORN, Benjamin F 108
EDWARDS, Captain 140 Miss 230 Newit 230 William 106
ELKS, William 105
ELLIOTT, John G 247
ELLIS, Elizabeth 220 Governor 118-120 215 Henry 57 59 John W 119
ENGLISH, Joseph 106
ENLOE, John 84
ERNUL, McG 127 157
ESTES, General 172
EVANS, General 217 George 55 57 58 62 70 73 76 84 98 220 223 James 98 Mr 50 Richard 92 108 172 223
FALCONER, George 83
FARMER, 188 Elizabeth 238 John W 113 Larry D 127 238
FLAKE, Reuben 105
FLANAGAN, Edward 228 Helen 229 John 228 Mary Wise 228 Mrs 228 Roy Chetwynd 228 Thomas 106 228
FLEMING, 150 203 E P 128 Harriet E 246 James L 204 James Leonidas 246 Joseph 148 Lula 246 R R 150 175 177
FOLEY, Sheriff
FORBES, A A 248 Alfred 231 Anastia 248 Annie 248 Arthur 22 70 71 93 95 96 126 Charles 57 James 133 Susan 221
FORNES, H C 193
FORREST, Eliza 230
FOWLER, John 106
FULFORD, Henry 105 Jordan 106 Stephen 105
FULLER, Ebenezer 53
GAINER, Joseph 58
GALLOWAY, John 169 William 105
GARDNER, Graves 236 Miss 236
GARRISS, Ancos 106
GASKILL, John Stanley 228 Miss 228
GASKINS, C F 124

GASTON, William 110
GATES, General 93
GIBBLE, Frederick 58 80
GILMER, J A 151
GLANAGAN, John 204
GLENN, Governor 249
GORDON, General 217
GORHAM, 27 74 223 General 87
　James 27 57 58 60 62 67 72 76
　79 83 87 93 223 John C 108
　Major 75 80
GRAHAM, Captain 143 W A 163
GRANDY,149
GRANGER, Miss 222
GRANT, General 148 217
GRAVES, E B W Mrs 232 N
　L 232
GRAY, Captain 135 J H 127
GREELEY, Horace 180
GREEN, James 78
GREENE, General 86
　Nathaniel 93 R 120 133
GREENVILLE,113
GRIFFIN, Colonel 133 135
GRIFTON,188
GRIMES,23 126 145 150-153 155
　198 Brigadier-General 150
　Bryan 120 122 159 181 182 193
　196 215 254 Captain 131
　Charles O'Hagan 255
　Colonel 133 134 147 149 150
　216 Dempsey 51 Denise 214
　Emily 254 General 179 217
　218 Helen Elise 255 J
　Bryan 194 195 199 200 202 260
　John Bryan 254 John Bryan
　Jr 255 Lieutenant-
　Colonel 126-129 Mary 221
　Mary Octavia 200
　Penelope 221 William 112 114
GRIST,33 Nancy 215 Richard 215
GUION, Judge 206
GURGANUS, Willie 108
HADISON, Harry 106
HALL, Levin 104
HAMMOND, Colonel 134 136
　Mrs 136 N M 136
HAND, Doctor 81
HANDCOCK, General 234
　James,234 Nancy 234
HANKS, Benjamin F 113

HANRAHAN, J A 127 131
　Thomas 113 W S 163
HARDEE, Elizabeth 225
　Isaac 225 Isaac Ensign 225
　Isaac Lewtenant 225 John 27
　29 31 42 43 45 54 55 57 58 78
　115 223 225 Mary Randall 225
HARDING, Elizabeth 251 F C 252
　Ford 227 H P 252 Henry 190 J
　B 252 Major 227 260 Major
　Henry 251 Mary 227
　Nathaniel 251 Susan 227 252
　W F 199 227 252 Fordyce
　Cunningham 227
HARDY, John 29
HARLAN, Mr 66
HARPER, Mary J 218
HARRINGTON, W H 258
HARRIS,109-112 154 Charles 116
　H F 110 233 T W 234
　Taylor 154 W H 196
HARRISON, William Henry 110
HART, Cora 253 W F 253
HASLIN, Dr 49
HATTERAS, 122
HATTON, Moses 104
HATTOWAY, David 106
HAVENS, B F 113
HAWKES, John 93
HAWKINS, Governor 104
HAYWOOD, Nancy 220
HAZEN, Colonel 85
HENDERSON, Bessie 152
HERRINGTON, Calven 105
HEWES, Joseph 62 76
HIGGS, E B 204
HIGHSMITH, William　105
HILL, D H 130 215
HILLIARD, Louis 181
HILLSBOROUGH, Lord 50
HINES, A J 123 124 142 147
　Captain 145 155 William 80
HODGES, 133 W J 143
HOELL, 133
HOGG, Thomas D 113
HOKE, 146 156 General 146 260
HOLDEN, 161 Governor 163 172
　242 W W 152
HOLLIDAY, Thomas 105
HOOKER, 192 General 216
HOOPER, William 59 62 76

HOPKINS, Rillie 226
HORN, 143
HORNE, W R 262
HORNER, 132 143
HOUSE, D E 192
HOWARD, William 102
HOWES, Joseph 59
HOYT, Gould 113
HUNTER, Isaac 95 John 78
INDIAN, 26
IREDELL, James 95
IRWIN, Henry 80
JACKEY, C E 127
JACKSON, 134 151 Allen 237 General, 137 J A 160 Richard, 172 Stonewall 137 216 244 Susan A 237
JAMES, 22 150 Charlie 250 D H, 261 F C 250 Fernando Godfrey, 249 J A 151 James B 250 John G 249 Lancelot 102 M A 150 Mangie 250 Mary R 249 Maryu R 249 Matthew 105 Mrs F G 252 Thomas 231 William 249
JAMESON, Robert 73
JAMISON, Robert 75
JARVIS, 179 183 188 Captain 145 Senator 191 T J 147 180 181 185 186 191 249 Thomas Jordan 256
JOHNS, Edith 263
JOHNSON, Aaron 263 Bushrod 217 Capt 65 67 Captain 122 G W 120 123 160 J H 160 President 162 170
JOHNSTON, 157 231 A D 193 Benjamin 104 Colonel 74 General 158 162 163 244 254 J V 193 Joseph E 260 Samuel 67 104 William 130
JOINER, Isaac 106
JONES, A W 145 Allen 88 Harriet E 246 Major 246 S M 199 Sallie Ann 186 Sallie Ann 231
JORDAN, A G 235 John 91 Thomas 108 Valentine 108 Valentine S 112 Violetta 235 W C 160

JOYNER, Aaron 248 Abram 245 Andrew 191 237 Annie 248 Captain 130 J P 131 Jacob 248 Jason P 125 John 104 108 109 Martha 245 Mary 248 Noah 87 108 Olthus Leeland 248 R W 131 157
K, H T 27 92
KEEL, Bettie 227 John 227
KENERLY, Rev Mr 135
KENNADY, Mr 74
KILLEBREW, George 105
KING, Abram 241 Allie 241 Allie V 241-245 Almeta 242 Bettie 245 Blanche 238 Ella 239 G B 191 George B 245 Henry T 191 Henry Thomas 237 John 241-245 Martha 245 Martha A 237 244 258 Mary 241 Mattie E 258 Mrs W M 239 Nancy W 241 Polly 241 R W 237 Richard Warren 258 Robert W 241 Robert Williams 243 Thomas 145 147 155 237 241 244 258 W M 180 239 256 William M 241 William May 242
KITCHIN, Governor 203 260
KITTRELL, Toney 172
KLINGMAN, General 130 135
KNOLES, John Jr 57
KNOWLES, John 58
KNOX, George 104 John 69
LAFLIN, 169 Bryon 170 Byron 172
LAMB, Colonel 84 Gideon 84 222
LAMBORT, William 81
LANG, B A 262 Mariah 262 Mary 262 Robert 262 W G 146 262 William 106
LANGLEY, D P 146 David 112 Godfrey 112 249 Mary R 249
LANIER, James 58 60 62 80 James Jr 78
LATHAM, 179 183 188 Charles 260 Church 128 Eunice L 238 James 57 58 67 80 Josephus 190 251 257 L C 181 186 192 259 Louis Charles 260 Martha 257 Mrs

LATHAM (continued)
  Mrs Louis Charles 261
  Nancy C 257 Thomas J 257
LAUGHINGHOUSE, Annie 260 C
  O'H 260 Carrie 227 Cas 142-
  144 Charles O'Hagan 227 Dr
  228 Edward L 260 Eliza 227
  230 260 Elizabeth Forrest 255
  George 260 J A 259 J J 148
  152 203 227 230 John 259 John
  H 260 Joseph 260 Joseph John
  259 Mary Octavia 255 Ned 260
  S V 152 Thomas 259 William
  J 260
LAWSON, John 17 27
LAY, Second Assistant Engineer
  132
LEACH, Colonel 49
LEARY, Harriet P 255 Thomas H
  255
LEATHEM, Rother 74
LEE, 151 158 General 148 157
  161 217 261 263
LEGGET, T Benjamin 105
LESLIE, John 53 59
LINCOLN, 190 Abraham 119 164
  General 85 President 119 134
  161
LINEBERRY, G E 198
LITTLE, Dread 106 Gray 135
  James 108 John 106 Josiah 78
  Mary Ann 226 Samuel 226
  Thomas 31 William 105
LOCKHART, James 62 John 58
LOFTIN, Julia A 256 Julia
  Parker 256 M R C 256
LOVEJOY, J M 233 Professor
  184
LUCAS, W H 192
LUKE, J M C 126
LYMAN, Major 174-177
LYON, Annie 248 J T 254
MACE, 33 William 29
MADISON, 122
MAGOWNS, Noah 105
MALLISON, Captain 106 107
MANLY, Charles 113
MANN, J S 203
MANNING, William 105
MARION, Robert L 255
MARTIN, Ann M 226 Betty 39

MARTIN (continued)
  Brigadier-General 127 Eliza-
  beth 39 General 134 Governor
  50 51 54 68 78 224 H W 226
  Josiah 51 Mary E 227
MASTERS, Joseph 254
MAY, Benjamin 55 58 59 62 76
  79 84 91 93 220 241 Benjamin
  Jr 221 Harriett 221 James 78
  221 James W 170 John 93
  Mary 221 Penelope 221 Polly
  241 Susan 221 William 221
MAYO, P H 192
MCADEN, Hugh 29 31
MCARTHUR, William 171
MCD, J 193
MCDONALD, Donald 74 General
  74 Gunner 132
MCGHEE, Bettie 214 Charles M
  214 Cornelia H 214
MCGLOHON, Fred 253 Mary 253
MCKINLEY, President 193 214
  259
MCLANE, Lieutenant 132
MCLAWHON, Loany 117
MCWAIN, Major 31
MCWHORTER, Z D 198
MEEKS, Simpson 106
MERRICK, 66
MERRILL, Wm H 120
MEYERS, John 112 113 R L 113
MILL, 33
MILLER, John 172
MILLS, Abraham 106 Dr 253
  Josiah 105 Thomas 106
MITCHEL, William 105
MOBLEY, T J 192
MONTEIRO, Alice M 254 Ella
  259 Miss 259 261
MOORE, 143 175 Allen 105
  Andrew J 238 261 Arcenia 261
  Arthur 76 Asia 105 B F 241
  Calhoun 143 D S 193 David
  261 David C Jr 261 David
  Columbus 261 Elizabeth 238
  Ella 239 Enoch 174 General 78
  81 Ichabod 238 J L 194 Jose-
  phine 245 Larry I 238 M B 163
  Martha A 261 Nancy W 241
  Samuel 245 Solicitor 249
  Thomas J 261 W A 181

MOORE (continued)
  William 47 48 105 106
MOORING, Catherine 244 G M
  150 Guilford Mortimer 244
  John 244 William L 244
MORDECAI, Samuel F 218
MORRILL, Captain 122 124
MOUND, Captain 89
MOY, George 42
MOYE, 41 Alfred 108 113 116 E
  A 155 Elbert 108 Elbert A 230
  Elbert Alfred 230 George 23 26
  17 45 49 53 57 78 George Sr 29
  Hortense 231 J G 252 John 96
  106 M T 123 Mary 230 Mattie
  E 258 Richard 91 95 W B 258
  William D 108
MURPHEY, Archibald D 115
MURRAY, Hugh 152 James 116
  170 184
NASH, Governor 87 88 98
NEAL, Ann E 219 Dr 219
NEGRO, 66
NELSON, Alfred 105 Edward 247
  Mary 247 Mr 66 Sarah 247
NEWTON, Allie V 241 Delphia
  242 W B F 139 Walter 139
  241
NOBLES, Benjamin 106 Jesse
  170 Samuel 105
NORCUM, Miss 261
O'BRYAN, Lawrence 225
O'BRYON, Susannah 225
O'HAGAN, C J 120 123 129 160
  172 184 227 234 260 Charles J
  197 Charles James 118
  Charles James Jr 230 Dr 193
  Eliza 230 260 Elvira 230 John
  P 118 Martha 230
OAKLEY, 190
ONSLOW, Captain 121
ORMOND, Roger 73 224
OSBORN, F A 128
PAGE, John 68
PAINE, Laz 57
PARKER, Archibald 108 G W 155
  241 Isaac 106 J R 192 Julia
  256 Mary 241 William 182 218
PARKSTON, William J 105
PATRICK, Cornelius 251 Elizabeth 251

PATTON, Colonel 85 221 John 81
PEARCE, Ada 252 B C 252
  James 106
PEARSCEN, Levy 104
PEARSON, R M 249
PEEBLES, Delphia 242
  Howell 242 Walter N 124
  William 106 William Jr 106
PENN, John 76
PERKINS, A M 248 Churchill 108
  112 120 163 169 190 Church
  175 David 57 58 80 95 Helen
  118 J J 229 W W 193
PETTER, 31 188
PETTIT, Mr 74 Nathaniel 104
PICKETT, General 145
PIERCE, Lazarus 78
PITT, 45 62 74 76 118-120 122
  157 Colonel 74 Robert 43
  William 41 43
POLLARD, Turner 106
POOL, John 119 163 W F 261
POPE, Avent 62 John 106 Simon
  70
PORTER, John 21 E E 138
POTTS, Joseph 113
PRICE, H F 125 126 157
PUGH, William 104
PURNELL, Thomas R 237
QUINERLY, S S 142
RAGSDALE, Amanda H 239
  Bettie 240 Professor 186 198
  Smith G 239 W H 184 194 199
  William Henry 239 W H 190
RAMSEUR, Brigadier-General
  134 General 216 217
RANDALL, Benjamin 48 Elizabeth 225
RANDOLPH, Fannie 220
RANSEUR, Major-General 152
RANSOM, M W 229
REACH, Charles 247 Sarah 247
REAMS, 150
REAVES, Peter 78
REDD, M L F 121
REID, David S 113
RENFROW, 175 J T 174
RESPESS, Captain 65 Thomas 65
RICH, 169 D J 170 172
RICHARDSON, W C 132
RIVERS, Richard Eaton 105

RIVES, Peter 58
ROACH, J R 143
ROBERSON, William 59 233
ROBERTSON, James 105
ROBESON, 82 Patrick 70 William 62 69 70 76 79 81 224
ROBEY, J T 193
ROBSON, William 58 60
RODGERS, Henry 106
RODMAN, W B 171 249
ROLLINS, J J 192 Reuben 105
ROOSEVELT, President 198 229 259
ROUNTREE, C D 124 147 155 Charles D 241 Mollie A 241 William 104
ROYSTER, Amanda H 239 W H 239
RUTHERFORD, John 42
SADLER, Captain 106
SAFFRE, Mrs 186
SALTER, 31 41 90 Captain 47 E 23 Edward 27 29 45 51 54 55 57 58 60 62 65 67-69 73 76 84 87 220 223 225 Edward Jr 220 221 Edward Sr 220 James 78 John 74 78 220 Robert 48 53 55 57 58 67 70-72 75 78 80-82 98 220 221
SATTERTHWAITE, Annie 260 Bryan 181 F B 113 120 215 260 Joseph J 260 Fenner Bryan 218
SAUNDERS, Absalom 108 F C Mrs 220 Mrs F C 23
SAVAGE, Edward 121
SCOTT, 118
SEIGEL, General 216
SELBY, John A 113
SERMON, Jethro 106
SEYMOUR, Horatio 180
SHARPE, Lieutenant 138 V B 139
SHELLEY, W H 120
SHEPPARD, 60 Alice 219 Annie W 219 243 B S 148 219 Benajmin 218 Elizabeth 219 Ella 219 Harper 218 Harper D 219 Henry 219 243 254 Henry Sr 218 Hernie 219 James G 219 James Glasgow 218 Lawrence B 219 Margaret 219

SHEPPARD (continued) Mary 219 Pattie 219 Solomon 60 64 Susan E 219
SHERIDAN, General 157 217
SHERMAN, 157 General 158
SHERROD, Pattie 250 252
SHINGLETON, Richard 106
SHIVERS, Benjamin 105
SHORT, Richard 172
SIMPSON, 47 53 82 90 101 Alice 225 Ann 225 Colonel 48 80 81 Elizabeth 225 Ichabod 53 58 John 224 250 252 John 27 41-43 51 54 55 57 58 60 62 65 67 69-71 73 76 78 83 84 90 93-97 223 John Hardee 225 Joseph 225 Mary Randall 225 Samuel 96 97 101 225 Sarah 225 Susannah 225
SINGELTARY, R W 132 160 T C 160 Captain 122 Colonel 126 128 G B 124 125 127 160 G B 118 George B 120 244 R W 120 122 124 126 127 131 T C 124 125 126 129
SITGREAVES, Mr 101
SKINNER, 188 193 198 Ella 259 Elmira W 258 Harry 192 193 198 200 258 Harry Jr 204 259 Henry 258 James C 258 John 95 William 258
SLADE, Lieutenant 144
SLAVE, 66 171 Madison 123 Merrick 66 Rose 90 91 Shade 91
SLOAN, Colonel 127 John 125
SMITH, Benjamin 106 Bryant 170 Captain 170 193 Claudius 247 Cora 253 D H 126 143 H L 172 Hardy 104 Henry 105 J T 130 193 John Richard 253 John S 126 M T 130 Mary 234 235 246 253 Mary V 235 Richard 18 Robert Williams 253 Theophilus 253 W H 235 William 253 William H 247
SOUTHALL, Sallie 231 263 Susan Sims 231 Thomas 263
SPAIN, Luther 105
SPIER, John 26 William 33 42
SPIERS, John 105

272

SPIVEY, James 81
STANCILL, Henry 170
STANSEL, Godfrey 57
STEPHENS, C 127 132
STEWARD, Mr 46
STEWART, Alex 50 Alexander 41 Mr 45
STOCKS, William 133
STOKES, 190 Col 124
SUGG, Allen 57 Benjamin H 248 252 I A 249 Mary 248 Nancy 248 252 Susan 252
SUMNER, General 88 223
SUTTON, Bettie 240 Elizabeth 240 H A 236 240 Hennie 236 Mrs H A 236
SWAIN, 223
TAYLOR, 118 William 66
TEACH, 23
TEAL, William 105
TELFAIR, Hugh 108
THOMAS, L 181
THOMPSON, C 195
THURMAN, A 261
TILLGHMAN, Wm 225
TILMAN, Captain 88
TIMBERLAKE, Mrs Julian 263
TINGLE, 193 J R 192 195
TISON, Aaron 57 John 57 60-63 69 105
TOOLE, 33 Henry I 112
TRAVERS, 33
TRAVIS, William 57 58 80
TRUSS, Joel 86
TRYON, Governor 47-49 221
TUCKER, Arden 106 TUCKER J A K 258
TURNAGE, A P 108 Ann E 219 Benjamin 219 Lewis 108 Martha A 237 244 258 Moses 104 108 244 Isaac 105
TURNER, Jacob 105
TYCE, 133 Allen 133
TYSON, Aaron 53 Abraham 45 Charles McGhee 214 Cornelius 221 Edith Johns 263 Isabella McGhee 214 Job 89 John 45 53 90 Lawrence Davis 213 Margaret Ann 219 Margaret Louise 213 Mary 221 Noah 234 Noah Eld 234 Richard Lawrence 213

TYSON (continued)
Sallie Ann 234 Sheppard Jr 218 Sherrod 213 Sherrod Sr 218 219 Sibbey 90 Susannah 225 Thomas 27 29
TRUSS, Polly 241
VANBUREN, Martin 110
VANCE, 130 179 Governor 152 251 257 Z B 130 181 191 256
VICHOUS, Benjamin 88
VINES, Allie 241 Charles 223 Mary 221 Polly 241 Samuel 104 228 241 244
WADE, 256 Elizabeth Hampton 256
WAIT, Samuel 109
WAKE, 74
WALKER, General 217
WALLACE, David R 184 W T 110
WALSTON, Harman 106
WARD, Allen 258 Benjamin 106 D K 206 Elmira 258 259 Robert 227 Sallie 227
WARREN, E J 113 114 172 184
WASHINGTON, 113 General 259 George 96 100 President 56 101 222
WESSON, Mrs Douglass B 263
WEST, Robert 26
WHEDBEE, Harry W 206 Judge 206
WHEELER, 161 162 Joe 162
WHICHARD, D J 181 186 191 David F 235 David J Sr 236 David Jordan 235 Hennie 236 J R 181 186 Solomon 105 Violet 115 Violetta 235 Willis 116
WHITE, Annie W 243 Burrel 106 C A 132 138 145 155 246 Captain 141 Charles A 243 Cornelia H 214 E F 145 J M 155 James 214 James A 243 James S 243 Louisa A 243 Luke 45 Lula 246 Noah Smith 81 Paul 70 Paule 70 71 Samuel 243 Samuel Tilden 243 Susie 23 26
WHITEHEAD, Captain 138 D F 160 H G 131 138 J T 127 130 160

WHITEHURST, 176 177 Alonzo 175 Mrs 175 Willoughby 105
WHITFORD, 138 143 Colonel 141
WIGGIN, Mrs Russell B 263
WILDER, W T 193
WILEY, Calvin H 116
WILKINS, J E 110
WILKINSON, Henry 17
WILLIAMS, 56 Dick 101 Dr 109 Edmond 55 58 Edmund 79 80 Elizabeth 220 Ella 219 Fannie 220 Garison 105 Harriet P 255 Harriett 221 J A 124 J T 155 219 J T 133 John 57 78 81 83 93 233 255 Nancy 220 Richard 101 219 Robert 26 82 83 86 93 95 109 219 233 255 W R 169 170 Willis Robert 169 255
WILLIAMSON, Hugh 93
WILSON, 113 E A 244 John 106 William 45
WINCHESTER, 150
WINDHAM, J McD 193
WISE, General 217 Mary 228
WISWALL, Howard 127
WITHERINGTON, I K 142
WOLFENDEN, Thomas 69 70 75
WOOTEN, Elizabeth Hampton 256 Francis Marion 255 Julia A 256 Robert L 256
WORTH, 161 Governor 172 Jonathan 163
WRIGHT, Bettie 200
WYATT, 122 Henry L 122
YELLOWLY, 109-112 122 130 183 Captain 130 Colonel 254 E C 110 116 123 124 130 160 186 Edward C 233 Lieutenant-Colonel 143 Major 142

www.ingramcontent.com/pod-product-compliance
Lightning Source LLC
Chambersburg PA
CBHW070727160426
43192CB00009B/1347